DATE DUE

TQM
in New Product
Manufacturing

TQM
in New Product
Manufacturing

H. G. Menon

McGraw-Hill, Inc.

New York St. Louis San Francisco Auckland Bogotá
Caracas Lisbon London Madrid Mexico Milan
Montreal New Delhi Paris San Juan São Paulo
Singapore Sydney Tokyo Toronto

Library of Congress Cataloging-in-Publication Data

Menon, H. G.
   TQM in new product manufacturing / H. G. Menon.
      p.   cm.
   Includes bibliographical references and index.
   ISBN 0-07-041532-3
   1. Production management—Quality control.   2. Total quality
management.   I. Title.
TS156.M435   1992
658.5′62—dc20   92-4782
                                                      CIP

1 2 3 4 5 6 7 8 9 0   DOC/DOC   9 8 7 6 5 4 3 2

ISBN   0-07-041532-3

The sponsoring editor for this book was Gail F. Nalven, the editing
supervisor was Stephen M. Smith, and the production supervisor was
Donald F. Schmidt. It was set in Century Schoolbook by
McGraw-Hill's Professional Book Group composition unit.

Printed and bound by R. R. Donnelley & Sons Company.

Contents

Preface

This book is written primarily for the industrial practitioner responsible for the management of quality (including managers, engineers, and technicians) and other people responsible for the creation of quality management systems. This book provides an overall total quality management (TQM) perspective so that these systems are not restricted to managing the quality of the end product. Managing the quality of a product from its inception is critical to manufacturing competitiveness. The process of improvement in quality through reduction of variation cannot be stressed enough and this ultimately leads to lower costs of production.

Most of the quality management systems discussed in this book were learned through my experiences with managing camshaft quality from inception to the problem-free product manufacturing stage. Most of the systems and standards described here are similar to those used by the Big Three automobile manufacturers, General Motors, Ford, and Chrysler, with special reference to the camshaft quality management system sucessfully being used by my employer.

Various aspects of the TQM systems are highlighted, including acquiring and stabilizing new machinery, gaging, data collection, and processing equipment. Statistical techniques valuable for the buying process are also discussed. Furthermore, experimental methods and statistical techniques for process control are detailed. When using equipment, the reliability of the equipment and manufacturing process is an important factor leading to satisfactory performance of the process. Inspection, though the least effective part of quality management systems, can almost never be eliminated and thus is discussed.

Much-needed stress is placed on developing the background for experimental methods, which provide strategies for optimizing process potential. Most people are scared by experimental methods because of the time and cost involved. Taguchi techniques provide a basis for efficient, time-saving strategies in experimental methods; these techniques are briefly introduced. Poka-Yoke techniques for 100 percent inspection are introduced as powerful tools for TQM. Other important strategies, such as total productive maintenance for ensuring reliability and performance of equipment, are also introduced.

Aspects of TQM such as short-run statistical process control, quality function deployment, and the accounting system known as computer-aided manufacturing–international (CAM-I) are discussed even though they were not actually used as a part of my employer's system. It is my hope that managers, engineers, and scientists appreciate the hands-on, user-oriented approach to total quality management described in this book and that they develop an understanding for the importance of implementing these methods from the very beginning of the manufacturing process.

I wish to thank Jernberg Industries for the support and input provided me as I prepared this manuscript, and especially the following people at the company: Mike Mills, T. Beecham, B. Giffune, P. Sautter, N. S. McMullen, A. Hazrat, O. Gonzalez, A. Flores, and Janet DiMascio. I must especially thank N. S. McMullen, A. Hazrat, and P. Sautter for reading the manuscript and providing other support in the production of this book. Rita McMullen deserves special thanks for her help in going over a part of the manuscript. I must also thank R. Madassery and Dr. Kurup for helping me with this project.

In addition, I wish to thank my parents for their encouragement during the time I worked on this book. Last but not least, I must thank the staff at McGraw-Hill, especially Gail Nalven, my editor, Stephen Smith, the editing supervisor, and Don Schmidt, the production supervisor, for excellent support and guidance through the various stages of the book production process.

H. G. Menon

TQM
in New Product
Manufacturing

Total Quality Management in New Product Manufacturing

A Strategy for Corporate Renewal

Although quality is recognized today as the most important part of a strategy to remain competitive, many people are confused about how total quality management (TQM) fits in as a management tool, finding many of the concepts of TQM abstract and mysterious. Better understanding of the concepts of TQM goes a long way in the process of implementing such a system. Creating a TQM model relevant to your environment is the path to continuous quality improvement and cost reduction, leading to a more competitive position. Furthermore, much has been said and written about TQM, but not much has been said about implementing such a system for a new product. With proper planning, it is much easier to implement a TQM system before all production systems are in place. Setting up a TQM system acts as the most powerful tool against your competitors. Implementing the TQM system correctly can act as a marketing tool in two ways:

1. It helps produce a better, more reliable product which better meets customer requirements.

2. It reduces manufacturing costs by minimizing variation in the manufacturing process.

The first step in the TQM process begins with top management's vision to see what has to be achieved in terms of quality and what improvement in product or service quality can achieve for the company. Any TQM system begun without this corporate vision is doomed to failure. Top management also has to act on this vision of quality and follow up words with action to ensure that the TQM process functions effectively.

When we talk about TQM, we are referring to a system that looks at far more than the product the company makes. TQM applies to the raw materials coming into the door, to the method used by the company to interface with its suppliers and customers, to the service it provides, and to the condition and management of its tools and machines. In short, every aspect of every business revolves around quality. Most job shops have stressed the importance of quality, and this is indicated by the shrinking supplier base. Secondary suppliers unable to meet the quality requirements of the primary customer become exsources. There are numerous tools available to ensure that the various parameters of quality requirements are met by the manufacturers. Demanding quality parts from your suppliers and developing the quality mindset throughout your company, starting from your floor sweepers to the occupants of the executive suites, is not just a part of doing business—it is the business. All the aspects covered by a TQM system and what it will do for you are illustrated in Fig. 1.1. This book will explain the various aspects of TQM for a new product and how to implement a TQM system. Many of the examples described in this book are from situations encountered while developing the manufac-

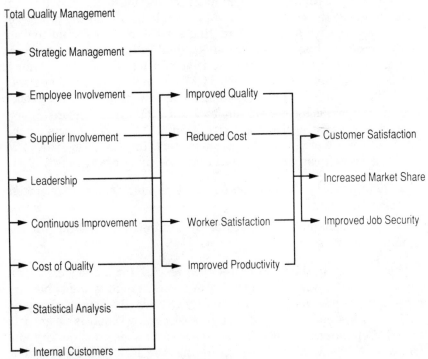

Figure 1.1   TQM systems and elements involved.

turing process for the camshaft used by one of the major automotive companies. Elements of the TQM system that could not be directly applied to the camshaft manufacturing process are also described so that all aspects of the process are covered.

With the skill level of manufacturing workers higher than ever before and workers getting better and better every day, quality provides the competitive edge for companies throughout the world. This can only be attained if companies

- Focus on customer needs more intently than ever before.
- Depend on employee contributions for the continuous improvement in product and processes.
- Strive to do things right the first time, and thus avoiding rework.
- Have the flexibility to change quickly as customer requirements change.

Quality can be attained by creating a problem-solving mindset based on facts, a process-oriented view based on prevention instead of inspection, an environment of continuous improvement driven by employee involvement, and an overriding priority of satisfying customer needs. Bridging the gap between talking about quality and implementing the quality systems and processes is the most important step any company can take for developing a TQM system. Implementation of TQM systems requires

- Quality leadership as the strategic objective, backed with a program, commitment, and resources necessary to do the job right the first time.
- Quality processes should be clearly defined, thoroughly understood, and fully installed. All the people in the organization should believe in the systems and should be active participants in the quality process.
- Empowering people to act in a way that they can meet the quality commitment of the organization.

Once the tools of TQM are implemented, a whole new culture of excellence is created, ensuring that the principles of excellence are adhered to by all areas and by all persons in the organization. To this end an information system has to be created to provide internal feedback and competitive comparison and to anticipate trends. Although the book attempts to deal with all aspects of TQM, special emphasis will be placed on the statistical and mathematical tools that are essential to its implementation, along with a special emphasis on manufacturing a new product.

The Product Used as Example— The Camshaft

To understand the TQM process, let me begin by describing the manufacturing process for the product with which we will be dealing. I will be using a metal-cutting process as the basis for all discussions; more specifically, a camshaft manufacturing process. Most of the quality planning and implementation processes described can be directly adapted to other manufacturing environments and, with suitable modification, to service environments. Usually, in service environments, service quality indicators, which are similar to the indicators used in measuring customer satisfaction in a manufacturing environment, are used to ensure that the customers' requirements are met. Service quality indicators have not been used extensively until recently, particularly since quantifying quality performance is difficult. The use of these methods has increased with competitive pressures.

This book describes the basic process of manufacturing the camshaft, which is shown in Fig. 1.2. The product from which the camshaft is manufactured is a forging, which is shown in Fig. 1.3. The camshaft is received in an as-forged condition, from which the camshaft is end-milled and center-drilled in the first operation. The second operation is drilling the spring pockets and the drive and oil holes. The third step is turning the four journals. The fourth step is spacing, followed by the fifth step, milling the lobes. The sixth and final step in the process of manufacturing of the camshaft is milling the keyway. Later in the book an actual flow diagram showing the manufacturing process is presented. Most of the examples used in this book were implemented while in the process of manufacturing the camshaft for the first time.

After milling the keyway, the camshaft is now termed partially machined and is ready for shipment to the customer, who grinds and heat treats the journals and lobes before the shaft is used in an engine. This product was not completely new for us, in the sense that we did manufacture the older version of the camshaft. The processing methods for this camshaft were completely changed by the new machinery and gaging systems adopted.

The Learning Process

Whenever a new product has to be manufactured, we usually go through a learning process, during which time the most important

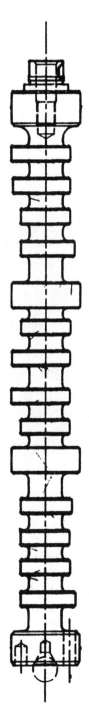

Figure 1.2   A finished camshaft.

Figure 1.3 A forged camshaft from which the finished product is made.

goal is to reduce process variation. It must be remembered that the reduction of variation is the key tool for continuous improvement even after the learning process is completed. As we learn about the product and the problems with our manufacturing methods, the number of defective parts decreases, thereby resulting in decreased production costs. This is shown in Fig. 1.4. The systems described in this book provide the means to determine where the process variation is the highest, the means to reduce variation in the process and to determine ways to prevent any defective parts as a result of the variation from

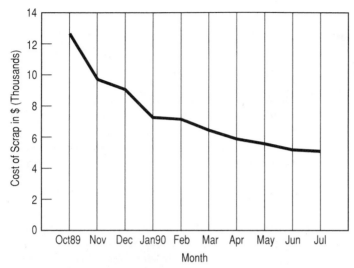

Figure 1.4 Example of learning curve: cost of scrap per month in dollars.

reaching the customer, and finally the means to reduce the common causes of variation so that no defective parts are produced. The book attempts to reduce the learning period in two ways:

1. By proper planning and implementation of the TQM system, the starting levels of scrap and rework can be much lower and approach the goal of "zero defects" using the statistical and other methods described.

2. Increasing the steepness of the learning curve using the various mathematical methods described here and decreasing the length of time for which high levels of scrap and rework are produced, that is, to increase the rate of learning to obtain a defect-free product.

   In short, once the systems are installed, you can proceed to the goal of zero defects at a much faster rate. Implementing a TQM system after all other systems are in place can be considerably expensive, but when implemented at the start of the manufacturing process, results in much improved quality. It is important to remember here that using good documentation facilitates the learning process, and all systems used must be followed up with documentation of their results. Good documentation can result in faster problem solving if a similar situation arises in the future.

   Throughout this book I have attempted to concentrate on the statistical and mathematical aspects of TQM in a metal-cutting environment, but not ignoring the other aspects of TQM in terms of technology and people.

Planning for Quality

Usually the first step in the manufacture of a new product is the manufacturing engineer deciding on a process sequence or process planning. In this context it is necessary to understand the concept of internal customer, which is discussed in Chap. 2. If possible the designer and the manufacturing engineer should interact to allow for better manufacture and assembly. During the decision-making process it is necessary to use the tools offered by quality function deployment for integrating the customers' requirement into the product design. At this stage of manufacturing, the planning for quality should begin and all critical features of the product and the quality-planning process have to be determined. If the product has to be designed, the designer should keep manufacturability in mind. Manufacturability software is a new and powerful tool which aids the designer in producing an easily manufactured product. Value engineering and simulation are two other powerful tools that aid the manufacturing process aiming for TQM. The techniques and systems for these are described briefly in this chapter. The various factors to be kept in mind when the process is being developed are described in Chap. 2, including a discussion on the principles of manufacturing accounting and the cost of producing a nonconforming part. The discussions on modern manufacturing accounting also lead to a discussion on CAM-I, the accounting system which is being accepted as the standard and is an important part of the TQM strategy. The initial sample run and the parameters that must be maintained form the basis for the next step in the process. The initial sample helps determine any failings of the manufacturing process and rectify the problems that may be encountered during that process. The parameters necessary for manufacturing the initial samples and parameters that need to be satisfied before sending the samples to the customer are dealt with in Chap. 2. The final analysis shows why reduction of variation is the key to improvement in quality.

The People Side of TQM

The use of TQM systems requires a basic change in the operating philosophy of managing people. Everyone in the organization has to understand that quality goes far beyond the issues of meeting the specifications of the customer. People have to be offered more than just a paycheck in terms of job satisfaction. For increased job satisfaction, it is necessary to create a culture in which employees can make a contribution to the whole process. The concepts of "big Q" and "small q" are explained, where the small q refers to meeting the customers' specifications and big Q deals with quality as an overall issue covering all aspects of customer satisfaction including price, reliability, safety, delivery, and courtesy. Improved job satisfaction can manifest itself in the form of training for the employees, leading them to assume increased responsibilities. The beginning of the TQM process using the concept of the big Q comes with a top management movement in this direction. This is followed by increased responsibilities for individuals or teams. The individual contributions can come as a result of the use of various statistical and problem-solving methods. The use of all the statistical and other methods described in the book requires all levels of management and workers to be trained in the TQM philosophy and the methodology to be used. Training ensures that all the tools available in the TQM system are correctly used, and that a team spirit is fostered in the company, with everyone working for continuous improvement of the process. Finally, the teachings of the TQM "gurus," including Deming, Juran, and Ishikawa, are discussed, while underscoring the shortcomings of the Crosby systems of quality management. Use of teams and team management for the problem-solving process is another important part of TQM philosophy and is dealt with in a later chapter. Sometimes it becomes necessary to use outside consultants to effect the massive changes that must come about in the basic organizational structure. The last part of Chap. 3 discusses the criteria for selecting and using consultants for managing change.

Machine Acceptance Criteria

The next step is to decide the type and number of machines to be purchased, retooled, or retrofitted to produce the new product. Once the necessary machines have been determined, it is necessary to determine the capability and reliability standards required to ensure that the machine can perform the necessary task. Numerous statistical methods are available to determine the capability and reliability of the machine. Depending on whether the machine is newly purchased or is retooled or retrofitted, parameters have to be set so that the machine performs satisfactorily. Setting these parameters becomes critical, especially in the case of machines purchased as turnkey projects. Machine capability and reliability parameters must be met before any kind of statistical process control (SPC) methods can be applied. The parameters and tests necessary before a machine is ready for production use are described in Chap. 4. Implementing these parameters with your suppliers and internally for any machines that are retooled should ensure no problems during production. Once the machine has been set up, it becomes necessary to implement a preventive maintenance program as a part of the machine acceptance criteria. Total maintenance management strategies are an important part of the strategy to maintain the capabilities developed, either by purchasing new machines or retrofitting or retooling existing machines. In the event the machine has to undergo major repairs or major modification, it is imperative that the process of accepting the repaired or modified machine should follow the procedures described above. Since total productive maintenance is an important part of the strategy to keep the machines running, the last part of Chap. 4 discusses this important facet of the TQM system. Productive maintenance management systems can be driven by various parameters, such as requirements set by the machinery manufacturer; requirements shown by SPC, failure modes and effects analysis, and design of experiments methods; and routine replacement of wear parts in the machinery. When dealing with machinery, the use and level of automation as a quality tool in addition to being a productivity tool is another important criterion in the machinery buying and acceptance process. The continuous improvement of the manufacturing process can be effected by evolutionary operation of processes and is described in this chapter, where process improvements are made by small changes in certain parameters that are likely to improve process performance.

Gage Acceptance Criteria

The next step is determining the gaging systems to be used. Although conformance to specification is regarded as a very small element in the TQM philosophy, all the systems revolve around creating an ideal environment so that parts do not fail to conform to requirements. Therefore it is really important to select appropriate tools with which to measure the parts. By designing statistically valid experiments, we can ensure performance of the gage when used as a part of our process. Most of the systems described will be for fixture-type gages, although in the beginning of the chapter various types of gaging systems available for dimensional measurement are classified. When buying gaging systems, specify the various resolution, accuracy, precision, repeatability, and reproducibility parameters. Although most fixture-type gagings usually only specify gage repeatability and reproducibility parameter requirements, it is important to ensure that the resolution, accuracy, and precision parameters are met. The necessary parameters must be specified prior to purchase, and most gaging manufacturers agree to meet the specified parameters. These parameters are described in detail in Chap. 5. Once the required parameters are specified, it becomes necessary to implement them and ensure that the supplier meets them. An important facet when using gaging systems is the calibration of gages and developing a history of gage calibration. The techniques for measuring gage performance and the possibility of accepting a part with a given master value are determined. Finally, criteria for evaluating an attribute gage for repeatability are discussed.

Failure Modes and Effects Analysis

Continually measuring the reliability of a machine, product, or process is an essential part of TQM. Without reliability for the machine, process, or product, the systems cannot function effectively. When acquiring new machines it is necessary to determine the reliability of the product created. There are many techniques for measuring the reliability of the process, the product, or the assembly. One of the most powerful is the failure modes and effects analysis (FMEA). This involves the identification of the potential failure modes and the effect of those failures on your customer. FMEA involves the analysis of the situations leading to the failure of the process to produce a product that meets the specifications of the customer. FMEA attempts to detect the potential product-related failure modes. It uses occurrence and detection probability criteria in conjunction with severity criteria to develop risk prioritization numbers for prioritization of corrective action considerations. The methods that can be used to evaluate a process are dealt with in Chap. 6. The methods used will be the same except that the new machine or equipment being designed would be considered the products. This is an important step in the process of debugging problems that may actually occur in the manufacturing process. The FMEA should be taken as a living document that continually changes as new problems are found during the manufacturing process and should be continually updated to ensure that we are currently tackling the most critical problem. Finally, Chap. 6 also deals with the other methods of establishing process reliability such as fault-tree analysis, worst-case analysis, and sneak-circuit analysis.

Supplier Quality Management

Another important aspect of total quality engineering is the use of preferred suppliers for various components, tooling, fixtures, and so on. The buyer plays an extremely critical role in getting quality products to the user, and this is discussed in Chap. 7. Preferred suppliers should be in a position to supply you with a quality product and should be committed to the goal of zero defects through the continual reduction of variation. The minimal requirements from such a supplier are machine capability data and statistical process control data for the parts supplied to you. A system should be developed for evaluating your suppliers and should be rigorously implemented to ensure that your production process is not hampered by your suppliers. The communication channels between the customer and the supplier determine the ability of the supplier to meet the increased quality expectations. Suppliers should also have systems set up to continuously improve their processes and attain the goal of zero defects. A detailed analysis of the process of developing the preferred supplier list and ensuring that the supplier meets your requirements is described in Chap. 7, along with the responsibilities of the buyer in developing such systems. A mathematical method for determining the preferred source of supply for a required product, called TOPSIS, is also described.

Problem-Solving and Continuous Improvement Techniques

Once all of these steps have been taken and the process for your new product is set up, numerous problems continue to arise. These problems have to be dealt with and a systematic method of attacking the problem has to be developed. In their simplest form, the steps involved are

1. Identify the problem.
2. Quantify the problem.
3. Identify the root cause(s).
4. Take actions to rectify the problem.
5. Quantify the effects of the action to determine whether the problem has been solved.
6. Set up systems to prevent the problems from recurring.

In the problem-solving process, it is important to involve all the people that can make a meaningful contribution in the form of teams. Strategies for forming and using teams in the problem-solving process are discussed in this chapter. Steps 3 through 6 should be repeated continuously until the problem is completely solved. The problem can usually be identified by using numerous tools, such as Cp/Cpk, Pareto charts analysis, process control charts analysis, and histogram analysis. Based on the quantification of the problem, experiments have to be set up to vary parameters to determine the ways to minimize or eliminate the problem. The very same tools that help determine that a problem exists can be used to determine whether the problem has been eliminated. Some problems may not involve use of extensive experimental methods but may involve simple solutions such as blowing out the chips under a clamp to eliminate offcenter drilling conditions. These methods are dealt with in detail in Chap. 8.

Another aspect to consider is the process of establishing a continuous improvement process. The continuous improvement process involves various factors coming together, including the leadership systems, quality systems, delivery systems, costing systems, and technological systems. Steps to improve the manufacturing process are critical, and are covered within the second part of Chap. 8. Many of the steps are similar to the problem-solving process. The continuous improvement model focuses on overall process improvement or on individual segments of the manufacturing process.

Continuous improvement models can be applied to service environments almost directly and improvements can be measured directly. There are numerous other continuous improvement models developed by various authors. The end result of all these methods is the constant improvement of process and quality. An extremely powerful tool for initiation of the continuous improvement process is comparison of your product or process to your competitors'. This comparison is termed *benchmarking* and leads to identifying the best in the business. Once identified, we try to emulate or exceed the best in the business.

Statistical Process Control

Once the changes resulting from all of the problem-solving methods have been implemented, the process has to be monitored using statistical process control (SPC), including sampling methods and plotting and interpreting X-bar and R charts. The use of computerized plotting methods is preferable to manual plotting, but the operator has to be able to interpret the chart. Using computerized plotting methods instantly gives numerous analyses, such as histograms and long-range process capability. Statistical process control is primarily used to:

1. Identify and eliminate the special causes for variation in your process.

2. Maintain the stability of your manufacturing process.

Numerous other methods are available such as p charts and c charts for attribute-type gages, X-bar and sigma charts, moving average charts, and X-bar and R_m charts for short runs. These are dealt with in Chap. 9. It is also important to remember to identify the key product characteristics and associated key control characteristics prior to applying SPC techniques to improve process performance. Key product characteristics and key control characteristics are such that when SPC methods are used, they result in a significant increase in customer satisfaction and reduce cost. Failure to meet these conditions can result in deterioration of the performance characteristics of the product. Certain powerful statistical methods such as CUSUM exist; these are not dealt with in this book, but they have important applications. The application of the various statistical tools is considerably facilitated by the use of data collection and SPC devices and software. These make the actual use considerably easier over manual computing skills. All of these aspects of a TQM system are explained in Chap. 8. Once the SPC systems are established, with all end-users trained, the next step in the process is setting up quality circles. Quality circles will fail without a reliable SPC system to measure the effectiveness of the suggestions implemented by the quality circles.

Design of Experiments

The next step in your TQM system is optimization of various aspects of your system such as tooling. Various experimental design and operations research tools are available to optimize the systems. If you specified certain performance requirements from your machinery manufacturer, he or she develops a process based on past experience. Tooling that is selected to meet your performance requirements may result in a less-than-optimum situation, and you may end up with considerably more expensive tooling. This situation calls for the use of an experiment. An *experiment* is defined as a considered course of action aimed at answering one or more carefully framed questions. This involves the selection of certain kinds of factors, deliberately varying those factors in a controlled fashion, and observing the effect of the action. This type of controlled experimentation to optimize the process and get an end product acceptable to the customer is the primary objective for experimental design. Chapter 10 attempts to deal with classical experimentation methods such as t tests, F tests, and ANOVA techniques leading to the determination of conditions for minimizing variation. Other techniques for experimentation, such as Youden square, fractional factorial, and blocked factorial experiments are also dealt with in this chapter. The last part of Chap. 10 deals with Taguchi techniques for quality engineering, and explains Taguchi's basic strategies, which helped the Japanese become powerful economic competitors. The numerous aspects of offline quality control, including parameter and tolerance design, are discussed, along with the concept of signal-to-noise ratios.

Inspection, Audit, and Poka-Yoke Systems

An inspection system is another aspect of a TQM program; it can almost never be completely eliminated. Chapter 11 attempts to deal with the conditions under which various levels of inspection become necessary, instructions for inspection, general principles of inspection, and acceptance sampling. Inspection techniques must use certain statistical parameters, so that the acceptance of parts is based on a statistically valid inspection. The statistical methods in an inspection plan are described in this chapter. After dealing with the concepts of inspection systems, it is necessary to create audit systems that help ensure that all the systems developed are in place and are working. Audit systems also ensure that any problem areas are highlighted and process improvement measures can be effected. Audit systems ensure that all the operating systems are working correctly. Finally, this chapter also deals with the concept of Poka-Yoke, or mistake-proofing the manufacturing process. Developed by Dr. Shigeo Shingo, Poka-Yoke devices and solutions come from the shop floor and are implemented with the help of engineering personnel to create systems for 100 percent source inspection. These devices can often be powerful tools in the process of reaching your goal of zero defects by preventing them at the source.

Selecting Automatic Inspection, Data Collection, and Analysis Systems

One important tool for total quality engineering is the use of computers for inspection, data collection, and statistical process control (SPC). Chapter 12 deals with the numerous parameters necessary while selecting a computer system and software for automatic data collection. With the bewildering array of data collection and SPC analysis software available, the choices can sometimes be extremely confusing. The determination of which questions must be asked prior to selecting software is critical to the satisfactory performance of data collection and process analysis systems. Chapter 12 also answers the questions that arise in dealing with the purchase of a computer system used for inspection, such as a coordinate measuring machine, where the computer system computes or can be set up to compute various dimensions.

Measures of Customer (Dis)Satisfaction

Finally, the most important aspect of your total quality engineering system involves measuring customer satisfaction. It is most critical to initiate customer feedback and steps to eliminate customer dissatisfaction if necessary. The goal of Chap. 13 is to ensure that the various measures of customer (dis)satisfaction, such as complaints, returns, and rejects, total zero. To accomplish this, it is necessary to develop the criteria to properly measure customer satisfaction and to take proper actions to ensure that the problems reported do not reappear or that the customer does not have a reason to return the product. The various methods available to measure customer (dis)satisfaction are dealt with in Chap. 13. Since it is the dissatisfied customer that often prevents you from attaining your goal of expanding your business, the important aspects of the measures of customer satisfaction or dissatisfaction are dealt with in Chap. 13. These tools are quite similar to service quality indicators, where the quality of the service provided to the supplier is the critical factor, unlike manufacturing, where quality of a tangible product is the critical factor.

The Final Analysis and Beyond TQM

Once all of these systems are implemented, we have a TQM system in place and we are on the road to continuous improvement with the ultimate goal of reaching zero defects. When properly implemented, the system results in minimal manufacturing problems and also problems related with the end product are detected prior to their occurrence. This leads us to just-in-time methods, the successful implementation of which depends on the successful use of TQM. Another direction of growth beyond TQM is building products to satisfy every need of the customer; this is termed as *Kansei engineering* and can be attained by creating manufacturing systems that are extremely flexible to the needs of the customer.

Conclusion

Most of this book explains how to apply the various tools for determining problems in a manufacturing system. Here it must be stated that certain features not applicable in the camshaft manufacturing process are described in the appropriate context. An example is the process of constructing X-bar and R charts for short runs within the context of SPC. Another example of techniques not used in the camshaft manufacturing process would be quality function deployment, since the customer has defined the requirements of the product exactly. The mathematical justification for using the methods described are not offered in this book. The final goal of this book is to lead you beyond the realm of TQM to what the Japanese in the auto industry call *miroyokuteki hinshitshu,* or products that are not just reliable but fascinate, delight, and bewitch the customer. In plain English this translates to "things gone right," and in the process engineering into products an intriguing look, sound, and feel while improving product reliability.

Once convinced of the benefits of TQM, many companies seek out the "gurus" for advice on improving their quality. If you do seek out a guru, then it is important to check out his or her credentials. The purpose of this book is to provide an alternative to the advice proffered by these gurus and to help you acquire tools to implement specific strategies customized for your unique problems. While the advice of the gurus and consultants can form an important part of the strategy, the importance of the various tools can vary depending on the product or service you provide. Using consultants can be extremely important in environments where certain notions about quality are ingrained in the value system, and effecting change is extremely difficult if not impossible internally. In such cases, these external consultants can be valuable catalysts for change.

2

Planning for Quality

Manufacturing Process Planning

One of the first requirements for producing a quality product is the process of manufacturing planning. There are numerous aspects to manufacturing planning for quality, including the process planning that ensures good manufacturing and quality practices, the process control practices, development of the pilot line for manufacturing the product, and the process certification. All required methods and documentation must be determined at the stage of manufacturing the product.

Once you have decided on the inputs that are transformed by the process into the required output, it is necessary to set up a feedback loop. The feedback loop relates information about the outputs back to the input stage so that the process can be analyzed. The usual method of setting up a feedback loop is shown in Fig. 2.1. Establishing a feedback loop is critical to the effective functioning of the process for producing a quality output and in turn the entire organization.

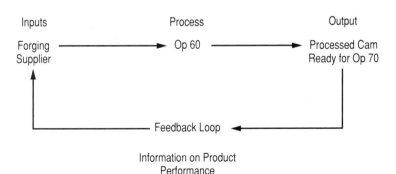

Figure 2.1   Using feedback loops.

Important questions to ask when defining the process are

1. Are the manufacturing and quality processes used good? To answer this question, any change in the process instructions must be documented and approved, and final functional features for the pilot run must be tested on a piece-by-piece basis.
2. Who's responsible for the process? By this, we mean the person who is responsible for the state and improvement of the process; this person should have access to the resources necessary to implement process improvements.
3. What are the boundaries of the process? Defining the boundaries of each process is dealt with in detail under process routing sheets.
4. What is the process flow? A flowchart is usually used to depict the flow of materials through the various operations and is also discussed under process routing sheets.
5. What are the objectives of the process? The person responsible for the process is responsible for stating the objectives of the process and this must be consistent with the organizational objectives.
6. Are the measurements taken on the process valid? There must be a valid measuring system for determining the performance of the process. In case of a manufacturing process, the measuring system is a gage or a set of gages.

Other important factors in manufacturing process planning are the control of engineering documents so that an outdated print or process sheets are not used for manufacturing the product. These engineering documents must be properly controlled and released. This involves the following steps:

1. Purchasing and tool design should not be performed before the design is finalized.
2. Process routing should be finalized and approved by quality assurance.
3. Critical equipment such as gage and masters must be certified.
4. Product development stage should be carefully controlled.
5. Incoming materials must be carefully controlled.
6. In-process controls must be in place.

The Internal Customer

The concept of the internal customer needs to be handled carefully when implementing a TQM system. This concept has to be understood by every member of the organization. The concept of internal customer refers to either the next person in the manufacturing line who handles the product, or the person who uses the feature created by a manufacturing operation. Internal feedback loops similar to the feedback loop from the customer have to be set up with the understanding that defects in the manufacturing process will not be tolerated by the internal customer. The series of feedback loops set up within the organization ensure that only products that meet the quality requirements are passed on to the next manufacturing operation, as shown in Fig. 2.2.

The traditional view of manufacturing planners has been to build in a factor for the losses due to scrap. This has a tendency to affect the quality of the manufacturing process, as shown later in this chapter. Increased variance decreases the quality of the product and thereby affects competitive position. Considering the continuous improvement efforts of competitors that manufacture similar products or services, it is necessary to understand the need for continuous improvement. This can be achieved by the internal customer getting the internal supplier the information needed to meet the quality requirements.

Preproduction or Pilot Runs

This is an issue that arises with the manufacture of a new product. The rationale for a preproduction run is to put lots of the product through the entire system to detect deficiencies of the entire process. The need for preproduction runs becomes necessary to determine whether the end product will meet the quality requirements of the customer.

The use of preproduction runs or pilot runs depends on various factors, the chief among them being:

1. Does the new product have untested quality or performance factors? In the case of the camshaft example, the key factor was the keyslot on the pilot, which had not been tried on a camshaft by our customer, as a locating point for grinding the lobes.

2. Are the machines and processes used either new or untried? When manufacturing a new product, usually new machines, retrofitted machines, or retooled machines are used. Therefore the sequencing of operations is often different from previous experience, meaning that the machines and processes have to be tested for performance.

3. Are there difficulties in the use of the new product? This can be detected by actually letting the customer use the product. One of the biggest problems with using the new camshaft was the keyway, which was the primary untested feature on the camshaft. After nu-

Feedback Loops Setting Up Internal
and External Customers for Camshaft
Manufacturing Process.

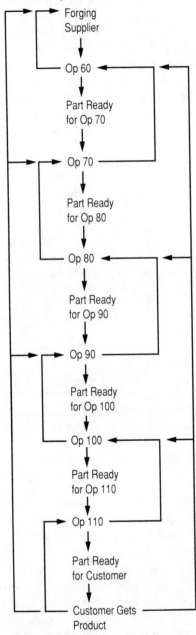

Forging
Supplier

Op 60

Part Ready
for Op 70

Op 70

Part Ready
for Op 80

Op 80

Part Ready
for Op 90

Op 90

Part Ready
for Op 100

Op 100

Part Ready
for Op 110

Op 110

Part Ready
for Customer

Customer Gets
Product

External Customer Input May Be to
Management, So Information
Is Passed On to the Actual Operation.

Figure 2.2 Internal customers
and feedback loops. (Lines and
arrows indicate feedback loops.)

merous tests and trials with the keyway, the key, and the sprocket that mounts the cam could a satisfactory design be reached.

To this end, the satisfactory performance of the product has to be determined. This may mean corrosion resistance, strength, life cycle, and so on, have to be determined to see if the minimum acceptable limits are met. In the case of the camshaft, most of the product validation tests were performed by our customers.

Process Routing Sheet

The first step in process development is the creation of a process routing sheet. The process routing sheet provides all the people involved with the product a pictorial description of each operation in the manufacturing process, provides specifications based on customer requirements, and gives current engineering change levels by which the process is being evaluated. In addition, the process routing sheet presents critical features of specific operations and the tooling associated with those operations. The requirements for such a sheet are the listing of part name, part number, customer name, operation number, and date the sheets were set up, along with all revision dates. Complete description of the operations involved and machine description must be listed on the sheet; the gaging used to ensure the process meets its requirements should also be listed. While developing the process routing sheet, it is also necessary to develop a process flow diagram, shown in Fig. 2.3. Figure 2.4 shows a sample process routing sheet for the camshaft example we will be using throughout this book. The final process routing sheets may be developed in multiple stages since the pilot part may actually be produced with current equipment while waiting for the actual manufacturing process to become available. Pilot runs attempt to use all the equipment that is currently available to avoid investment in new tooling, since the effort may be to weed out any flaws in the product which prevent or hinder processing.

Quality Function Deployment

Originally developed by Dr. Yoji Akao, quality function deployment (QFD) is a planning tool that allows a company to predict the features that a customer wants in a product, through the use of market research and then translates them into required engineering specifications. QFD is more directly related to consumer products where the manufacturer has greater control on product design; it may not be directly applicable to manufacturers who do not have direct control on the design of the product, for example, to a supplier of parts to an au-

PRODUCTION FLOWCHART

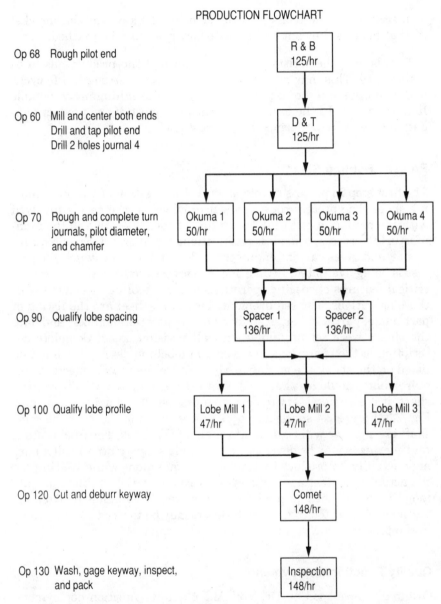

Op 68   Rough pilot end

Op 60   Mill and center both ends
        Drill and tap pilot end
        Drill 2 holes journal 4

Op 70   Rough and complete turn
        journals, pilot diameter,
        and chamfer

Op 90   Qualify lobe spacing

Op 100 Qualify lobe profile

Op 120 Cut and deburr keyway

Op 130 Wash, gage keyway, inspect,
        and pack

Figure 2.3 Flowchart showing process flow.

tomotive manufacturer, since the end product is clearly specified by the customer. But the use of customer input would help determine a better processing sequence, so that the user is better satisfied with the product. Using QFD can result in key cost reductions and a more successful product. While most manufacturing customers will specify the

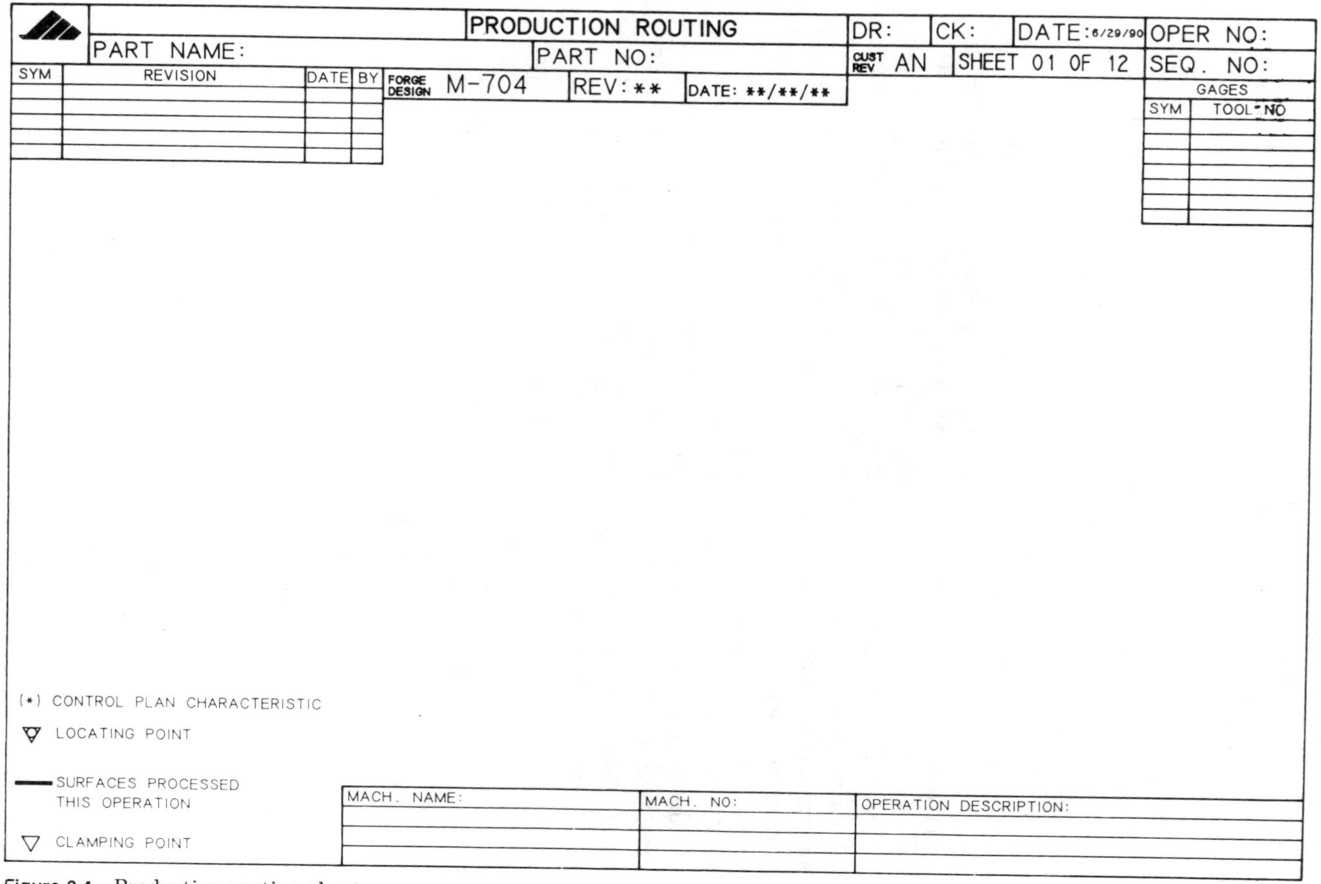

PRODUCTION ROUTING

PART NAME:

PART NO:

SYM	REVISION				

DATE BY

FORGE DESIGN M-704

REV: ** DATE: **/**/**

DR: CK: DATE: 6/29/90

CUST REV AN SHEET 01 OF 12

OPER NO:

SEQ. NO:

GAGES

SYM	TOOL NO

OPERATION DESCRIPTION:

MACH. NAME:

MACH. NO:

(∗) CONTROL PLAN CHARACTERISTIC

▽ LOCATING POINT

— SURFACES PROCESSED
THIS OPERATION

▽ CLAMPING POINT

Figure 2.4 Production routing sheet.

dimensional requirements, certain requirements have a much higher priority than others, and other specifications may not be put in writing but are expected by the customer. Identifying these customer requirements prior to product design helps translate them into quantified design characteristics that are then implemented. QFD also helps to choose the appropriate manufacturing process and to build in product reliability, while reducing cost and meeting the quality requirements. QFD is a method of responding to the customer requirements. Deployment of QFD systems along with the parameters of design for manufacturability and assembly results in optimal quality.

The effective implementation of QFD requires three ingredients to come together: correct and timely information, a well-defined and disciplined manufacturing process and knowledgeable people. The use of QFD tools for continuous improvement, leading to meeting the strategic objectives of a top-down TQM system is shown in Fig. 2.5. All the stages of a product's life cycle during the initial design stage and engineering product cost and performance to meet the desired goals are shown. QFD matrices are set throughout to focus on customer requirements. Effective utilization of these matrices requires computer-aided engineering, project management tools, and communication tools such as simulation models and market analysis models.

Pilot projects are an essential part of the QFD implementation process, with the size selected so that a good sample results. Using a very large sample may be risky and success is jeopardized. On the other hand using a small sample may risk all the functions not being in-

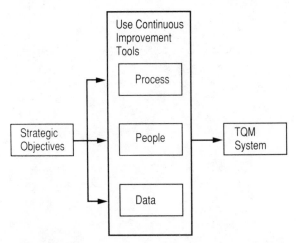

Figure 2.5 Using QFD techniques for implementing TQM systems.

cluded. A pilot run ensures actual production conditions being simulated without overextending in a new manufacturing situation.

The key QFD issues for improving competitive position are cost, responsiveness, timing, prevention, and strategic planning. To help address these issues, it often becomes necessary to define what the customer wants. Certain characteristics may not be specified in the design requirements but have to be factored into the manufacturing process since the customer expects them. One of the problems we faced was the gripper marks left by the chuck jaws on the end chamfers of the camshaft, which tore the engine lining when being put in the engine. The gripper marks on the chamfer were not removed during the grinding process, and neither was there any specification on the drawing disallowing that. This meant that to satisfy the customer we had to redesign the grippers so no marks were left on the chamfers.

Once the customer requirements are defined, the next step in the process is prioritizing those requirements based on present performance gaps, quantifying them if possible. Once this is done then these customer requirements have to be translated into design requirements using target values rather than engineering limits. Used carefully, QFD can be important in designing engineering parameters into the product. QFD methods are an important part of the overall TQM strategy.

Design for Manufacturability and Assembly

Effective manufacturing systems require effective interaction between design and manufacturing functions, and this is one of the biggest bottlenecks in the TQM system. Traditionally design has more often than not ignored the needs of manufacturing, with the result that once the concept is in the hands of manufacturing, they have to keep going back to design for changes and fixes to make the product more manufacturable. Another question in setting up the process is how the flexibility of the process can be enhanced while keeping the reliability and maintainability of the system. The answer to these questions lies in the use of numerous techniques offered by simulation, computer-aided design, and design for manufacturability and assembly (DFMA). The last of these three is perhaps the most critical and fastest-growing tool in process planning. The new concept is to concurrently run both design and manufacturing processes, so that we may identify the appropriate manufacturing or assembly system and at the same time relate this to a careful structural analysis of the product design for its overall efficiency for the chosen manufacturing or assembly method. The way to go about this is to break down the walls between design and manufacturing, and when a new project is undertaken, all the related departments compare notes, creating continuous feedback that curbs late fixes and helps get the product out in time. This helps reduce the cycle time from conception to production. DFMA helps attain the most efficient method for manufacturing the product and is sometimes termed *concurrent engineering* or *simultaneous engineering*.

Implementing DFMA may mean that the design departments of numerous organizations that out-source the manufactured product work closely with the suppliers so that the required manufacturing efficiencies may be attained. One of the biggest roadblocks to the successful implementation of simultaneous engineering is the failure of users to understand that DFMA has more to do with people and communication than with engineering. DFMA sees all the engineering functions, from design until final inspection, in the context of a total process. DFMA integrates the process of product design and the process of manufacture at the same time. It also attacks the engineering problems but does not limit the focus to the detailed assignment and measurement of individual tasks. DFMA helps reduce the cycle time from conception to production.

The biggest obstacles to concurrent engineering are middle management and lack of computerized tools. Many of the middle managers who head engineering and design fear losing control as a result of using these techniques, because lines for reporting become blurred. In larger companies the fact that the computers are not linked to provide interaction between departments can mean that communication between departments is managed using paper only, considerably slowing the effectiveness of the DFMA system. However, with the implementation of newer computer communication systems, this obstacle is almost disappearing.

Another factor in the failure of DFMA systems is the fact that a supplier may have almost no control on the design of the product but be supposed to come up with a manufacturing system based on the design. Many larger corporations are overcoming this by letting the supplier come up with the entire idea from design to engineering to manufacturing, and others are involving the vendors of purchased parts in the design stage. Once simultaneous engineering techniques are adopted, the biggest benefit is the reduction in time to market without compromising quality.

Value Engineering

Value engineering is another powerful tool in the TQM process. The purpose of this technique is to reduce the excess cost of design, and it is based on the premise that many existing designs can be improved substantially since the original design has substantial excess costs. In a limited way the goals of value engineering are similar to the goals of design for manufacturability and assembly—to effect changes in the design to reduce the net cost of the product. Value engineering uses Pareto analysis to make the most cost-effective changes to the process to find the problems that give the biggest increase in savings. The sequence of steps involved in the value engineering process is

1. Define the problem.
2. Get information.
3. Define and evaluate functions.
4. Create solutions.
5. Test solutions.
6. Recommend solutions.

The basic principles of value engineering are similar to the problem-solving and continuous improvement methods described in Chap. 9. While defining the problem, it is often necessary to quantify the goal in dollar values and savings. The solution with the biggest cost savings potential should be given the highest priority. Once the problem, quantified in cost terms, is defined, pertinent information must be obtained from all possible sources, including engineering, purchasing, and marketing. Based on these evaluations, solutions must be created. If possible, come up with multiple solutions to the problem in question. Evaluate each solution to determine which is the most cost-effective to implement. Based on the evaluation recommend a solution. A more detailed analysis of these methods is described as a part of Chap. 8.

Computerized Simulation

Another powerful tool in the planning for quality is computer simulation of real-world process over time. These simulation models provide a new way to ask and answer "what-if" questions, and they define the interrelationships of the various elements of the manufacturing facility. Executing the model causes time to advance just as the plant would actually operate. Statistics are automatically collected to report bottleneck operations, equipment usage, levels of work-in-process inventories, and factory throughput for the various products. Some of the newer simulation packages offer the facility for finite-capacity planning and scheduling systems that offer no compromise to the manufacturing manager in level of detail or precision of the models. This kind of experimentation can actually be done extremely fast and help balance the trade-offs among high utilization of facilities, work-in-process inventory levels, and shipping dates to the customers which a modern manufacturing manager is under constant pressure to achieve. These models can become powerful tools in the TQM process.

Control Plan

Based on the process sheet, the next step in the quality management system is the control plan. Once the process for manufacture has been decided upon, a control plan has to be worked out. The main reason for determining the control plan is to establish a system of features to control so that the end product meets the requirements of the customer. The control plan requires identification of the method of gaging for a particular feature, the method of monitoring (like X-bar and R charts) and what to do in case a nonconformance to specification occurs.

Identification of issues related to implementation of a control plan

The first step in the TQM system is planning the manufacturing process and determining the control plan to work with. Once the process is decided upon, the form shown in Fig. 2.6, based on the process sheets, is filled out. The information collected includes the dimensions to be checked and the methodology for gaging the dimension under consideration, including the type of gage to be used and the type of charting to be used, such as X-bar or R charts. The control plan also tells what to do in case a nonconformance is detected. Documenting and following the control plan helps avoid situations leading to nonconforming parts being made, and in the event nonconforming parts are made, then avoiding situations where these parts reach the customer, leading to further complications. Any time nonconforming parts are made it is necessary to isolate these parts and tag them so they are not accidentally shipped to the customer. Accidental shipping of nonconforming parts to the customer is probably one of the biggest causes for customer complaint, with the supplier discovering the situation only after the parts have been shipped. In this book most of the effort will be dedicated to prevent situations leading to nonconforming parts and establishing systems that detect process problems prior to the parts being produced. The above goals will be attained by studying the variations in the process and developing methods to minimize the effect of these variations. In implementing the control plans, certain basic statistical tools will be required. The tools needed in the TQM system are the indices that measure machine capability. The indices

Figure 2.6 Control plan.

CONTROL PLAN

Pg. __ of __

CUSTOMER: _____
PART NO.: _____
PART NAME: _____

DRAWING NO. & REVISION: _____
CUSTOMER REV. NO.: _____
DATE: _____

CONTROL CHARACTERISTICS: _____   METALL.: _____   MFG: _____   ENG: _____   Q.A.: _____

A   E   I   M   Q
B   F   J   N   R
C   G   K   O   S
D   H   L   P   T

CONTROL STATION	CHARACTERISTIC	EVALUATION/ANALYSIS METHOD	FREQUENCY/SAMPLE SIZE	REACTION TO NONCONFORMANCE

of machine capability and the underlying assumptions during the evaluations of machine capabilities are discussed below.

Indexes for measuring process capability

The indexes of capability are statistical tools that take the information contained in a histogram and reduce it to a single number. These indexes are based on the tolerance specified for the part, and when all the parts fall within the dimensional variation, then a histogram is formed which has the ideal bell shape, where 99.73 percent of all parts fall within a range of plus or minus three standard deviations. Figure 2.7 shows a normal distribution around the mean, and for this type of distribution the calculations are valid. It must be remembered here that these calculations are only valid if they are applied to normally distributed data. The calculations for determining these parameters when the distribution is skewed are not dealt with in this book. These tools for measuring the capability of the machine, including the type of distribution, forms the basis for measuring the performance of the processing equipment.

The Cp (process capability) index.   This is the ratio of the tolerance to six standard deviations. This can be stated mathematically as

$$Cp = \text{tolerance}/6\sigma$$

Based on the value of tolerance obtained, the following conclusions can be drawn about the process:

$$Cp > 1.33 \qquad \text{Process is capable.}$$

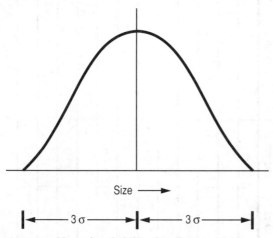

Size ⟶

$$|\!\!\longleftarrow\!\!-3\sigma\longrightarrow\!\!|\!\!\longleftarrow\!\!-3\sigma\longrightarrow\!\!|$$

Figure 2.7   Normal probability distribution: histogram.

1.33 > Cp > 1.00   Process is capable but should be monitored.

Cp > 1.00   Process is not capable.

If the mean of the measurements is not at the midpoint of the data, then the Cp values become less precise and can be made more capable by shifting the mean. Suppose a part has a given critical dimension with a tolerance of ±.005 in, and we want to hold our parts to half that tolerance, that is, we wish the parts to be within ±.0025 in; then the characteristic must have a value of 2.0.

The Cpk (process performance) index. This index is the measure of the data based on the worst-case view of the data, and takes the centering of the data into consideration. The computation of Cpk values can be stated mathematically as:

Cpk = Lesser of   (USL − mean)/3σ or   (mean − LSL)/3σ

where USL = upper specification limit and LSL = lower specification limit. Let's tabulate the results obtained by computing the Cpk values:

Cpk < 0   Mean is outside specification limits.

Cpk = 0   Mean is at one of the specification limits.

0 < Cpk < 1 Part of the 6σ limits fall outside the specification limits.

Cpk > 1 6σ limits fall completely in the specification limit.

Cpk is a measure of how well a machine's process capability hits the target. This means that if our machine has to produce a part with a dimension of 1.435 in ± .005 and if the tolerance held is ±.0025 in but the part size has a mean value of 1.440, then 50 percent of the parts fall outside the specified limits and may be oversize. So Cpk is the parameter that measures how centered the process is around the required mean. In an ideal situation Cp and Cpk will be the same. The value of Cp is always greater than Cpk and can almost equal the value of Cp, and so Cpk is the more important measure of process capability. Since Cp and Cpk are two of the most powerful tools that will be continually used throughout your TQM system, these concepts will come up repeatedly in this book as various aspects of using Cp and Cpk are discussed.

One important thing to remember is that Cpk is not a valid measure for a statistically one-sided characteristic, such as true position, runout, or surface finish, and in this case Cp must be used. Here the Cp's are computed by using the ratio of tolerance divided by three standard deviations. Another problem encountered with the calculations described above is that these computations are not valid if the distributions are not normally distributed. The methods for calculating Cpk for distributions that are not normally distributed are described later in this book.

Estimating scrap and rework—normal distribution

One of the most important tools handed to us by the use of statistics is in estimating the percentage of scrap and rework produced by the manufacturing system, especially for normally distributed systems. For computing the scrap and rework, the first step is to compute the values of

$$(\text{LSL} - \overline{X})/\sigma \quad \text{and} \quad (\text{USL} - \overline{X})/\sigma$$

Based on the numerical values computed, we need to look up the areas that lie outside the specification limits of both the numbers computed above. The tables for areas outside the specification can be obtained from *Statistical Quality Control* by Grant and Leavenworth. Suppose the area outside the normal distribution curve as obtained from the computation of (LSL − mean)/σ is A_1 and the area under the curve (USL − mean)/σ is A_2; then the fraction of scrap produced by the process is computed by the relationship

$$\text{Scrap and rework rate} = A_1 + 1 - A_2$$

$$\text{Rework rate} = 1 - A_2$$

$$\text{Scrap rate} = A_1$$

This is also based on the assumption that parts over the upper specification limit are reworkable and parts below the lower specification limit are scrap, in addition to the assumption of a normal distribution. However, in case of internal diameters, the situation is reversed and smaller diameters are reworkable, while diameters over the upper limit are scrapped.

Estimating scrap and rework—nonnormal distribution

The next problem that arises is how to compute the scrap and rework on a nonnormal distribution. Data that do not conform to the definition of normally distributed data forming the classic bell-shaped curve around the mean can be classified into three categories:

1. Roughly normal data
2. Data that conform to Camp-Meidell conditions, or the data have a

mean equal to the mode and the frequency distribution decreases continuously around the mean

3. Data that do not conform to either of the conditions stated above

Now the computation process is slightly different. The following numbers are calculated:

$$(\overline{X} - LSL)/\sigma \quad \text{and} \quad (USL - \overline{X})/\sigma$$

Computation for the area under the curve for roughly normal data that conform to Camp-Meidell conditions are available. The sum of the areas outside the specification limit gives the percentage of scrap and rework generated by the process.

Chi-squared goodness of fit and kurtosis

Other measures of capability are the chi-squared goodness-of-fit test, the test for skewness of the normal distribution curve, and the measure of flatness of the normal distribution curve, which is termed *kurtosis*. The various types of skewness and kurtosis are shown in Figs. 2.8 and 2.9. The numerical measure of the skewness of a distribution is as under:

$$\text{Skewness}_p = 3(\overline{X} - M_e)/s$$

This measure is termed the *Pearson coefficient of skewness*, and $\overline{X}$ is the mean, M_e is the median, and s is the standard deviation. If the measure of skewness is zero, then the distribution is said to be nor-

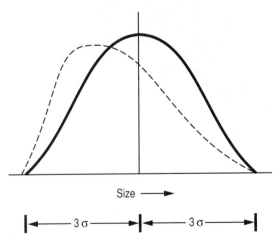

Size ⟶

|← —— 3σ —— →|← —— 3σ —— →|

Figure 2.8 Normal probability distribution: skewed distribution.

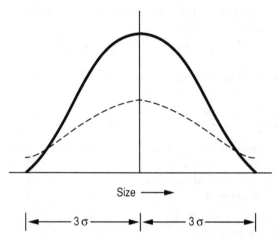

Figure 2.9 Normal probability distribution: platykurtic distribution.

mally distributed; depending on the sign, the calculated skewness is said to be positive or negative. The indexes calculated for machine capability for normally distributed data are not valid for a skewed distribution.

Similarly, the numerical measure of kurtosis is

$$\frac{\Sigma(x - \overline{X})^4}{ns^4}$$

where x is each individual piece of data, $\overline{X}$ is the mean, n is the number of pieces of data, and s is the standard deviation. Positive values for kurtosis indicate leptokurtic distribution, while negative values indicate platykurtic distribution. When the resulting histogram is flattened out it is termed platykurtic, while a distribution with an extremely narrow spread is termed leptokurtic.

Manufacturing Accounting

All the above discussions on scrap and rework raise the question of cost base accountability for the costs incurred. Before any discussion on modern techniques being developed in accounting, it is necessary to discuss conventional manufacturing accounting. The primary areas addressed in conventional accounting are cost-monitoring systems and cost-reduction systems. The bases for cost monitoring are collecting and analyzing actual costs to conventional costs and comparing them to a predetermined standard. In the process, attention is placed largely on continuous improvement of the cost structure to reduce cost of the product. Cost control requires systematic methods to develop standard costs, tracking and controlling actual costs to reach the levels of the standard. Cost-reduction programs require competitive product development and target cost development, cost data sharing, and price structure and cost estimates. Cost-monitoring and -control systems are required, since the cost of doing business, including labor, material, and overhead, cannot be controlled without an effective system that monitors how costs are incurred.

Standard cost development

These costs are developed on the basis of labor, material, and overhead costs. Each of these costs has a basis for development of standard costs. Standard costs for labor are developed on the basis of time and motion studies, taking into account direct and indirect labor. Material costs, on the other hand, are developed on the basis of direct and indirect material content of parts and components produced. Calculating overhead is more complicated and, depending on the manufacturer, may depend on the direct labor cost, direct material cost, machine hours, physical output, or any combination of the above methods. A standard labor routing sheet with standard labor allowances for each operation must be used. These standard costs must be reviewed annually, along with overhead costs and the bill of material.

Actual costs

Once the standard costs are determined, then it becomes necessary to record the actual labor hours and material used and convert these data into actual costs. Similarly, actual overhead costs should be computed. Any cost increases due to overtime labor hours should be budgeted and should be carefully managed. Based on these computations, methods should be established to identify and rectify situations where actual costs vary from standard costs. Attempts should be made to identify any trends that exist and to rectify them. A tolerance range should be established to determine when increases in cost variance are unacceptable. Day-to-day cost changes can be plotted on X-bar and R charts to establish control on the costs. Analysis of variance can also be a powerful tool in control of costs. Manufacturing accounting decisions should be made on the basis of statistical process control (SPC) techniques described later in this book.

Collection and processing of cost data

The collection and processing of cost data provides the financial interface for the TQM process. These activities can be expressed as a set of nine financial activities, using the example of a typical machine shop.

1. *Estimate cost and price.* These costs are developed based on either an existing process plan or a manufacturing plan developed for the quote. These estimates are based on the standard labor, standard machine, and vendor costs. The other costs involved in the process, such as engineering, taxes, and shipping and handling, can be classified as miscellaneous costs. This estimate is based on the type of part, the quantity produced, and operations needed, based on a knowledge of the operation sequence, operation type, setup time, run time, machine group, machine time, whether or not it is a bought-out (purchased) item, estimated vendor costs, and tooling, fixture, and material costs. The estimated vendor costs, labor hours, machine hours, cost of materials, tools, and estimated price is also arrived at this stage.

2. *Process labor vouchers.* This refers to both the engineering and production labor. Production labor can be calculated from the labor cards filled out by the operators and contains information about the machine hours and pieces completed and also helps determine the work in progress for the job. The performance of the operation determines the performance to plan and cost. Labor costs and machine costs can be directly calculated from the vouchers. Other indirect charges can be determined as a function of labor and machine hours. Correctly determining labor and machine utilization is a large part of getting an accurate job cost.

3. *Buying materials.* This is the next step in the process of accounting at machine shops. This includes buying raw materials, tooling, and other items necessary to produce the product.

4. *Sending the parts to outside vendors.* Many tasks cannot be performed in a single job shop, either due to cost constraints or availability of appropriate equipment. Shipping the parts or the material to outside vendors with detailed instructions for processing may be necessary.

5. *Material receiving.* This function coordinates and identifies all incoming materials, tools, general stock, consigned material, and parts returning from vendors. Once the quantity received and accepted is recorded, the actual schedule, inventory data, and status data for individual lots using outside services can be updated.

6. *Receiving invoice from vendor.* This information is entered in accounts receivable and contains the actual charges of supplies or services delivered to the shop. Actual cost data may be fed into the job cost in the form of adjustments to the cost estimate, which is used to relieve work-in-process inventory.

7. *Invoice shipment.* This involves shipping finished parts to the customer and recording the number of parts shipped. Based on the

number of parts shipped, the invoice is generated. This forms the planning control system and helps monitor any returned goods.

8. *Relieve work in process based on parts invoiced.* This step tracks the work-in-process costs based on maintaining current production costs and relieving those pieces based on invoiced pieces. The direct labor costs and the direct machine costs will be calculated from the labor voucher against a particular lot.

9. *Compare actual costs against standard costs.* This is the final step in the process of estimating actual costs. The standards can be measured based on motion studies, averages from previous production runs, or based on similar parts, and becomes the tool for performance measurement and cost control. The accuracy of the standard can be revised over time.

The steps described above constitute the traditional approach to accounting in a job shop. A chart showing the interface between planning and control and accounting in the job shop is shown in Fig. 2.10.

Cost-reduction efforts

Based on the analysis of the data, the manufacturer should focus attention on continuous cost improvement, based on systems for scrap

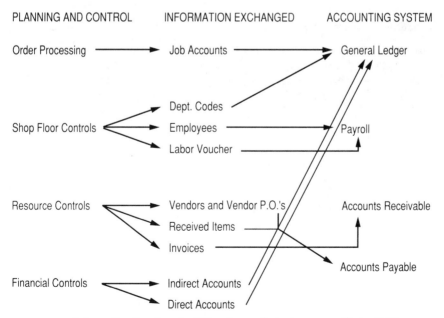

Figure 2.10   Information flow in a traditional manufacturing accounting system.

reduction, productivity improvement, inventory reduction to approach just-in-time levels, supplier optimization, capital optimization, and standardization. Similarly, efforts should be made using simultaneous engineering techniques to develop a competitive product development and pricing. Based on all of these, a pricing structure and cost estimate should be developed.

The cost accounting system using standard costs and actual costs has certain drawbacks and limitations in the modern manufacturing environment. Most modern manufacturing environments with high levels of automation do not relate to the older systems where labor force accounts for 80 percent of the manufacturing costs and costs were directly proportional to the direct labor. With most modern manufacturing systems, labor costs do not account for more than 25 percent of the cost. Existing systems based on standard costs and actual costs attempt to relate the process changes and improvement in terms of labor savings. Moreover, the existing systems fail to account for scrap and rework, which is the same as not producing. Downtime does not eliminate the cost of wages, electricity, heat, interest on borrowed money, and so on. Another problem with traditional accounting systems is the failure to account for increased uptime as a result of automation. Automation only shows up as a cost. This analysis shows the need for an accounting system which overcomes the shortcomings of traditional accounting.

Modern manufacturing accounting

Modern manufacturing requires accounting to be an integral part of the TQM system strategy. Manufacturing accounting requires us to work around the limitations of traditional cost accounting where cost is directly related to direct labor costs, with everything else lumped into overhead. In fact, when quoting for new jobs, cost estimates are based on a direct proportion to labor costs. All other costs are based on purely arbitrary ratios and are more often than not misleading. Process improvements are quantified into labor cost savings, while any other savings, if considered at all, are based on arbitrary measures. Cost of not producing is not taken into account. Cost of downtime, scrap, rework, and so on, is not accounted for in traditional cost accounting but becomes an important part of the cost in manufacturing accounting. The accounting for this is done by assuming good products are produced 80 percent of the time, but in reality the downtime is actually more than 20 percent and these add to the cost in wages, electricity, interest, and raw materials. Most manufacturing systems quantify automation as a cost, but automation fails to show up in the benefits column of our accounting system. Automation reduces nonproductive time by improving quality and by reducing machine downtime for product changeover. Manufacturing accounting based on the computer-aided manufacturing—international, CAM-I, standard uses time as the basis for determining the cost of the product. This manufacturing accounting standard is based on the fact that all costs for a given period of time are constant and are not purely a function of the labor costs. Material costs are assumed to be constant, since defectives use as much material as a good product. Time is the only variable and controllable factor, and it measures how long it takes to produce a good product. Process improvements result in decrease in time taken to produce a quality product. Finished goods inventory cannot therefore be considered an asset as accounted for in traditional cost accounting, but is seen as a sunk cost tying down cash flow. One of the biggest disadvantages of manufacturing accounting is its inability to deal with intangibles, such as the return on investment in automation or the risk in not making an investment in overcoming production bottlenecks. In-plant cost and benefits of a particular decision can be worked out easily, but the business consequences of not taking the decision cannot be accurately judged. Most manufacturing accountants agree that these intangible costs have to be integrated into manufacturing costs, but disagree how these costs can be accounted for.

Cost of quality

Another aspect of manufacturing accounting is measuring the costs associated with producing a nonconforming part, termed the *cost of quality*. Cost of quality is perhaps the most commonly used technique in industry, since this measure does not involve a detailed knowledge of accounting systems and gives the members of the organization a quantified measure of the losses to the organization as a result of the scrap and rework generated that is simple to understand. The first step in measuring the scrap costs is identifying the amount of scrap generated by each operation of the manufacturing process. An example is shown in Fig. 2.11 showing a pie chart of the actual fraction of the number of scrap cams produced. In Fig. 2.12, the pie chart shows the fraction of the cost associated with fraction of scrap created by that operation. We use the pie chart showing the cost of producing the nonconforming part as the basis for determining which problem to tackle on priority basis. The cost of quality is the criterion we use to determine the most important problem to tackle. Cost of quality is dealt with further in Chap. 9. This type of quantification can also take the form of a Pareto chart, where the factors resulting in the highest cost for producing a nonconforming part are identified with the intent to tackle the highest-cost problem. The use of a Pareto chart is described

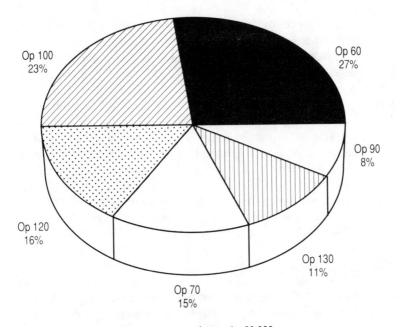

Op 100
23%

Op 60
27%

Op 90
8%

Op 120
16%

Op 130
11%

Op 70
15%

Total pieces manufactured = 20,000

Figure 2.11   Scrap report: actual pieces (= 597).

later in Chap. 9. The main advantage of using cost of quality as a tool for management is that a dollar value is associated with the scrap produced, giving the means to attack the problem causing the most losses. It is important to also identify problems that can be easily solved, compared to the one whose solutions are long and drawn out.

Based on the assessment of cost of quality, it is necessary to develop a suitable corrective action consistent with the goals of the organization. Cause-and-effect analysis can be used to determine the best method to correct the problem and prevent it from recurring.

Requirements for Running Initial Samples

Once the process planning process is completed, one of the first requirements is to manufacture initial samples and check all the features as per customer specifications. The parts should be made to the approved drawings and engineering specifications from specified materials using regular production tooling, with no operations included that will not be included in the regular production processing, unless authorized by the customer. One of the requirements for any such tests is to ensure that the gaging used meets the gage repeatability

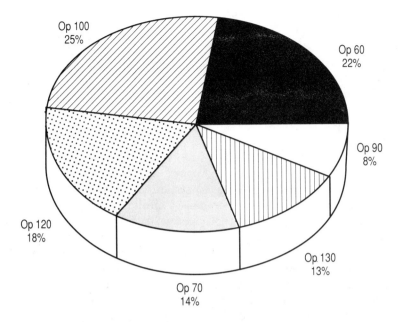

Number of cams produced = 20,000

Figure 2.12   Scrap report, January 1991: total cost = $4731.70.

and reproducibility specifications. If the part does not meet the specification report, then it must be noted on the sample inspection report and efforts must be made to rectify the situation as early as possible. The initial sample should include the following documentation with the samples:

1. Correct quantity and types of samples as requested by the customer

2. Marked print referenced to the layout report including any deviations, waivers, and so on

3. Copies of all laboratory test data

4. All tooling aids, such as fixtures and templates, when requested by the customer

5. All inspection reports, including samples

6. Process control plans

7. Failure modes and effects analysis

8. Data sheets, X-bar and R charts, capability studies

9. Process routing sheets

10. Flow diagrams

A change in any of the following parameters will result in getting a new sample to be detailed: any changes in subcontractor or sources, moving existing tooling to a new plant, changes to an optional material, any significant change in method of manufacture, using multiple locations to manufacture the part, and manufacture of additional or replacement tooling.

Instructions for Operations

Once all of these conditions have been met, another important requirement is to ensure that process instructions are documented. These written documents must encompass techniques being used to provide products of a consistent, acceptable quality level, including in-process statistical process control system. The methodology for interpreting the process control charts is dealt with in a later chapter. These documents must be updated and signed and made available for review. Any changes in the process, or the revision of the prints by the customer, requires an update of the process routing sheets and the process instructions so that the product specifications are met. This is the beginning of the process of establishing a TQM system. A sample instruction sheet used by our operators on one of the manufacturing processes is shown in Fig. 2.13.

Why Reduction in Variation Is the Key

While it will be repeated throughout this book, it is important to remember that the goal of using all these systems and processes is the continual reduction of variation. TQM systems can only succeed if the system is continually geared toward reduction of variation and is the path to continuous improvement of the process. Even though all the parts meet the specification, an extreme variation in the process may prevent you from meeting the quality requirements from time to time.

Before justifying the significance of reduction in variation, it is important to describe the history of manufacturing systems. Since the beginning of mass production, the goal always was to meet the specification most of the time. Many companies still pay lip-service to statistical methods and do aim to meet the specification most of the time. If the part met the specification, it was classified as a good part and passed on to the next operation. If the part failed to meet the specification, then it was classified as bad and either reworked or scrapped. The output was maintained at a high level by producing a certain percentage over the required level or accepting marginally defective items.

Reduction in variation leads to parts that are more alike and reduces the probability of producing defectives. Getting these parts

D&T—Op 60

PRESET GAGE:

1. Use the preset gage to set all tools.

GAGE:

2. Check required by the operator (6 pieces per hour, unless otherwise specified, to be recorded). Ensure that 6 consecutive pieces are recorded.

Dimension	Tolerance	Gage
1. Ball to ball (BB)	±.010	Electronic/fixture
2. Ball to pilot face (BPF)	±.010	Electronic/fixture
3. Ball to journal face (BJF)	±.005	Electronic/fixture
4. Stock distribution (SD)	±.007	Electronic/fixture
5. Spring pocket 1 (SP1)	±.007	Electronic/fixture
6. Spring pocket 2 (SP2)	±.007	Electronic/fixture
7. Thread		1 in 10 pieces for depth with go gage
	100% check	$\frac{2}{3}$ turns
8. Journal 4 hole	±.015	Electronic/fixture
9. Journal 4 hole location	±.005	Omni gage

3. Master your gage 3 times/shift. While mastering the gage watch for *master reversal error* at the bottom of the screen. If *master reversal error* occurs do not use the gage until it has been checked out.

MACHINE:

4. Before setting up drills/inserts/taps, etc., be sure to clean holders, etc.

5. Ensure that all clamps are working properly. If not, inform your foreman immediately.

6. In the event of a crash (station does not back out before the turnion indexes, etc.) inform the quality control department before running the machine.

7. Do not attempt any kind of rework on a part once it has been unclamped.

8. Check stop for stock distribution once a shift to ensure that it is not worn out.

9. Report any abnormalities on the machine such as noise or vibrations immediately.

10. Clean chips at regular intervals to ensure smooth operation of the machine.

11. Follow the sequence provided on the next sheet to determine which drill to move.

Figure 2.13   Operating instructions for operation 60.

closer to the nominal results in a more reliable process increases customer satisfaction, because the customer knows what to expect. Process output will be known with certainty, and any changes to the process will be more predictable.

Let us consider the example of the camshaft forging with an axial length of $x \pm .02$ in. Suppose the process is centered on the mean and we have a process capability of .34. From the calculations for scrap and rework, we now have a situation where 33 percent of the parts are below the lower specification, while 33 percent of the parts are over the upper specification. This means that we now require a total tolerance of $\pm .06$ in and we can only manufacture the part to the specification of $x \pm .06$. This means that we have to increase the design of the part to $(x + .04) \pm .06$, so that the minimum length requirements will be met. If all the other dimensions were similarly affected, we would be adding .04 in to all the dimensions on the forging. This increases the cost of production in two ways:

1. Increase in material used.
2. Increase in the cost of metal removal, as the .040 in extra stock has to be removed.

In the original manufacturing process, whenever a situation arose leading to non-cleanup on the forging during the machining process, the immediate response was to add material to the affected dimension. Understanding process variation and developing means to reduce this variation leads to decrease in stock on the forging. The above calculations were made with the assumption that the process is targeted around the process center. Should the process not be centered, then the increase in stock on the forging for metal removal may be considerably higher.

Taguchi Loss Function—A Different Approach to Defining Quality

The Taguchi loss function recognizes the needs of the customer to have a product that is consistent, piece to piece, and the producer's need to manufacture a low-cost part. Taguchi recognizes these seemingly opposing needs in terms of the loss to society, which consists of the cost of manufacturing the product and the cost to the consumer from using the product, in terms of the costs of repair and other costs. A detailed discussion on the Taguchi loss function is dealt with later in Chap. 10.

The People Side of TQM

What Is the People Side?

The success or failure of TQM systems depends on the people working within the organization. The traditional concepts of managing people using discipline as the basic tool has to give way to motivating them to contribute to the process. The employees have to feel respected and valued to make a meaningful contribution to the process. Once this attitude is ingrained among the employees, the contributions and cost savings resulting from the TQM systems will amaze you.

Another problem with the management vision of quality is that many organizations are steeped in the traditional view of quality, which defines quality as conforming to customers' requirements in terms of the final product specifications. This view of quality, which is often termed the *little q,* must change. Every element of the business has to view quality as its overriding goal, and the quality of every element of the business contributes to the overall customer satisfaction. This means that quality starting from supplies received from suppliers to every aspect of the business contributes to the quality of the final product. Every aspect of the customer's requirements, including price, service, reliability, safety, delivery, and courtesy, are important to the organization. This big picture is often termed *big Q.* TQM is about change, and about instilling the values of a big Q attitude throughout the organization. The people are the most important element of the failure or success of the TQM program. Each employee has to define progress in terms of meeting the customer's requirements. Failure of management to consider employees as valuable partners in the process of quality management can lead to system failures.

The people side of TQM involves the use of two powerful tools— training for problem solving and using a team approach to problem solving. The team approach to problem solving fits better in the context of problem-solving methods and is discussed later in this book. This chapter deals with the training requirements for various levels of personnel that will be required to successfully implement a TQM system.

The Vision Thing

Before going on to the various aspects of training, it is pertinent to discuss what the vision required of top management is all about. Considerable stress is placed on the leadership vision for successful implementation of the TQM strategy. Quality can only be driven by a clear and focused direction from management. The economy is in a state of flux and turmoil. The pace, magnitude, and complexity of change is much bigger than ever before, and in this environment the leadership has to have the ability to see what is possible beyond the present in terms of satisfying the needs of the customer. This is the decisive element in leading the organization and stimulates the organization to grow and change. This vision has to be transmitted to all organization members so that all the people are pursuing the same goal.

When the top management vision is translated into reality, considerable change and innovation has to be effected. All parts of the business must be integrated to support the vision and allow the organization to move quickly. The primary goals of this strategic vision include continuously improving quality, reducing time, increasing flexibility, and empowering the people. Improvements to each of these parameters cannot be effected on just a segment of the business, and the basic equation of improvement must change to include every element of the business, revolving around the TQM objective. This type of a holistic strategy can lead to business integration and overall improvement in quality.

The vision to see beyond the present must include managing technology to this. Managing technology involves comparing the levels of technology used by you to that of your competitors, creating a technology investment strategy, and comparing your technology levels to emerging technologies, with a firm understanding of your customer needs. This means understanding how the competition is moving and implementing systems to measure your effectiveness. Harnessing technology to corporate vision for competitive advantage is often referred to as leveraging technology. The actual techniques are termed benchmarking, and are described later in the book.

Besides all of these systems and parameters to manage the vision of TQM is the need to create a participative management where everyone is involved in the process of implementing or creating systems that meet the organization's vision. No leader can implement or meet his or her vision alone; every element in the organization has to be driven by the corporate vision.

The final element is developing external relationships conforming to the corporate vision. External elements include all suppliers of goods and services to the company, the quality of which must be managed.

Training for Quality

One of the most important facets of the TQM system is the participation of every level of personnel within the company to the quality process and getting appropriate inputs from them. This process can be accelerated and improved by providing appropriate tools to all levels of personnel. While the rest of this discussion ponders the importance of direct quality training, there are other aspects of training, such as cross training in other functional departments to ensure a better understanding of other related functions.

Why train your people?

Before beginning your training programs, it is necessary to ask the question, what is the purpose of training? The answer could be one or several of the following:

- Foster an attitude of change.
- Make all employees view the business from the customer's point of view.
- Demonstrate management commitment to continuous improvement.
- Develop skills in workers, leading to solutions to problems.
- Encourage employee decision making.
- Encourage group problem-solving skills.
- Provide the tools necessary to provide quality service to customers.
- Build a team spirit among the workers.

Who should be trained?

This one factor will be the critical variable in determining how successful the TQM system will be. Training should not be short-term, but should be a continuous reinforcement of the learning process. Depending on the level of the personnel in the organization, different levels of quality education and training are required. Basically, organizations can be divided into four levels:

1. Top management, including owners, presidents, and vice presidents

2. Middle managers, including department chiefs and plant managers

3. Engineering, design, and R&D personnel

4. Supervisory personnel and operators

Some of the training offered will overlap or be omitted, depending on the defined organizational responsibility. For example, some of the training offered to the engineering personnel may be offered to the SPC facilitator and the supervisors, but not to the operators. Offering a common course which introduces the concept of quality control, including aspects such as zero defects, continuous improvement, and other general concepts of quality such as nonconformance is critical to creating a uniform mindset throughout the organization. The training offered has to be put to use within the organization for running a successful quality management system. The teachings of one of the TQM gurus such as Deming or Juran can be used as the basis for introducing the TQM system and this is dealt with later in this chapter. The level of training and other training-related issues can be decided using a systems approach, as shown in Fig. 3.1.

Four important considerations in determining a training program are

1. Clearly define the objectives of the training program.

2. Develop a training program to match the objectives of the training program.

3. Training programs should not be exclusive of either technical or behavioral content.

4. Get the input of the participants, in a formal or informal manner, to improve the quality of the training program.

The various types of training programs that should be considered essential to the successful implementation of the total quality management program are as follows.

1. *Leadership.*   This training has to be different from conventional training, since management has to be trained to share decision-making responsibilities. They have to forget the conventional route of managing employees through discipline. This also means that the top management has to go out and emphasize the importance of the contributions of the employees and show their appreciation for them. Many members of top management teams have an inherent reluctance to share power by delegating decision-making authority lower down the organization ladder. Without a top management vision,

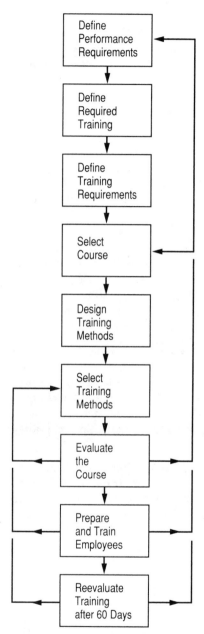

Figure 3.1 A systems approach to TQM training.

there can be no total quality management. The leadership training programs should attempt to teach the leaders of the organization these skills, the most important being the vision of seeing quality as an issue of conforming to requirements, and seeing what a TQM strategy can do.

Another problem leadership faces is the resistance to change. Leadership must instill the understanding that business cannot continue as it always has. Nurturing change is another important task for top management. Change has to come about as a result of understanding the importance of the use of statistical methods for managing quality. Top management has to have a strong conviction in the effectiveness of using statistical methods as the basis for improving efficiency and reducing waste.

2. *Strategic planning.* This is an important skill top and middle managers have to learn. The strategy of the company should revolve around the quality management systems, and planning should be such that a quality product results. Conventional strategic plans have revolved around the methods to increase market share, increasing sales, increasing profitability, and such. These goals are automatically attained by using TQM strategies in your planning process. TQM strategies improve your competitive position and, in turn, result in a cost-effective, quality product and a resulting increase in market share. The strategic planners should see that an overall quality management strategy automatically leads to improved profitability, increase in sales, and market share.

3. *Supplier involvement.* The first step in involving suppliers is training your own buyer to demand and expect only quality product from your suppliers. The next step in the process is to train the supplier in the TQM philosophy adopted by your company and what is expected of them. Many of the larger companies do offer such training to their suppliers. The numerous techniques to manage supplier quality are dealt with in Chap. 8.

4. *Internal and external customer satisfaction.* Normally, the manufacture of a product requires the use of numerous steps. At each point the person getting the input is the customer and should be treated as any external customer to the organization would be treated. Most external customers will not accept anything less than zero defects, and all personnel should be trained in the concept of internal and external customer.

5. *Statistical analysis.* This may consist of numerous aspects, from simple graphing, histograms, Pareto analysis, and X-bar and R charts to complex statistical methods such as design of experiments. Training in these methods has to be offered to all levels of employees. Depending on the level of the personnel, suitable levels of training may be offered to them. Many larger organizations do offer training to the employees of their suppliers as a part of getting the supplier to meet the quality requirements.

6. *Cost of quality.* The concept of cost of quality has been dealt with earlier, and by the most commonly accepted definition is the cost associated with producing a nonconforming part. Usually the information is documented by someone in the accounting or quality control department. All levels of personnel should be trained in interpreting the charts depicting cost of quality so that they can understand how much it costs to produce a nonconforming part. The understanding of cost of quality charts often leads to operator endeavors to correct numerous problems either by bringing them to engineering's attention, or, if possible, fixing them themselves.

7. *Continuous improvement.* For remaining competitive, it is necessary to improve the processes continuously. Training for continuous improvement is an important part of the TQM strategy, and the sequential steps for effecting continuous improvement are dealt with later in this book. Many of the statistical tools offer operators important skills in identifying problems with the process and offering suggestions to improve the process. A very important part of the continuous improvement process is training the machine operators to correctly identify problems and suggest possible solutions.

8. *Employee involvement in a team environment.* While employee involvement in the decision-making process is not a new concept, employees working as teams is new in most American work environments. To avoid bitterness among the team participants, each member must be trained in team dynamics and how to work effectively with team members.

The first step in the process of implementing a TQM training program is to determine which of the areas described above require maximum attention. This can be attained by interviewing the employees at all levels.

Top management training

The first step in the process of implementing a TQM system is the orientation of the top management in the dynamics of TQM with an indepth analysis of reasons for failure of such systems:

- Failure to bridge the gap between training and implementation.
- Partial training, where only some of the members of the organizations are trained in the use of statistical process control.

Top management must also be trained in the executive management's roles and responsibilities, required long-term investment and strategic and operation planning, and the difference between management commitment and endorsement of TQM. The leadership or the top management is critical to the success of the TQM process for the following critical reasons:

1. They are required to provide the vision to unify all the quality improvement projects.
2. They are the chief motivators during the massive changes in philosophy as a result of applying TQM.
3. They have the power to change manufacturing systems and parameters before a crisis stage is reached.
4. They have the ability to allocate resources necessary for solving the problems and effecting continuous improvement.
5. Priority for continuous quality improvement at the levels offered to manufacturing, R&D, and marketing can be attained only if the top management wishes for it.
6. Only the leadership can allocate adequate training time for every level of the organization.

Middle management training

The next level in the organization that must be trained is the middle management. Middle management should be trained similarly to top management, with less emphasis on strategy and more on the overall management of quality. Considerably more emphasis is placed on tools and techniques of TQM and SPC. The actual implementation of the methods is dependent on this level of management having a clear understanding of the techniques available for use.

Training technical personnel

Once middle managers are trained in the tools of TQM, the next step in the process is training the technical personnel, who, depending on the organizational responsibility, should be trained in every aspect of TQM. The various courses in training will depend on the responsibilities. Design and verification personnel would have to be trained in CAD simulation, prototype building, design, and development tests. Manufacturing engineering and process verification would have to be trained in various aspects of SPC, reliability tests, problem-solving techniques, and so on. Technical quality assurance personnel would have to be trained in coming quality assurance methods, including SPC, product process control, and supplier process monitoring. Depending on the manufacturing process and the product, it may be necessary to offer certain specialized training to the personnel. For example, in case of electronic components, it is necessary to statistically analyze the results of burn-in tests; this is not applicable to other products.

Operator training

Finally, training the operators is a critical aspect of the successful implementation of the TQM system. Operators should be trained in SPC and actual operation of the machinery and the gaging systems used. The SPC training must essentially be in the form of programmed learning where the operators are taken through SPC in simple incremental steps. Depending on the size of the organization, an SPC facilitator or trainer may be used. Using a separate SPC facilitator offers considerable advantages over letting one of the technical personnel or supervisors train the operators, since for any training to be effective it is necessary for it to be a continuous process. The classroom training should be repeated at regular intervals for all levels in the organizations so that the initial enthusiasm for using the SPC methods is not lost. The operators should also be trained in basic problem-solving skills, where they learn to define the problem, identify the root causes, and take action if necessary to rectify the problem in systematic, scientific fashion as far as possible. This problem-solving course can be used to help operators highlight any problems that arise to the technical personnel who may be adequately equipped to solve them.

At each level of the organization, appropriate problem solving should be practiced so that the training sessions do not remain in the classroom. It may be necessary to form teams of a company steering committee consisting of a cross section of employees that gathers information from various work areas, provides recommendations to the committee, and is empowered to implement the recommendations.

How to implement training programs

There are numerous aspects to training that must be determined by top management, including where the training should be held, how much information should be imparted at various levels, and how fast information should be given. The material and content of each of the courses offered at various levels should be determined, and this is a part of the strategic planning for quality. The steps needed for quality training are defining the requirements; identifying the training requirements based on which course content is selected; designing instruction; and selecting methods and training aids such as notes, video displays, tape recording, and so on. Care should be taken to reinforce the training through repetition.

Customizing training programs

Many canned training programs are readily available, but more often than not the examples used are not related to the actual manufacturing process. Most of these canned programs use combinations of slides, video tapes, and workbooks, but are often not relatable to your own manufacturing environment. This is particularly true for operator-level training for SPC. When the operator is not able to relate to the training program, then getting him or her to use the methods will be extremely difficult. From our own experience, the best method for training operators is programmed learning, where the operators are answering simple multiple-choice questions or fill-in-the-blanks to enhance the learning process. I used a sample dimension from our shop floor as an example for creating an easier understanding of the SPC mechanism.

One more direction to look into is the possibility of using an outside consultant to implement the SPC programs. This is advantageous when the conventional wisdom of quality management has to be changed to a TQM philosophy. But this may not work as well as expected because the outside consultant may not have a good evaluation of the system existing within the company. However, if a decision is taken to hire an outside consultant, then it is usually a good idea to check if his or her views of TQM match yours, what he or she expects to change as a result of TQM systems being adopted by the company, and how these systems should be implemented. Besides this, it is also useful to check the consultant's reputation and performance with other clients. Using a consultant on a continual basis may not prove cost-effective, so more often than not the sensible course to take is to start off with an external training program followed by internally developed training programs. The importance of reinforcing the learning process by repeated training cannot be overemphasized. Besides reinforcing learning, the use of repeated training tells employees that they are important for the organization.

Where to train

This is an important question, usually decided by the level of the person in the organization and the resources of the company to develop and implement training programs. These are important considerations, but the attempt here will be to answer the question of whether the quality management program should be conducted in-house or outside the company. The key benefits of using in-house training, whether conducted by an internal or an external trainer, are

1. Reduced training costs.
2. Reduction in time taken for travel.
3. Flexible training schedules with the trainees being able to change the times depending on the tasks being performed on the shop floor.
4. Trainees can continue performing most of the day-to-day tasks.
5. Workers learn more about the quality orientation of the company and relate information learned to the actual working environment.
6. The distractions are fewer. This may not be true if the trainees are asked to attend to shop-floor problems right in the middle of the training sessions.
7. Training can be matched to class size and composition. Training outside the company may require sending people at different levels to different training programs.

The Teachings of the Gurus

No discussion on the planning for quality and quality training is complete without talking about the teachings of the gurus, since they provide us with the basic theory for developing TQM systems. While there are many gurus, the main four I will talk about are Deming, Ishikawa, Juran, and Feigenbaum. All have made important contributions to the development of the quality process. Another important quality theorist is Crosby; his philosophy has shortcomings, but it is nevertheless used by many corporations in the United States. These shortcomings are discussed after the other gurus. Methods developed by other gurus such as Taguchi and Shingo are dealt with in later chapters in this book as a basis for developing your TQM system. Let's now deal with the teachings of the four main gurus.

W. Edwards Deming

This is the man often credited with inventing quality. While this is not true, he definitely had the impact necessary to create an environment in which quality is the overriding factor in the manufacturing process. He was responsible for developing Japanese quality to levels it has attained today.

The basis for his philosophy is founded in reducing variation, which requires everyone to participate in the process and in turn requires leadership. The leadership should function in such a way as to effect improved performance of workers and machines, leading to simultaneous improvement in quality and productivity and pride in workmanship. To this effect he gives us "14 points," which call for fundamental changes in the way business is done, the way an enterprise is managed, and the way people are treated. These points and a brief explanation are given below:

1. *Create constancy of purpose toward improvement in product and service.* One of the basic failures of management is its inability to take the long-term view. The goal is to provide a framework of consistent action on a day-to-day and long-term basis. This allows for innovation, redesign, training, education, and research to improve quality.

2. *Refuse to accept defects.* Most of our companies function at the lowest level of quality control—detection of defects. Refusing to accept defects involves creating an environment for preventing defects. Creation of this environment leads to continuous improvement.

3. *Cease dependence on mass inspection.* Inspection is usually a process of checking goods without the intention of ever making them better. It must be understood that inspection can neither improve nor guarantee quality. Deming recommends an all-or-none inspection policy and provides statistical proof for it.

4. *End the practice of awarding business on the basis of price tag.* Require suppliers to provide statistical evidence of quality. Price is perhaps the most important criterion for determining the supplier for a particular product. Mathematical evaluation of supplier quality should be the basis for accepting a supplier. The suppliers must also be required to provide statistical evidence of quality.

5. *Find problems.* This means creating a situation where the process is being continually improved. He recommends a plan-do-check-act, or PDCA, cycle to effect the continuous improvement process shown in Fig. 3.2. It is always economical to continually attempt to decrease the difference between customer needs and process performance.

6. *Institute methods of training on the job.* This is perhaps the most critical and often the most neglected aspect of the TQM process. Without a commitment to employee growth and development, the organizational performance actually goes down. This type of training may take the form of classroom training, on-the-job training, and instructional materials. Proper training gives workers a share in the philosophy and goals of the organization.

7. *Give all employees all the tools to do the job right.* This refers to

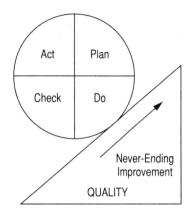

Figure 3.2   Deming's PDCA cycle.

the supervisory personnel, who act as the link between the top management and the employees. Supervisory personnel must attempt to create an environment that encourages learning, development, problem solving, trust, and fostering pride in their work, while emphasizing quality.

8. *Drive out fear, so everyone can work effectively.* Productivity and morale of workers who are continually worried about the disciplinary actions of management will be low. Coercion should be recognized as a management tool to be avoided. Performance of the workers in an environment also affects the physical and emotional well-being of the employees, which in turn leads to poor performance.

9. *Break down barriers between departments.* Encourage different departments to work together on problem solving. Using teams is perhaps the only way many complex problems in todays' manufacturing environments are solved. Unless barriers between departments come down, many of the problems cannot be effectively solved. In fact, many modern manufacturing techniques, including simultaneous engineering and quality function deployment, can only be achieved by using a team approach.

10. *Eliminate numerical goals, posters, and slogans that ask for new levels of productivity, without providing specific improvement methods.* Slogans only represent management's desires and fail to motivate the employee. Any posters used should display the continuous improvement process.

11. *Eliminate work standards that prescribe numerical quotas.* Use statistical methods to continuously improve quality and productivity. Work standards are classical industrial engineering techniques, but by quantifying the expected productivity, good supervision and training are prevented. Further problems may arise from setting the requirements too high or too low. Too high quotas

increase the defectives due to the pressure on the worker to meet the quota. Low quotas may result in the worker having nothing to do for the last hour, and this may affect the performance of other workers who have to work to the end of the shift to meet the quotas.

12. *Remove all barriers to pride in workmanship.*   Pride in work provides the impetus to perform better and to improve quality. Problems at work should be attended to as soon as possible so that the worker does not become disinterested in the task and as a result the quality suffers.

13. *Provide ongoing education and retraining.*   This helps define new jobs and responsibilities, readying employees for future jobs and preventing burnout.

14. *Clearly demonstrate management commitment to all of the above every day.*   Everyone in the organization must be committed to the process of transforming the organization. Change creates problems and the management must be committed to solving these problems.

Dr. Deming's methods have revolutionized Japanese manufacturing and have been adopted universally throughout Japanese companies. Many American companies are trying to adopt his methods due to the enormous success he had in Japan.

Kaoru Ishikawa

He is the leader in Japan's quality effort, and from the beginning most of his efforts relate to providing the road map for application of Dr. Deming's methods. His theories are based on a revolution in the way we think about management. His philosophy can be summed up in the phrase, "The practice of quality control is to develop, design and produce a quality product that is most economical, most useful and always satisfactory to the customer." Note that this style of quality management stresses the importance of customer satisfaction in the quality improvement process. He also introduced the concept of internal customer, which refers to the fact that the next process performed on a product is the customer for previous processes and that it is the worker's job to satisfy the next customer. He also stresses the importance of quality improvement by continually making small improvements by using data and statistical tools for analysis of these data. This can be achieved by providing tools for quality improvement at all levels in the organization through training.

Joseph M. Juran

Juran stresses the importance of understanding the fact that quality is not just a function of one department, such as the quality control department, but is a function of the entire organization. He feels that upper management must lead the drive for quality, making three major breaks with tradition by effecting:

1. Annual improvements in quality year after year.

2. Hands-on leadership by the upper management to establish new policies, goals, plans, organizational measures, and controls throughout the company.

3. Massive training in quality for the entire management team, not just the quality department.

Armand V. Feigenbaum

The concept of total quality control was developed by Dr. Feigenbaum and has become the phrase used to describe Japanese quality management systems which are an integral part of the just-in-time techniques. His concept deals with the entire organization with integrated controls to ensure customer quality satisfaction and economical costs of quality. All aspects of the business, including engineering, purchasing, finance, marketing, and manufacturing have to function as an integral part of the quality management system. Total quality control recognizes the advantages of having separate functions perform separate functions, but also recognizes the flaws with such a system. Quality improvement can only be effected by the integration of efforts from each of these departments. Total quality control is the basis for ongoing organizational quality control and provides the basis for systematic engineering to effect process improvements.

All of these theories have certain advantages for developing the quality management systems within your company, usually combining the theories of these gurus, taking what is needed, keeping our own organization structure in mind. So most of this book is written taking into account that when implementing your own total quality management system, many of the human factors involved, such as training for operators, may depend on individual perspectives. Training operators, for example, in problem solving would be meaningless if the operator has no comprehension of the manufacturing process. In some cases, it may therefore become necessary to train the operators in the basic functioning of the machine prior to any training in problem-solving methods. It is a fact of life that even on the shop floors of many of the larger corporations there are many operators who do not comprehend anything beyond loading and unloading the machine, with the responsibility toward the quality of the product left to the supervisor or the inspector.

Phillip Crosby

The primary basis for Crosby's theory rests on the four absolutes he states as the foundation for a quality system. Many organizations in the United States accept his theories as gospel, but there are inherent flaws in his theories on quality, and the acceptance of his theories may often be a formula for disaster. Before going on, the four absolutes are

- Definition of quality as conformance to requirements.
- The performance standard is zero defects.
- The measurement of quality is price of nonconformance.
- It is always cheaper to do the job right the first time.

To attain these absolutes of quality, he recommends a quality improvement program which includes:

1. *Management commitment.* To make it clear where management stands on quality.

2. *The quality improvement team.* To run the quality improvement program.

3. *Quality measurement.* To provide a display of current and potential nonconformance problems in a manner that permits objective evaluation.

4. *The cost of quality.* To define the ingredients of the cost of quality, and explain its use as a management tool.

5. *Quality awareness.* To provide a method of raising the personal concern felt by all personnel in the company toward the conformance of the product or service and the quality reputation of the company.

6. *Corrective action.* To provide a systematic method of resolving problems that are identified through previous action steps.

7. *Zero defects planning.* To examine the various activities that must be conducted in preparation for formally launching a zero defects program.

8. *Supervisor training.* To define the type of training that supervisors need in order to actively carry out their part of the quality improvement program.

9. *Zero defects day.* To create an event that will let all employees realize through a personal experience, that there has been a change.

10. *Goal setting.* To turn pledges and commitments into action by

encouraging individuals to establish improvement goals for themselves and their groups.

11. *Error-cause removal.*   To give the individual employee a method of communicating to management the situations that make it difficult for the employee to meet the pledge to improve.

12. *Recognition.*   To appreciate those who participate.

13. *Quality councils.*   To bring together the professional quality people for planned communication on a regular basis.

14. *Do it over again.*   To emphasize that the quality improvement program never ends.

The drawback to this approach is the first statement that quality is conformance to requirements, which is often termed as the "goalpost syndrome" and has the drawback of considering only the designers and the manufacturers, but failing to meet the customers' requirements. Most customers require the product they purchase to be close to the nominal all the time. The elements involved in a manufacturing process are shown in Fig. 3.3. Crosby's philosophy tends to suggest that conformance to quality requirements is enough, but you must remember that the competition is striving for continuous reduction of product variation about the target or nominal values. While many American corporations have religiously adopted Crosby's philosophy, the inherent drawback of his system can be the source of many problems. There is an inherent reduction in the cost of the product as the variation decreases and an increased ability for the manufacturers to meet the customers' requirements. Crosby completely fails to address this issue.

Once again it is necessary to discuss the issues of big Q and small q

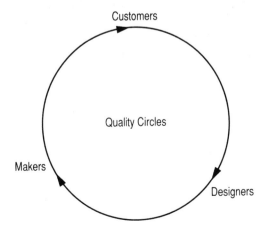

Figure 3.3 Elements of a manufacturing process.

in why Phillip Crosby fails to provide us with an adequate quality philosophy. The small q refers to conforming to product specifications. People often get slowed down by the trees of specifications, and as a result fail to see the forest of broader quality issues. Big Q, on the other hand, encompasses everything a customer wants or expects when purchasing your product or service and includes every aspect of your business, including price, service, reliability, safety, delivery, courtesy, and all else. Only when big Q becomes the basis for managing your company can you aim to become the most successful in your industry. TQM is the system to give you the corporate vision of quality, which can then be translated into specific goals. TQM requires the company to change its philosophy and management culture, defining progress in terms of the customer's needs, and making employees valued partners in the process. Application and use of TQM techniques is not dictated by the size, industry, or sector it is in. Crosby's philosophy is based entirely on the small q premise.

Using Quality Consultants to Effect TQM Systems

Using external consultants to effect TQM systems can offer important advantages to the process of change that is inevitable as a result of implementation of TQM systems. One of the biggest problems encountered in this process is the hierarchical structure of organizations, with senior management with fiefdoms of their own. The problems with effecting changes internally may be the deeply entrenched "battle lines." External consultants can provide the neutral middle ground for breaking down the traditional organizational barriers. Carefully selected, consultants can also become an important part of TQM awareness training, education, and implementation. Using TQM systems involves sophisticated automated computing tools, the training for which can be facilitated by these outside consultants. Using outside consultants, if necessary, must be done with extreme care, since a wrong selection may result in a disastrous situation.

4

Machine Acceptance Criteria

Types of Machinery Used

Machinery used in the manufacture of a new product can be classified into three basic categories:

1. New machines

2. Retrofitted machines

3. Retooled machines

Each of these categories needs to be dealt with separately.

Prior to determining the suppliers, specifically suppliers of machinery, the methods described in Chap. 8 must be used to determine the preferred suppliers. Many of the requirements specified in Chap. 8 may have to be modified to ensure that the suppliers chosen are able to meet all the commitments made in terms of delivery and price and commitment to the goal of zero defects. With a worldwide supplier base, commitment to delivery and sometimes the prices due to fluctuations in exchange rates must be considered. So extreme caution has to be exercised in selecting the supplier to deliver the equipment.

It is pertinent here to mention that many machinery manufacturers are represented by various companies in the United States, and this complicates the situation. Companies that manufacture the machinery may have the highest-quality machines, but the technical competence of the representative also comes into play, since the representatives are responsible for completing the various aspects of tooling and programming and setup of the machine, especially when the machine is purchased as a turnkey project. Lack of competence on the part of the representative may result in a disastrous situation both in terms of quality and delivery. Care should be taken to evaluate the representative as well as the machinery manufacturer when considering a major investment in machinery.

Statistical Tools for New Machinery Purchase

The process of purchasing a new machine is entirely different from buying a retrofitted machine or retooling an existing machine. The process is compounded by the fact that the product to be manufactured on this machine is new. So extra care has to be taken when treading into the territory of buying a new machine for manufacturing a new product. There are numerous elements in the organization involved in the decision-making process for acquiring a new machine. Design and manufacturing engineering are involved with the development of the process, in determining the machines to acquire, and if necessary, design of the machine. Manufacturing engineering has to determine the viability of the process design, determine the cost effectiveness of the process, and also determine whether it is going to be a turnkey project or not. The purchasing department is concerned with the cost of the buying process and other elements, such as ability of the supplier to meet delivery commitments. With modern machinery the quality department has to specify the statistical specifications that must be met by the supplier. Simultaneous engineering, described earlier in this book, is the required mechanism to ensure all these factors are dealt with prior to placing the purchase order.

The process we went through to purchase a four-axis, two-turret lathe for our camshaft project will be used to illustrate the process of buying of new machine tool on a turnkey basis and specifying the tests to ensure that you get the desired capabilities. The lathe was required to manufacture an automotive camshaft involving turning four journals and the pilot diameter, with the tightest tolerance on the axial dimension being $\pm.001$ in and radially $\pm.0005$ in. All of this has to be accomplished between centers, and the tightest requirement of runout between centers is .001. The journals have a chamfer on both sides. Figure 4.1 shows a sample part in the machine used in the runoff process prior to accepting the machine. While a machine tool is used as an example, the methods described herein should in no way be construed as only applicable to machine tools. These tests can be basically modified to apply to any machinery-buying process.

The first step in the process is to specify the statistical and reliability tests to be used to determine the capability of the machine. The requirements we specified were as follows:

1. We will require Cpk values on all the dimensions to be greater than 1.4 measured over 50 pieces. (Mathematically, Cp values are

Figure 4.1 The machine for which purchasing standards were developed. A part finished by the process is shown.

greater than or equal to the values for Cpk, so it is preferable to specify this Cpk requirement instead of Cp.) The value of Cpk is defined as the lesser of:

$$\frac{\text{USL} - \text{mean}}{3\sigma} \quad \text{and} \quad \frac{\text{Mean} - \text{LSL}}{3\sigma}$$

where USL and LSL are the upper and lower specification limits, respectively, and σ is the standard deviation. Cp is defined as the ratio of the tolerance divided by 6 times the standard deviation:

$$\text{Cp} = (\text{USL} - \text{LSL})/6\sigma$$

(Some people prefer a much higher Cpk value for a new machine.) Also, in case of runout checks you have to specify Cp's greater than 1.4 instead of Cpk's, which are not valid for one-sided checks. Checking the data collected from the 50 pieces sampled for normality would be an important precaution, since the calculations described above are only valid if the sample data are normally distributed. If the data are not normally distributed, then it is necessary to use Pearson curves or Johnson transformations to determine the capability of the machine.

2. We will also require the machine to run continuously without any failures for a period of 2 hours and during that time to produce

parts dimensionally within the customer's specifications. (Here the machinery manufacturer is at liberty to set the machine at the lower limit of the tolerance and let the part grow to the upper limit over a 2-hour period to ensure the reliability of the machine and tooling.) The 2-hour runoff should attain the production rate specified by the manufacturer and agreed to by the customer (which in our case was .77 minutes).

These tests are designed so that a decision on the acceptance of the machine may be made in a short period of time without worrying about modifying processing to get the desired results. The first test is intended to show the ability of the machine to manufacture the parts to the required tolerances, while the second test is a measure of the reliability of the machine. These clauses should be included in the purchase order along with a part print of the part to be manufactured. At this stage a few critical items to consider are as follows.

1. Most manufacturers will also specify what tolerances they are willing to meet prior to buying the machine. It would be helpful to clarify this at the start and include one of the dimensions to the manufacturer's tightest specifications allowed on tolerances. This will help determine whether the manufacturer is meeting the required specifications. (If you find that the machine at this stage is not capable of meeting your requirements, looking at alternative machinery is in order.) It may also be pointed out that it will be necessary to specify checking the capability along all the axes available for a machine tool to the tightest possible tolerance to ensure that no problems occur during use. This specification is the most critical, even though you may not use it, since this assures you that you are getting exactly the machine you specified.

2. It is also important to specify the gaging methods to be used to determine the capability of the machine. Usually, stating that "We will provide a gage with a gage repeatability and reproducibility lower than 10 percent using the standard 3 operator/3 trial/10 parts method" (described in the next chapter) should be adequate for most purposes. (We also specified that the various angles would be checked using a comparator, while the surface finish requirements would be checked using a profilometer.) If a fixture-type gaging is not available, then it is important to specify exactly the gaging to be used.

3. Most manufacturers will offer you additional features such as a tool touchsetter to eliminate the need for manual offsets, especially in case of a machine tool. Here it is pertinent to mention that state-

ments such as "The accuracy of sensor repeatability of the tool touchsetter is .0001 in and has a continuous machining accuracy of .0008 in" should be carefully examined for the parameters under which they are valid. It is also necessary to specify the parameters under which such additional features will be tested prior to purchasing the machine. The performance of these added features often becomes a major problem when they fail to perform to your exact requirements.

4. Many of today's machines have more than one station and depend on the same set of tools. In the case of machines, such as a dial indexing machine or a trunion indexing machine, it may be necessary to treat each station as a separate machine. These machines are primarily designed for high-volume production runs and so require extra care as far as performance requirements go. These machines automatically take care of machine reliability studies, since each station is treated as a separate machine. However, these machines are considerably more difficult to do capability studies on, since the tooling variance over the whole production range has to be minimal. This means that if a machine has six stations, the tooling must be capable over 300 pieces. Sometimes this may create a situation where the machine has to be run one station at a time. Reliability studies would then be conducted after setting the machine at the low limit or the high limit of the specification (as the case may be), as discussed earlier.

5. In the case of furnaces used for heat treatment, the rules to be used would be a sample of 10 pieces drawn over five heat treatment cycles and tested for properties such as hardness and microstructure. Purchases of furnaces have to be treated differently from those of other machines, because of the greater variability in the process and the longer time frame that is necessary for satisfactory performance of the equipment in actual use.

6. Another aspect to consider when buying expensive pieces of machinery is the level of automation that is desired. There are numerous benefits to considering automation of material handling, the gaging system associated with the machine, and so on. Automation of material handling may reduce downtime since the machine no longer depends on the operator to get parts. Automation of gaging systems to automatically offset the machine control results in a lower rate of scrap since the offset is not operator-dependent. The numerous aspects to automation are dealt with later on in this chapter. But when making the purchasing decision, the machinery maker should, if possible, also supply the automation equipment. This helps prevent the machinery manufacturer from blaming the

automation equipment manufacturer for failing to meet the quality commitments as far as their machine goes and vice versa. When considering purchasing machine tools and related automation, it is often necessary to look for manufacturers who can provide the entire job on a turnkey basis.

The statistical tools come into use once the machine is built and the manufacturer of the machine should come up with a chart showing the operation description and the characteristics associated with it. An example of a table used can be seen in Fig. 4.2. The table was filled out by the machinery manufacturer and the machines were set up according to the table. Numerous manufacturing problems were detected as a result of the trial run by the machinery manufacturer. After numerous changes to the process, the machine was deemed ready for runoff. Continuous use of the table provides a good history for the machine and duplication of experiments is avoided. This is true for all experiments you may conduct later on to optimize tooling use in the machine.

Once the machine is manufactured according to the parameters specified, then we can use the tests specified to verify whether the machine is suitable for our purpose. In our case the machine was capable on all counts except the #7 chamfer, where the Cp was found to be .94. Careful examination showed that the odd-numbered chamfers showed capabilities considerably lower than the even-numbered chamfers. This indicated the possibility that something was moving in the machine while turning the chamfer. Investigation showed that the tailstock was moving .002 in when the chamfers were being cut. Once the problem was identified it was relatively easy to rectify it, and by modifying the process and taking a second pass on the chamfer, the Cps and the Cpks were in the acceptable range.

The other problem identified was that the machine was not capable of cutting the pilot diameter within a tolerance range of .001 in. This problem arose from the fact that while the pilot was being cut, the journal was being simultaneously cut, resulting in an uneven surface finish on the pilot. This affected the capability of the machine and could be rectified by stopping the other turret while the pilot was being cut.

Once the manufacturing problems were rectified and the tooling problems solved, it was fairly easy to get the machine to make parts to print for the 2-hour runoff. Initially some of the tooling used did not appear to give the required minimum life. By suitably modifying the machining parameters and some of the inserts to higher grades, this problem could be easily rectified.

Regression analysis is a powerful tool for analyzing the growth in

Customer:									
Part Name: CAMSHAFT									
Part Number:			Total Time:		0.77	MINUTES			
Date:			Material: 5150 STEEL						
Machine:			Holding Equipment: SPEEDGRIP DRIVING CENTER						
Sta. #	Operation Description	SFM	Dia.	RPM	IPR	IFM	Cut Length	Cut Time	Idle Time
	ENGAGE TAILSTOCK, CLOSE	-	-	-	-	-	-	-	-
	DOOR, START SPINDLE, INDEX	-	-	-	-	-	-	-	-
	TO TOOL #1	-	-	-	-	-	-	-	0.1
		-	-	-	-	-	-	-	-
1	ROUGH TURN .925-.930 DIA.	600	0.94	2438	0.026	63.4	0.85	0.01	-
1	TURN 1ST JOURNAL AND 2 CHAM	600	1.807	1268	0.026	33.0	1.14	0.03	0.01
1	TURN 2ND JOURNAL AND 1 CHAM	600	1.807	1268	0.026	33.0	0.93	0.03	0.01
1	TURN 3RD JOURNAL AND 1 CHAM	600	1.807	1268	0.026	33.0	0.93	0.03	0.01
1	TURN 4TH JOURNAL AND 2 CHAM	600	1.807	1268	0.026	33.0	1.16	0.04	0.01
	INDEX TO TOOL #2	-	-	-	-	-	-	-	0.06
		-	-	-	-	-	-	-	-
2	FACE FRONT OF FIRST CAM LOBE	600	1.29	1777	0.01	17.8	1.2	0.07	-
		-	-	-	-	-	-	-	-
	INDEX TO TOOL #3	-	-	-	-	-	-	-	0.06
		-	_	-	-	-	-	-	-
3	CHAMFER CENTER TWO	-	-	-	-	-	-	-	-
	JOURNALS AT CENTER OF CAM	1178	1.807	2490	0.005	12.5	0.42	0.03	0.016
		_	_	-	_	-	-	-	-
	INDEX TO TOOL #4 (WORK REST)	-	-	-	-	-	-	-	-
	POSITION UNDER CAM. WAIT FOR	-	-	-	-	-	-	-	-
	SPINDLE STOP	-	-	-	-	-	-	-	0.07
		-	-	-	-	-	-	-	-
	DISENGAGE TAILSTOCK, OPEN	-	-	-	-	-	-	-	-
	DOOR	-	-	-	-	-	-	-	0.05
	UNLOAD/LOAD NEXT PC	-	-	-	-	-	-	-	0.13
		-	-	-	-	-	-	-	-
	TOTAL CUT TIME	0.24	MIN	-	-	-	-	-	-
	TOTAL IDLE TIME	0.53	MIN	-	-	-	-	-	-

Figure 4.2 Chart showing sequence of processing the camshaft.

the part size. The best-fit straight line is a good indicator of whether the machine is capable of manufacturing the parts within the required tolerances and gives a pictorial view of how the parts being manufactured are growing. The use of regression analysis gives us a pictorial view of growth in the part size over 50 parts, unlike histogram which gives a view of the distribution. While no requirements for regression were specified, we did get a feel for the increase in the part size for the pilot from the regression chart over 30 pieces, shown in Fig. 4.3. The calculations used to compute the regression line are based on the assumption that the growth in part size is a straight line and fits the equation

$$Y_i = aX_i + b$$

From this we get the relationships

$$\sum_{i=1}^{n} Y_i = a \sum_{i=1}^{n} X_i + nb$$

and

$$\sum_{i=1}^{n} X_i Y_i = a \sum_{i=1}^{n} X_i + x \sum_{i=1}^{n} X$$

Solving the two simultaneous equations we get the values of a and b:

$$a = \frac{\sum X_i Y_i - (\sum X_i)(\sum Y_i)}{\sum X_i^2 - (\sum X_i)^2/n} = \frac{\sum (X_i - \overline{X})(Y_i - \overline{Y})}{\sum (X_i - \overline{X})^2}$$

$$b = \frac{1}{n}(\sum Y_i - a\sum X_i) - \overline{Y} - a\overline{X}$$

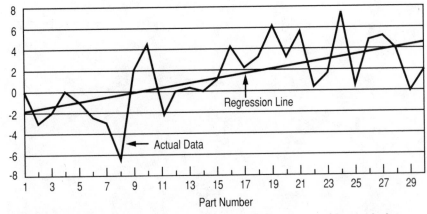

Figure 4.3 Using regression analysis to determine if there is a problem with the manufacturing process.

In spite of all this you may end up in a situation where the machinery manufacturer uses the most expensive tooling available, and this may not be the most optimum for your process. It may result in the process having to be changed several times before you get your process ready for your needs, but these tests ensure that the machine you get does not have any major problems.

In conclusion, it appears that most machinery buyers are buying machines as turnkey projects and correcting the processing problems themselves. This results in a considerable amount of wasted time in an effort to correct the process on the part of the buyer. Setting the correct standards at the time of purchasing any machinery and following through to ensure that the standards are met prior to installing machines in their plant would be the first step to manufacturing competitiveness in the world.

Statistical Tools for Retrofitted and Retooled Machines

In the case of retrofitted or retooled machines, basically the same rules apply as for a new machine. The machine capability index standards may be less easy to attain, and so the specifications have to be lowered. Many manufacturers of retrofitted machines may not agree to the same standards as required for a new machine. Appropriate standards must be set in negotiation with the retrofitters prior to ordering the machine to avoid any confusion. Some manufacturers of retrofitted machines may agree to the same standards as required for a new machine. These suppliers should be preferred over suppliers who do not agree to meet the requirements for a new machine. It is usual to specify the following:

1. Cpk > 1.78 over 50 consecutive pieces with no adjustment to the machine or failures.

2. The machine should run consecutively for 2 hours without any failures, and all parts should be within print specifications.

The specifications required are the minimum for using SPC. Wherever possible, the Cpk and Cp should be set at the levels specified for a new machine. If the machine fails to meet these minimum specifications, it may be necessary to check 100 percent of the parts produced on the machine.

Total Productive Maintenance

Once the machines used for the processing of the camshaft were accepted, it became necessary to develop a maintenance management system to prevent the systems from deteriorating and losing capability and finally leading to major failure. Input from various sources, such as FMEAs, SPC data, and recommendations of machinery manufacturers, were taken into consideration to effect preventive maintenance. Many times pressures of production can result in delaying scheduled maintenance with the net result that maintenance becomes corrective maintenance. Strategies for maintenance management should include planning for regular maintenance and audit schedules to ensure good preventive maintenance management practices are followed. Some of the biggest problems encountered to proposed plans for preventive maintenance are high cost. This can be avoided by presenting data from cost of poor quality and downtime resulting from lack of preventive maintenance.

One of the biggest problems with any maintenance management system is the fact that every element of the business is involved in the process. This aspect is particularly critical since maintenance costs make up 15 to 40 percent of the production costs, making it imperative that you keep the manufacturing equipment operating with minimal downtime. The designer has to be involved in the design stage to prevent high rate of failure and variable cycle time. This means he or she has to design maintainability or ease of maintenance into the system so that in the event of a machine breakdown, the downtime is not excessive. If the machine is extremely compact, then the various parts of the machine may not be easily accessible and other parts may have to be dismantled prior to fixing the part in question, increasing the downtime. Machine operators have to be trained in simple maintenance methods. Productive maintenance should be continuously implemented with the goal of reaching zero breakdowns. Any system of total productive maintenance (TPM) requires training at all levels within the organization, showing them the basic techniques for preventing equipment problems from happening in the first place. The prevention of breakdowns may involve simple things like making sure that a certain pocket is cleaned at regular intervals. Properly implemented, the productivity of the machine can increase by 150 percent. TPM is a powerful tool for effecting efficient use of human resources, equipment, and materials.

Maintainability

An important consideration in the total maintenance management system is the need for designing maintainability into the processes and equipment. Maintainability is the ability of the maintenance personnel to put a piece of equipment into working condition as soon as possible. This is particularly true for equipment being used for manufacturing, where the availability of the machine determines the profitability of the product. Availability of the machine is defined by

$$A = \text{MTBF}/(\text{MTBF} + \text{MDT})$$

where MTBF is the mean time between failures and MDT is the mean downtime. For improving the maintainability of the equipment, it is often necessary to determine a maintainability program, where all the tasks required in the maintainability program are identified, goals for maintainability are set during design stage, and we determine through evaluation and test if the goals have been met. Control must also be exercised on the suppliers to ensure that the maintainability models for our systems are not disturbed. FMEA, which is described later in this book for measuring reliability, can also be used to determine the maintainability of the equipment. Controlling suppliers becomes an extremely critical factor in keeping equipment maintainable. Care should be taken to ensure that defective spare parts from suppliers do not affect the maintainability of equipment. Another factor affecting maintainability of a machine is ease of access to the various parts of the machine. If numerous covers have to be removed prior to reaching a part then the mean downtime skyrockets for each failure. In a machine shop using an extremely compact machine is a surefire formula for disaster, with chips getting into various parts and further affecting the performance.

Automation as a Tool for Improving Quality

A primary concern when acquiring machines is the type and level of automation to be used alongside the machine. Most automation is entered into with the view of improving productivity. While no one can deny the importance of automation in improving productivity, it can also form a powerful tool in the TQM process. Automation refers to all types of automation, including loading and unloading processes, gaging automation, robotics, and automatic tool changers programmable controllers. One of the biggest problems faced with the manual loading and unloading systems as well as manual gaging systems is the difference between operators and the way they load the machines and gages. Human operators may not repeat themselves exactly each time. This may lead to higher process variability. Any inconsistencies in operator judgment may also result in process problems. In the machine purchasing example above, we purchased tool management software which automatically monitored the tool load, and when it exceeded a predetermined value, the tools were automatically switched over. Each turret had three sets of tooling for our process. This meant that the operator had to change inserts once at the beginning of a shift, which was then touchset with an automatic touchsetter as shown in Fig. 4.4. Once tools were touchset, tool changes were only necessary every 24 hours. This definitely improved productivity and was a definite quality advantage over other methods of processing parts. The tool load monitor, automatic tool change system, and automatic touchsetter resulted in reduced process variability. This was amply demonstrated by the increase in scrap rate that occurred when the automatic tool touchsetter had a breakdown and the operators had to use an external tool touchsetter. Another use of automation is in the use of adaptive controls when incoming material properties vary. Adaptive controls can also be used to reduce the variability of the end product in the event of incoming material variability. Automated in-process gaging may signal the out-of-range dimension, and automated feedback to the controls may reduce variability considerably. Automation in gaging processes leads to automated SPC processes and automated input to the machine controls. The most important and critical use of automation is when the product requires 100 percent inspection, especially in cases where any defective product results in safety issues. Products such as medical drugs or life and limb parts in cars may require 100 percent inspection. Depending on the importance of the inspection process, relying on human inspection more often than not results in rejected parts being mixed up with the good parts. Using an automated inspection process results in an improved inspection process.

When using automation systems, the primary concern is evaluating

Figure 4.4   Automatic in-process gaging for presetting tools.

their performance. Performance of the automation system is not easy to evaluate, since most automation systems are designed to perform extremely well under idealized conditions and problems arise when used under actual production conditions. Another problem with evaluating any automation system is that performance evaluation has to be designed for each system. Usually, for automated gaging such as a built-in gage for presetting the tools, repeatability can be checked. In most other automation systems repeatability is the primary criterion for determining the performance of the system, and suitable tests should be designed to ensure this.

Evolutionary Operation of Processes

Once all the equipment has been decided upon and the required machinery purchased, there comes a time when it is necessary to begin production, though not all systems have been optimized. There are numerous possibilities for improvement, but each change has only a potential for causing improvement. These changes are therefore not considered worthy of spending additional engineering resources investigating them and delaying production.

Once the production begins, the process produces two things:

1. Items for sale

2. Information about the process

The information about the process, if properly collected and analyzed, can form an alternative on-line experiment instead of using the off-line experimental methods, which can be expensive in terms of experimentation, laboratory, and experimenter costs. EVOP attempts to use the actual operator to conduct the actual experiment by varying the operating conditions in a series of steps. EVOP is the technique of making small incremental steps in the operating conditions until optimal operating parameters are arrived at.

When an experiment is conducted, the experimental design attempts to maximize the amount of information by minimizing the effects of noise. In EVOP, the same results are obtained by repeating the experiments, varying the experimental criteria slowly until the effects of the signal appear through the noise. Here it is assumed that the experimentation costs nothing, since the process is producing the product for sale. The experiments must usually be kept simple so that the change in the variables do not produce scrap. The technique uses small variations and preferably uses the favorable variants. EVOP experiments are designed to optimize the use of material or quality rather than minimize labor costs. Usually the savings obtained from using EVOP methods are not spectacular, but take the form of small increments.

Gage Acceptance Criteria

Selecting Types of Gages

Once all the machines have been decided upon, the next step in the process of new product management is the gaging. Gaging should be treated as a process in itself that follows the manufacturing process. This chapter will deal with mostly fixture-type gaging and the statistical tools to be used in determining the performance. Gaging should be treated as a part of the process for manufacturing the part. Selecting the type of gage to be used is one of the first decisions to be made. The main types of gaging used in the metalcutting process are as follows.

Attribute gages. These are more commonly referred to as go–no-go gages. Using these types of gages should be avoided as far as possible, since they do not quantify the feature being checked and should be used only to check clearances, or when actual dimensional measurement is difficult and the accurate measurements of the features under consideration are not critical to the performance of the part. Usually these gages are used for drilled hole diameters, tapped hole pitch, and minor diameters. We use an attribute gage for lobe widths where the tolerances are ±.015 in.

Micrometers and verniers. These gages are useful when the volume of production is small and cost of making fixtures is not justified. There are numerous types of micrometers and verniers and other standard gages that offer flexibility for a wide variety of parts. Another powerful yet flexible measuring system is a height gage, which has been extended in some cases to emulate a coordinate measuring machine.

Fixture-type gages. These are specially designed to gage particular dimensions of particular parts. The gaging mechanisms may use indicators, electronic transducers, or noncontact-type gaging such as lasers or air pressure to help determine the dimension. Depending on the application, noncontact gaging may offer better accuracies. We have used air pressure to measure inside diameters, but using air for outside diameters has proved difficult due to wear of the ring holding the air nozzles. Similarly, the use of lasers often requires an extremely clean part, so lasers work better in a laboratory-type environment. In metalcutting it is often not possible to clean the part of coolant prior to gaging, especially with a high production volume, and this may affect the measurement.

Optical comparators. These are powerful gaging tools using optical techniques. A comparator can be used to measure a wide variety of dimensions, including lengths, angles, diameters, and radiuses. One of the problems with using optical comparators is the speed of measurement, and this affects their use in production machining. Some of the newer models are automated for gaging specific features for production machining, but conventionally comparators have been used as inspection tools.

Coordinate measuring machines. Coordinate measuring machines (CMMs) use contact gaging to determine the dimensions of a wide range of parts and characteristics. Newer models are programmed to work faster than the older models and have been used for production machining, but, similar to comparators, have been used as inspection tools. With the development of closed-loop manufacturing systems where dimensions are directly input to the machine, many companies have moved the CMM to the shop floor. Certain special criteria may be required when deciding on purchasing such an expensive piece of gaging equipment. The criteria can be used for comparators or vision systems after suitable modification. These criteria include

1. Ability to measure parts to the accuracy levels desired, and the ability to perform satisfactorily in the work environment. Most modern CMMs are placed out on the shop floor to allow for faster gaging and hence are exposed to fairly rough environments.

2. Ability to measure all types of jobs. This type of universality ensures that the equipment is not obsolete when the job for which it was purchased is completed. Certain types of dedicated CMMs are available for camshafts. These are not useful except for measuring the features of the specialized jobs, and you may be required to have a CMM for certain specialized jobs that are being performed by you.

3. Flexibility for changing and extending measuring tasks. If a variety of probes are provided, then CMM can adapt to the changing tasks.

4. Speed of measuring. This is important, because very often a slow CMM can increase the downtime of the machine. The criteria that must be measured are the travel speed, angular speed of the rotary table, recording and data communication speed, and computing and storing speed.

5. Meeting the safety requirements for both workers and machine. While the human being working with the machine must be protected, it is also necessary to ensure that the probes and other sensitive parts are well protected.

6. Permit on-line statistical analysis. The CMM must be linked to a statistical package which can automate the analysis. This must include the ability to input the data into the standard SPC network.

Depending on the application, the type of gaging to be used is determined. Once the type of gaging is determined, the next step is to specify the parameters to be met by the gaging manufacturers, including the gaging accuracies, resolution, and gage repeatability, and reproducibility of the gage. These parameters to be specified and tested prior to accepting the gage are described below for fixture-type gages but can be modified for other types of gages.

Specifications for Gage Acceptance

The prime considerations in buying gages are as follows.

Accuracy

The accuracy of a gage is the extent to which the average of many measurements made by the gage agrees with the standard value as measured by the best available method. The accuracy of the gage must be measured over the whole range of the gage. This is often termed as *linearity*. The percent difference from the actual value is termed the *percent nonlinearity*. For most applications, the accuracy of the gage must be less than 10 percent. This must be specified prior to buying the gage to avoid situations where accuracy criteria are not met.

One more important factor to consider in purchasing gages is to ensure that the masters are made correctly. This is very important for accurate performance of the gage. Verifying documents provided by the gage manufacturer from an alternative source is critical to determining the accuracy of the gage.

Resolution

Resolution or sensitivity is the measure to which the gage can sense the variation of the quantity to be measured. This means that you cannot use an indicator with .001-in divisions when the measurement has to have an accuracy of .0001 in. Most electronic columns and computerized gages can be adjusted to the required level of sensitivity and so do not become an important part of specifications except in case of indicator-type gages.

One factor to remember here is that many manufacturers provide one mean master instead of a min/max master. This situation should be avoided, since the resolution of the gage is not checked each time a gage is mastered. If for any reason the resolution of the gage is affected, using a mean master alone may not be a good idea. For this reason any computer system and accompanying software that use only the mean master for calibrating the gage should be avoided. In computer systems, the inaccuracies of resolution resulting from using the mean master alone can be less easily detected; in fact, operators may not detect this problem for a considerable length of time. When ordering gaging systems it is often necessary to specify a min/max master prior to ordering the gage so we can be sure that the resolution of the gage is never more or less than it should be.

Gage stability

This is the measure of the total variation in the measurements obtained with a gage on the same master or master parts when measuring a single characteristic over an extended period of time. Here it is important to differentiate between gage stability and statistical stability. Statistical stability includes all aspects of the gages' stability including the gage repeatability, reproducibility, and accuracy. The traditional definition of gage stability is that a gage has greater variation in accuracy, resulting in lower gage stability. Statistical stability is determined by the use of control charts, which can measure the causes affecting measurement and separate the common and special causes of variation. Typically, the master is measured over periodic intervals, the value obtained on measuring the master or set of masters is recorded, and the value is plotted on X-bar and R charts. The methodology for interpreting the stability of these charts is discussed later in the chapter on statistical process control.

Gage linearity

Linearity of the gage is determined by selecting parts which lie throughout the operating range of the gaging instrument. The accuracy is determined by the difference between the master measurement and the observed average measurement. The slope of the regression line that fits the accuracy average versus the master part value multiplied by the process variation of the parts will represent the linearity of the gage. The following possible reasons will explain nonlinearity of the gage:

1. Poor calibration of the gage at the upper or lower end.
2. Error in the master either due to incorrect design or manufacture or due to wear and tear.
3. Worn gage.
4. Incorrect gage design.

Gage repeatability and reproducibility

This is the most important consideration prior to ordering a gage. Various methods are available to determine the gage repeatability and reproducibility (R&R). *Repeatability* is the variation obtained when one person using the same instrument measures the same dimension two or more times. *Reproducibility* is the variation in measurement averages.

Method for Conducting a Gage R&R Study

Described below is the gage R&R test for a gage:

1. Select five or more parts checked to be within the required specifications. We usually use fixture-type gages to check more than one feature on the gage, and so care should be taken to ensure that all the features under consideration are with the specification limits for the part. Gages are usually designed to be accurate within those specification limits.

2. Prepare the parts for gaging by washing, deburring, and numbering. Cleaning these parts is necessary, since the attempt here is to determine the variability of the gage and any extraneous factors that may affect the repeatability or reproducibility of the gage(s) should be avoided.

3. Select two or more operators and have them become familiar with the gage prior to beginning the study. The operators should be

fully versed in operating the gage, including loading, taking measurements, and unloading the gage. In certain gages we may need the part to be loaded in a particular fashion, and all the operators taking part in the gage R&R study must be well versed in the use of the gage. Setting up stops for parts for a gage R&R study may be an effective method to avoid the effect of runout on a part.

4. Each operator evaluates the parts in random order. Complete randomization can be attained by writing the part numbers on small slips of paper and having the operator draw a slip from a box and the number of the part drawn is gaged. Other methods, such as using the random number table, may be used to determine the sequence, but the method described above is the simplest to use. This may not be possible in the case of a gage connected to a computer where the software package comes built in with the ability to compute the gage repeatability and reproducibility, but here the operator cannot usually change the value of the measurement. The computer computes the size of the part to be evaluated.

It is important that the operators do not see the readings of the other operator or their own readings for the times they gaged the part previously. Looking at the previous reading on the part or readings of the other operators tends to bias the readings, especially if the gages are connected to electronic columns or dial indicators where the operator has to interpret the readings to some extent.

5. Readings for gage R&R studies should be one decimal place more accurate than the actual gaging. This should be specified to all the operators right from the beginning and they should estimate the extra decimal place from the display if possible.

6. Record the readings as shown in Fig. 5.1.

7. Compute the differences between each of the operators. Fill in all the totals and calculate the averages indicated. Compute R_1.

8. Calculate the upper control limit and compare the individual ranges of this value. Discard points out of control and recalculate R_1.

9. Calculate R_3, which is the difference between the largest and smallest operator averages. Figure 5.2 gives the value of the multiplying factor $1/d_2$ for number of operators: SDM = $(1/d_2)(R_3)$ variance = $(SD)^2$. This is the operator variation.

10. Similarly, calculate the gage variation or the repeatability of the gage where R_1 is the average of the sum of the ranges of each of the individual operation. This gives us SDR = $(1/d_2)(R_1)$.

11. The combined standard deviation of the gage R&R is the square root of the sum of the squares of the two standard deviations calculated above.

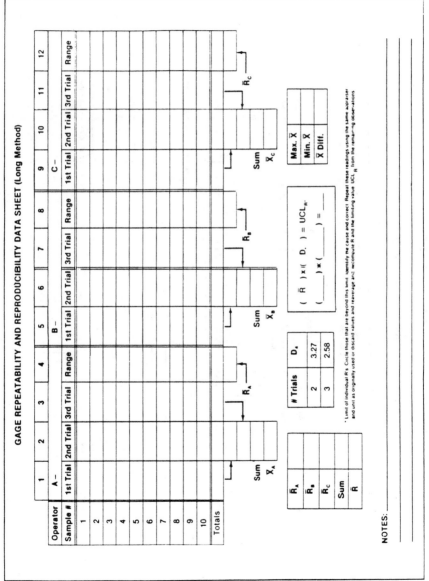

Figure 5.1 Gage repeatability and reproducibility data sheet (long method).

85

Gage Repeatability and Reproducibility Report

Part No. & Name _____	Gage Name _____	Date _____
Characteristic _____	Gage No. _____	Performed By: _____
Specification _____	Gage Type _____	

From Data Sheet

$\bar{R}$ = [ ] $\bar{X}_{Diff}$ = [ ]

MEASUREMENT UNIT ANALYSIS

REPEATABILITY - EQUIPMENT VARIATION (E V)

$E V = (\bar{R}) \times (K_1)$

$= (\_\_\_) \times (\_\_\_) =$ [ ]

TRIALS	2	3
K_1	4.56	3.05

n = number of parts
r = number of trials

REPRODUCIBILITY — APPRAISER VARIATION (A V)

$A V = \sqrt{[(\bar{X}_{diff}) \times (K_2)]^2 - [(E V)^2 / (n \times r)]}$

$= \sqrt{[(\_\_\_) \times (\_\_\_)]^2 - [(\_\_\_)^2 / (\_\_\_ \times \_\_\_)]}$

$=$ [ ]

OPERATORS	2	3
K_2	3.65	2.70

REPEATABILITY AND REPRODUCIBILITY (R & R)

$R \& R = \sqrt{(E V)^2 + (A V)^2}$

$= \sqrt{(\_\_\_)^2 + (\_\_\_)^2} =$ [ ]

% TOLERANCE ANALYSIS

$\% E V = 100 [(E V) / (TOLERANCE)]$

$= 100 [(\_\_\_) / (\_\_\_)]$

$= $ [ ] %

$\% A V = 100 [(A V) / (TOLERANCE)]$

$= 100 [(\_\_\_) / (\_\_\_)]$

$= $ [ ] %

$\% R \& R = \sqrt{(\% E V)^2 + (\% A V)^2}$

$= \sqrt{(\_\_\_)^2 + (\_\_\_)^2}$

$= $ [ ] %

NOTE: All calculations are based upon predicting 5.15 σ (99% of the area under normal curve)

* A negative value under the square root sign causes the appraiser variation to default to zero

Figure 5.2 Gage repeatability and reproducibility report.

12. Finally, to calculate the percent tolerance consumed by the repeatability and reproducibility, we use the following formula: %T.C. = [(5.15) (SDRR) + tolerance](100).

Most gaging manufacturers should agree to a gage R&R of less than 10 percent, which is generally the acceptance standard among gaging manufacturers. The parameters under which the gage has to have an R&R of less than 10 percent are usually three operators, three trials, and ten parts. The short form of the gage R&R involves the use of two operators, two trials, and five parts; the format used for this is shown in Fig. 5.3. Most users and gaging manufacturers use the long form of gage R&R as the standard, since this is a more accurate indicator of the percentage of the tolerance consumed by the gage. The entire set of calculations computerized is shown in Fig. 5.4. Besides the long form of gage R&R, there is also the ANOVA method, and many users

VARIABLE GAGE STUDY (SHORT METHOD)

P/N: _____   Date: _____   Gage: _____

Procedure : Select 2 operators and 5 parts. Number the parts 1 to 5.
Both operators measure the parts in a random order.

P/N	Operator A	Operator B	Range (A-B)
	Sum of Ranges		

Average of Ranges

Gage R&R = 4.33 X $\overline{R}$ =

Acceptance Guidelines

Under 10% gage R&R: Gage is acceptable for use
10 to 30%: May be acceptable based on criticality of application
Over 30%: Not acceptable

Figure 5.3 Variable gage study (short method).

GAGE REPEATABILITY AND REPRODUCIBILITY REPORT

PART # & NAME:	CAM 25533156	GAGE NAME:	BENCH CENTER	DATE:	02-18-89
CHARACTERISTIC:	PRO1-100	GAGE #	400-071-100	PERFORMED BY:	HGM
SPECIFICATION:	RUNOUT +/- .0015	GAGE TYPE:	FEDERAL INDICATOR		

GAGE SETTING: 0.00000   GAGE TOLERANCE: 0.00000 0.00150

	OPERATOR A: NSM				OPERATOR B: HGM				OPERATOR C: OG			
SAMPLE #	1ST TRIAL	2ND TRIAL	3RD TRIAL	RANGE	1ST TRIAL	2ND TRIAL	3RD TRIAL	RANGE	1ST TRIAL	2ND TRIAL	3RD TRIAL	RANGE
1	0.00005	0.00005	0.00005	0.00000	0.00005	0.00005	0.00005	0.00000	0.00000	0.00010	0.00010	0.00010
2	0.00005	0.00005	0.00010	0.00005	0.00005	0.00000	0.00005	0.00005	0.00010	0.00010	0.00010	0.00000
3	0.00015	0.00005	0.00010	0.00010	0.00005	0.00005	0.00005	0.00000	0.00010	0.00010	0.00010	0.00000
4	0.00005	0.00010	0.00005	0.00005	0.00005	0.00005	0.00005	0.00000	0.00010	0.00010	0.00010	0.00000
5	0.00005	0.00005	0.00005	0.00000	0.00000	0.00000	0.00005	0.00005	0.00010	0.00000	0.00010	0.00010
6	0.00005	0.00010	0.00005	0.00005	0.00005	0.00000	0.00005	0.00005	0.00010	0.00000	0.00010	0.00010
7	0.00005	0.00005	0.00005	0.00000	0.00000	0.00005	0.00005	0.00005	0.00000	0.00010	0.00010	0.00010
8	0.00005	0.00005	0.00005	0.00000	0.00000	0.00005	0.00005	0.00005	0.00010	0.00000	0.00010	0.00010
9	0.00005	0.00005	0.00005	0.00000	0.00005	0.00005	0.00000	0.00005	0.00010	0.00010	0.00000	0.00010
10	0.00005	0.00005	0.00005	0.00000	0.00005	0.00005	0.0^005	0.00000	0.00000	0.00000	0.00000	0.00000
TOTALS	0.00060	0.00060	0.00060	0.00025	0.00035	0.00035	0.00045	0.00030	0.00060	0.00060	0.00070	0.00060

GRAND TOTAL   0.00180   0.00115   0.00190
GRAND AVERAGE 0.00006 =XA   0.00003   0.00004 =XB   0.00003   0.00006 =XC   0.00006

```
          RA: 0.000025                    MAX: 0.000063
          RB: 0.000030    UCL RANGE: 0.00010    MIN: 0.000038
          RC: 0.000060                    X DIFF: 0.000025
         SUM: 0.000115
  R AVERAGE:  0.00004
```

MEASUREMENT UNIT ANALYSIS: % TOLERANCE ANALYSIS

REPEATABILITY-EQUIPMENT VARIATION(E.V.):   0.00012   % E.V.   7.79444

REPRODUCIBILITY-APPRAISER VARIATION(A.V.): 0.00006   % A.V.   4.26906

REPEATABILITY & REPRODUCIBILITY (R & R)=   0.00013   % R.R.   8.88697

Figure 5.4 Computerized gage repeatability and reproducibility report.

are switching to this method since the factor d_2 is an approximation and any error associated with this approximation can be eliminated. The mathematical calculations involved in using the ANOVA method are fairly complex; ANOVA is covered at the end of the chapter.

Once a gage is accepted, the gage has to be continuously monitored. For this, the system to be used is X-bar and R charts. The methodology is explained in detail in Chap. 7. The process used is to gage the master prior to mastering the gage. If the gage is mastered say five times a shift, then the mean and the range of the five readings are plotted on X-bar and R charts. The average of the variation from the actual value forms the mean, and the range is continuously plotted and the long-range process capability is calculated. The charts should be checked for a pattern. This system of calibrating a gage is termed an *active gage calibration system* and, depending on the results of the charts plotted, you may either increase or decrease the frequency of calibration. This type of charting helps monitor the likelihood of the gage drifting over a period of time and helps evaluate error of measurement from time to time.

Numerous sources of error can occur in most measuring instruments. The error in a measuring instrument is defined as the difference between the measured value and the true value. The errors may be caused by various factors such as nonlinearity, hysteresis, and sensitivity to environmental factors such as temperature and electrical fields. Errors may also be magnified by improper fastening of mechanical linkages, loose clamps, poor electrical connections, and so on. Another critical source of error may be improper design. One problem of improper design we had was using a gage for our center-drilling operation that was based on locating the camshaft on the forged journals, because that was the method of manufacture. Here repeatability and reproducibility were lost because of the inconsistencies of the unmachined journals. The rest of the processing of the camshaft is based on processing the camshaft between centers. The main problem with the gage is that the variation in journal forging size, runout, and mismatch makes it impossible for the gage to determine the axial distances accurately. So it is necessary to compromise in certain cases where the gaging process cannot accurately duplicate the manufacturing process. The processes following the process under consideration must also be kept in mind.

Gaging Systems and Calibration

Any good gaging system must have the following characteristics:

1. *Gage storage.* Any gage that is not currently being used must be stored in an area where accessibility is limited. Limiting general access to the area where the gages not in use are kept is perhaps the easiest way to attain this, since many modern gages are not small enough to fit in a cabinet. The smaller gages should, however, be locked in a small cabinet that shows how many of each gage type are available at a glance.

2. *Gage serialization.* This is another important feature of a gaging system. In a large shop, this is often the only way to keep track of the gages available for use. Gage calibration software to continually monitor the calibration system does not allow for overlap of gaging numbers. But usually a machine shop has all types of gages, including verniers, micrometers, and go–no-go gages, besides the fixture-type gages with computers attached to them. This means

that developing a good serialization system is necessary to ensure that the gage is properly calibrated.

3. *Gage function.*   Besides a numbering system, it is necessary to determine the gage function, including the level of accuracy for each gage. Certain jobs may require a greater level of accuracy than offered by a particular gage, and this would make that gage unusable for the job. Accuracy charts help match gages with appropriate jobs.

4. *Gage responsibility.*   This is the final element of a good gaging system, and the responsibility for this task must be clearly assigned and defined. One individual must have the responsibility and the authority for keeping control of the gage location and use for a particular function. These gages must be signed out by the user, which may be the inspector or the operator. The person responsible for keeping track of the gages must ensure that the gage is returned to the storage area after use.

Developing a Calibration System

The first step in developing a gage calibration system is selecting good software for the job, which must include the following functions. It must have a database to track when each gage in the system is due for recalibration, an active gage calibration package, and, if possible, an attached statistical package to track the calibration. These can be obtained in the market as ready-made packages. Once this is done, the next step in the process is classifying gages by type, environment, location, and so on, depending on shop variables that may affect the calibration.

The second step in the process is to determine an acceptable tolerance range in which you will allow the gages to work. This range is what the system tries to achieve after resetting the calibration of the gage. For example, a gage that must read a range of ±.0005 will have an acceptable tolerance range of +.0001. This means that the gage must have an accuracy tolerance level 10 times greater than the dimensions the gage is checking.

The next step in the process is setting the recall level, which has to be set depending on the safety factors, sophistication of the calibration system, policy, criticality of the part dimension, and any other pertinent considerations. Once this is established, then data can be gathered to determine the frequency of recalibration of the gages in question. Based on the data, the frequency of calibration can be set and changed when necessary. Drift of gages due to wear is often not linear. Historical data can determine whether the goal is being reached and if the calibration frequency can be decreased.

Calculations in a Gage R&R Study

The calculations involved in the measurement of gage R&R (standard form) are

Repeatability [equipment variation (E.V.)]: $E.V. = (5.15 \times R)/d_2$

Reproducibility [appraiser variation (A.V.)]:

$$A.V. = ([(5.15 \times X_{diff})/d_2] - [(E.V.)_2/(n \times r)])^{1/2}$$

Repeatability and reproducibility (R&R): $R\&R = [(E.V.)^2 + (A.V.)^2]^{1/2}$

d_2 is a constant factor that depends on the number of parts and number of operators:

No. of parts	No. of operators			
	2	3	4	5
1	1.41	1.91	2.24	2.48
2	1.28	1.81	2.15	2.40
3	1.23	1.81	2.12	2.38
4	1.21	1.77	2.11	2.38
5	1.19	1.75	2.10	2.36
6	1.18	1.74	2.09	2.35
7	1.17	1.73	2.09	2.35
8	1.17	1.73	2.08	2.35
9	1.16	1.72	2.08	2.34
10	1.16	1.72	2.08	2.34

Calculations for ANOVA Method of Gage R&R

The ANOVA method of calculations requires the determination of several factors, from which the gage R&R values are obtained. The ANOVA method of determining R&R is generally considered to be the standard, though many people do not like to use it because the method involves considerably more calculations. The availability of computer programs that can do all the calculations described below has increased the use of the ANOVA method.

$$n = \text{number of parts}$$

$$r = \text{number of trials}$$

$$k = \text{number of operators}$$

$$T = \sum_{h=1}^{n} \sum_{i=1}^{k} \sum_{j=1}^{r} (X_{hij})^2$$

Effect of parts:

$$\text{SSP} = \sum_{i=1}^{n}\left(\frac{X_i^2}{kr}\right) - \frac{T^2}{nkr}$$

$$\text{MSP} = \frac{\text{SSP}}{(n-1)}$$

Effect of operators:

$$\text{SSO} = \sum_{j=1}^{k}\left(\frac{X_j^2}{nr}\right) - \frac{T^2}{nkr}$$

$$\text{MSO} = \frac{\text{SSO}}{n-1}$$

Effect of interaction between operators and parts:

$$\text{SSOP} = \sum_{i=1}^{n}\sum_{j=1}^{k}\left(\frac{X_{ij}^2}{nr}\right) - \sum_{i=1}^{n}\frac{X_i^2}{kr} - \sum_{j=1}^{k}\frac{X_j^2}{nr} + \frac{T^2}{nkr}$$

$$\text{MSOP} = \frac{\text{SSOP}(n-1)}{(k-1)}$$

Gage R&R calculations will vary depending on whether the interaction between the part and operators is judged to be significant. This determination is based on the factor

$$F = \text{MSOP/MSE}$$

This factor is compared to the F-chart value for the number of parts, trials, and operators to determine the significance of the interaction. If the F-value calculated is greater than the value from the table, then the interaction is significant, while if it is less than the interaction, it is deemed not significant.

Interaction significant

Repeatability [equipment variation (E.V.)]: $\text{E.V.} = 5.15\,(\text{MSE})^{1/2}$

Reproducibility [appraiser variation (A.V.)]:

$$\text{A.V.} = 5.15([(\text{MSOP} - \text{MSE})/r] + [(\text{MSO} - \text{MSOP})/nr])^{1/2}$$

Repeatability and reproducibility (R&R):

$$\text{R\&R} = 5.15(\text{MSE} + [(\text{MSOP} - \text{MSE})/r] + [(\text{MSO} - \text{MSOP})/nr])^{1/2}$$

Interaction not significant

$$SS_{pool} = SSE + SSOP$$

$$MS_{pool} = SS_{pool}/(nkr - n - k + 1)$$

Repeatability [equipment variation (E.V.)]:   E.V. $= 5.15(MS_{pool})^{1/2}$

Reproducibility [appraiser variation (A.V.)]:

$$A.V. = 5.15[(MSO - MS_{pool})/nr]^{1/2}$$

Repeatability and reproducibility (R&R):

$$R\&R = 5.15(MS_{pool} + [(MSOP - MS_{pool})/nr])^{1/2}$$

Other Methods for Measurement System Assessment

Two additional methods of assessing a measuring system deserve mention. The first uses a control chart method. The second method expands on the average and range method to include the "within-part variation." These graphical methods serve the purpose of determining whether the measurement process is adequate for the manufacturing process variation, and they can help determine whether all the gages are doing the same job, the operators are doing the same job, if the measurement system variation is greater than the process variation, and finally, determine how good the data are obtained by using the given measuring system. Based on the charts, the signal-to-noise ratio is calculated to determine the discriminating power of the gage. Details of these calculations can be obtained in *Evaluating the Measurement Process* by Wheeler and Lyday.

Gage Performance Curve

The performance of the gage is charted to determine the probability of accepting or rejecting a part of some ideal master value. The ideal gage performance is shown in Fig. 5.5. Actual gage performance usually resembles Fig. 5.6. Based on the curve obtained for the gage, we determine the percentage probability of rejecting a part from the equation

$$P_a = \int_{LL}^{UL} N(X_T + A, s^2)dn$$

and using the standard normal curve, the probability of accepting the part is

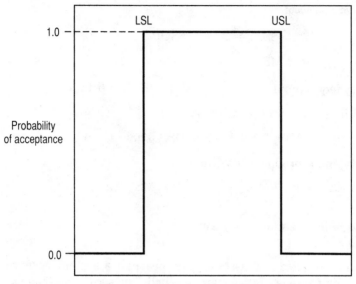

Figure 5.5   Gage performance under idealized conditions.

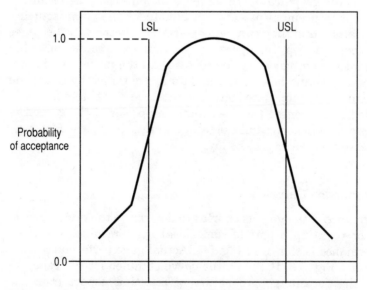

Figure 5.6   Gage performance under actual conditions.

$$P_a = \phi\left[\frac{UL - (X_T + A)}{s}\right] - \phi\left[\frac{LL - (X_T + A)}{s}\right]$$

where UL is the upper tolerance limit, LL is the lower tolerance limit, s is the gage R&R divided by 5.15, X_T is the mean assuming the distribution is normal, and A is the accuracy with some variance s^2. Based on the calculations, the probability of accepting a part of a given master value is determined.

Attribute Gage Study

The problem with determining the acceptability of the gage for use in the measuring process is that an attribute gage can only determine whether a part is good or bad, but it does not attempt to quantify how good or bad a part is. The simplest technique would be to select a mix of good and bad parts and, using two operators, measure each of the parts twice. Care should be taken to ensure that operator bias is eliminated by using a completely randomized technique. The simplest method of randomizing the test would be to let the operator check the part by drawing a number from a box with pieces of paper numbered from 1 to 20. Care should be taken that the operator cannot see the readings of the other operator or the readings taken in a previous run. Based on this test, if all the readings taken agree, then the gages are acceptable for use. If all the measurements on all the parts do not agree, then attempts should be made to reevaluate the gage and/or improve it. The method described above is usually termed the short method.

A long method for evaluating the performance of the gage is available. It uses the gage performance curve to determine the repeatability and accuracy. This method can be used for single- and double-limit gages. For a double-limit gage, only one of the limits needs to be explained. The long method involves the use of several parts for which the master values are known and the parts are checked repetitively and by many operators to determine the total number of accepts and rejects, keeping the rules of a completely randomized experiment in mind. The probability of acceptance of each of the parts must be calculated and, based on this, the gage performance curve can be plotted. The accuracy is then determined by subtracting the master value with a probability of acceptance of .5 from the lower limit:

$$\text{Accuracy} = \text{lower limit} - X_T \quad (\text{at } P'_a = .5)$$

The repeatability of the gage, on the other hand, is determined by subtracting the master value for which the probability of acceptance is .005 from the master value for which the probability of acceptance is .995 and dividing the difference by the adjustment factor of 1.08:

$$\text{Repeatability} = \frac{X_T(\text{at } P'_a = .995) - X_T(\text{at } P'_a = .005)}{1.08}$$

To determine whether the accuracy is significantly different from zero, the following statistic is used:

$$t = 31.3 \times \text{accuracy/repeatability}$$

For 20 parts we would have 19 degrees of freedom and the calculated value is greater than 2.093 (.025, 19); thus the calculated value is significantly different from zero.

6

Failure Modes and Effects Analysis

Reliability Analysis

One of the most important characteristics of any product is its reliability. Reliability is an important aspect of customer satisfaction. This aspect is dealt with later in Chap. 13. Most customers want a long service life for products purchased with long times between failures. As products became more complex, traditional design methods were not adequate to ensure low rates of failure. From this evolved the need for designing reliability into the product. *Reliability* is defined as the probability of the product to perform as expected over a given period of time, for a given set of operating conditions, and a given set of product performance characteristics.

To ensure the reliability of a product, it often becomes necessary to develop a reliability program, the chief elements of which are a reliability program plan, a method to monitor and control suppliers, a failure reporting system, analysis of the failure, a means of implementing corrective action, a failure review system, reliability modeling, allocation and prediction, and failure modes and effects analysis. When the products become more complex, then it becomes necessary to add other types of tests to determine the reliability of the product. In our case we used all these methods only to evaluate the reliability of the equipment used to manufacture the products.

One extremely important consideration when performing reliability studies is the safety of the product or the process. Criticality of a product, component, or process is affected severely if any human safety considerations are involved, and most of the reliability tests including FMEAs and other methods can form the basis for safety studies too, although they are not extensively used as a safety tool.

Failure Rate

Most products follow a very familiar pattern of failure. These failures can be classified into three basic categories. The first category includes a high rate of failure during the initial stages as a result of errors in design or manufacture, or due to misuse. The second category is the failure of the product due to inherent limitations in design, or accidents, or poor maintenance. The third and final category consists of failure due to wear out after it has performed satisfactorily for the period recommended by the manufacturer. These three periods of failure can be represented by an exponential distribution, and the probability of survival of the product or the system is quantified as

$$P = e^{-t\lambda}$$

where P is the period of failure-free operation, t is the time specified for failure-free operation, and λ is the failure rate.

Requirements for Reliability

In the case of the four-axis, two-turret lathe, we specified that the machine must be set up to continuously produce parts within the given specifications for the camshaft for a 2-hour period without any machine failure, including electrical, tooling, or any other systems. The acceptance of the machine was subject to meeting a certain requirement for reliability of the machine. So the definition of reliability as used commonly is fairly simple, but care must be taken to define what failure constitutes, especially when purchasing equipment, since the supplier's and customer's definitions of failure may differ. So precise, quantified statements must be used to define reliability. This reliability should also be quantified in terms of the interrelationships between the subsystems, reliability of previous subsystems, relative complexity, and relative criticality of the failure. This means that using our engineering judgment, it is necessary to determine the criticality of the failure. If a certain failure occurs, then if the machine becomes inoperable, the criticality is higher than if the failure leads to only a slight inconvenience for the operator. Finally, based on the definition of the part, assembly, or machine under consideration, we have to get the reliability of each subsystem and the factors involved in reliability and compute the appropriate reliability relationships for each part, class, or module of the product. Based on these studies, a basis can be attained for selection evaluation and control of parts. This also helps to develop a parts application study, an approved parts list, critical components list, and a system for changing the operating parameters. In the care of the lathe, changing the operating parameters refers to lowering the cutting load on an insert when it is found to break at a higher load condition. This also leads us to a formal system for managing the FMEA based on the probability of the defect occurring, probability of the customer noticing the defect, and the probability of the defect being shipped to the customer.

Relationship between Part and System Reliability

Assuming that failure of a part is independent of the failure of the other parts of a system or a machine, and the failure of any part in the system will cause the system to fail, the probability of failure can be calculated by the equation

$$P = P_1 * P_2 * \cdots * P_n$$

This formula is useful to begin our calculations, but it must be refined as more and more information becomes available about the interdependence of the parts. Each of the individual probabilities can be assumed to be an exponential distribution. Since each of the probabilities of failure is a fraction, the probability of failure for the system will actually be greater than the probability of failure of the individual components or parts.

The simplest mechanism for overcoming this is the use of parallel system, which means critical parts are set up so that if at least one of the parts operates, then the system does not fail. Designing parallel systems to increase the reliability becomes critical when risk to human lives is involved. By using n systems in parallel, the reliability of the system is now computed as

$$1 - (1 - P)^n$$

which has a value greater than P.

Purpose of an FMEA

Once the process has been established and the machinery has been acquired and set up, we now require a method to determine the reliability of the process. The next step in the process is determining the failure modes and the effects they have on the customer. This study needs to be conducted before the production process begins and in most cases prior to acquiring the necessary machinery and gaging. The purpose of a process FMEA is to identify the potential causes for failure in the process and the means to prevent those failures from occurring. The basis for an FMEA is to compare the design characteristics relative to the planned manufacturing or assembly methods, to ensure that a product meets the expected customer requirements. Corrective actions can be initiated once a failure mode is identified. The FMEA justifies the reasons for a process being set up the way it is.

The purpose of the FMEA is to analyze the probable causes of product failure, to determine how the problem affects the customer, to identify the probable manufacturing or assembly process responsible, to identify the process control variable to focus on for prevention and detection, and to quantify the effect on the customer.

The FMEA should be looked upon as the manufacturing engineer's analysis of all possible things that could go wrong with the process the way it is set up. This can be treated as a formalization of the thinking associated with developing the process.

Customer expectations are higher than ever, as are the regulatory requirements, and the attitude of the courts toward product problems is considerably tougher than ever before. So the use of process FMEA is more important than ever before. The important thing to remember here is that the FMEA should be treated as a living document and should be continually updated as the production process begins and new problems not anticipated by the manufacturing engineers become apparent. The method is a measure of the reliability of the process to produce a quality product meeting the expectations of the customer. These methods highlighted here have to be used in conjunction with SPC to emphasize the importance of defect prevention over defect detection.

Process FMEAs should be updated with each new or revised process to maximize the benefits that can be obtained from the methods. The use of process FMEA is often necessary on high-warranty products, low-reliability products, products with extreme manufacturing complexity, or products where the probability of not meeting the customer expectation or engineering specification is high. But performing FMEAs on every step in your manufacturing process can help avoid considerable grief at a later date. Of course, the most important aspect of all this is to follow up on any concerns that appear critical. Any process action or design changes taken to prevent the problems appearing once the product has reached the customer should be reflected in the evolving FMEA.

The process or product FMEA can provide the following functions, summarized below:

1. A systematic review of component failure modes to ensure that any failure produces minimal damage to the product or process.

2. Determining the effects that any failure will have on other items in the product or process and their functions.

3. Determining those parts of the product or the process whose failure will have critical effects on product or process operation, thus producing the greatest damage, and which failure modes will generate these damaging effects.

4. Calculating the probabilities of failures in assemblies, subassemblies, products, and processes from the individual failure probabilities of their components and the arrangements in which they have been designed. Since components have more than one failure mode, the probability that one will fail at all is the sum of the total probability of the failure modes.

5. Establishing test program requirements to determine failure mode and rate data not available from other sources.

6. Establishing test program requirements to verify empirical reliability predictions.

7. Providing input data for trade-off studies to establish the effectiveness of changes in a proposed product or process or to determine the probable effect of modifications to an existing product or process.

8. Determining how the high-failure-rate components of a product or process can be adapted for higher-reliability components, redundancies, or both.

9. Eliminating or minimizing the adverse effects that assembly failures could generate and indicating safeguards to be incorporated if the product or the process cannot be made failsafe or brought within acceptable failure limits.

Developing an FMEA

The use of a process FMEA for a manufacturing process close to the one currently used at Ford Motor Company is described below. The information necessary to complete the FMEA shown in Fig. 6.1 is described in the following paragraphs.

The initial task is to identify the process under study, along with related information such as which division is responsible for initiating and effecting the concerns identified by the FMEA. Other divisions and suppliers affected by the problems identified by the FMEA should also be determined. The end user of the product should also be identified, along with the scheduled production release, showing the earliest release date. The engineer responsible for developing and implementing the FMEA and the supervisors who are affected by the problems highlighted by the analysis should be identified. The first date on which the analysis was initiated should be noted. All this information has to be gathered prior to developing the process FMEA.

POTENTIAL
FAILURE MODE AND EFFECTS ANALYSIS
(PROCESS FMEA)

Company Name: _____

Part or Process Name/No._____

Design/Mfg. Responsibility_____

Other Areas Involved_____

Suppliers and Plants Affected_____

Model Year/Vehicle(s)_____

Engineering Release Date_____

Page _____ Rows _____ through _____

Prepared By_____

FMEA Date (Orig.) _____ (Rev.) _____

Key Production Date_____

Process Description / Process Purpose	Potential Failure Mode	Potential Effect(s) of Failure	S e v	Potential Cause(s) of Failure	O c c u r	Current Controls	D e t e c	R. P. N.	Recommended Action(s)	Area/Individual Responsible & Completion Date	Action Results				
											Actions Taken	S e v	O c c	D e t	R. P. N.

Figure 6.1   Failure modes and effects analysis report.

The next step in the process is to identify the process failure modes. Each possible failure mode should be identified by continually asking the questions, "What could go wrong with the process?" and "How could the part fail to meet specifications?" It is necessary to answer these questions without considering the engineering specifications. For an assembly, the typical answers would be bent, corroded, distorted, misaligned, poor surface finish, cracked, omitted, and so on. Similarly, for a manufacturing process, the answ~rs would be oversize, undersize, missed operation, and so on.

If a failure occurs, and the problem identified by th~ ~ustomer, the question to ask would be, "What is the result of the failvːe mode identified?" In case of an assembly the typical answers would oə air leaks, chatter, failure, high operating efforts, and so on. In case of ⁺he manufacturing process for the camshaft, the next question would be, "Who will the customer be?" This means if we have a hole missing on journal 4, for example, this would be found by the next processing operation, but a missing tapped hole would not be found until the camshaft is already in the engine. The first problem, while not acceptable, would not be as calamitous to the customer as having to tear down an engine to put in a camshaft that has a good tapped hole.

If the characteristic is controlled statistically, then it is necessary to identify it as such. The method used to control the characteristic should also be identified, meaning if a p chart or X-bar chart is used, it should be identified as such.

The next question to ask and answer is what the processing variables are that lead to the potential failure mode. Typical answers to such a question in case of an assembly would be assembly error, inadequate controls, misalignment, or a damaged part. In our manufacturing example, the typical causes would be broken drills, improper tool setup, and so on.

The next step is to identify the controls existing in the process that are intended to prevent or detect the problem. Once all the required information has been gathered, it is necessary to estimate the probability of occurrence of the problem. The probability of the problem can be estimated based on the variable process control charts and be ranked from 1 to 10 based on the probability of occurrence.

Criteria	Capability within	Ranking	Statistical proportion outside specification limits
Remote probability	± 4σ	1	1/10000
Low probability	± 3σ	2	1/5000
Low probability	± 3σ	3	1/2000
Low probability	± 3σ	4	1/1000

(*Continued*)

Criteria	Capability within	Ranking	Statistical proportion outside specification limits
Low probability	± 3σ	5	1/500
Moderate probability	± 2.5σ	6	1/200
High probability	> ± 2.5σ	7	1/100
High probability	> ± 2.5σ	8	1/50
Very high probability		9	1/20
Very high probability		10	1/10+

The occurrence ranking is a very important basis for attacking a problem, and regardless of how little an effect it has on the end product, corrective action should be taken to ensure that the ranking of the problem is reduced.

The next step in the process of developing the FMEA is to rate the severity of the problem or the effect of the problem on a scale of 1 to 10. The severity will be changed by actions to change the design of the product or the process.

Criteria	Ranking
Customer not affected and/or cannot notice	1
Minor problem, slightly annoys customer	2, 3
Moderate customer annoyance	4–6
High customer annoyance	7, 8
Very high severity ranking	9, 10

If the barrel diameter of the camshaft is .001 in smaller or larger than specified, the customer will probably not notice it because it will be removed during the grinding process and so will have a ranking of 1, whereas burr on the lobes created while milling would probably cause a minor annoyance to the customer and could have a rank of 2. The severity is not critical since they will be removed by the grinding process. On the other hand, a missing tapped hole would not be detected until the part is in the engine and so would have a ranking of 10.

The next step in the process is to rank the probability of detection. SPC is a valid detection method. These are also ranked on a scale of 1 to 10. The basis for classification is described below.

Criteria	Ranking	Probability of defect being shipped
Remote likelihood	1	1/10,000
Low likelihood	2	1/5000
Low likelihood	3	1/2000
Low likelihood	4	1/1000

(Continued)

Criteria	Ranking	Probability of defect being shipped
Low likelihood	5	1/500
Moderate likelihood	6	1/200
Moderate likelihood	7	1/100
Moderate likelihood	8	1/50
High likelihood	9	1/20
Very high likelihood	10	1/10+

Based on multiplying the occurrence, severity, and detection ranking, we can calculate the risk priority number. The problems with the highest risk priority number should be tackled first. Any problem with a high occurrence probability should also be tackled on a priority basis.

Based on the risk priority number, specific, quantifiable actions should be determined and acted upon to bring the probability of occurrence down. Once any corrective action is taken, the risk priority number should be recalculated. The FMEA should be treated as a living document and be continually updated. When this is done, the FMEA is a powerful tool for determining process reliability.

FMECA

There are other techniques for determining the reliability of a piece of equipment, a part, or an assembly. Failure modes, effects, and criticality analysis (FMECA) is a technique where potential failures are identified in terms of failure modes and the effect of each failure mode on the failure of the entire system is studied, followed by a review of systems to prevent and detect the type of failure under consideration. In FMECA the criticality of the component in terms of the product performance or the well-being of the operators is taken into consideration. The component or assembly may be critical because it is inherently hazardous or past experience has shown it to be sensitive or damaging. A single-point failure is one in which an accident could result from loss of one component, human error, or another single, untimely event. The design action taken to prevent occurrence of this type of failure is determined and after the design changes are made, their efficacy is checked.

The criticality of the component can be determined as either a failure resulting in a potential loss of life, failure resulting in a project failure, failure resulting in reduction of operational availability, or failure resulting in excessive unscheduled maintenance. Criticality ranking can be used to determine:

1. Which items should be studied more intensively to eliminate the hazard that could cause failure and thus requires a failsafe design or a design for reduction of failures or damage.

2. Which items require tight quality control and protective handling.

3. Special requirements to suppliers concerning design, performance, reliability, safety, and quality assurance.

4. Acceptance standard for components received from suppliers and a parameter for which they should be tested.

5. When special procedures, safeguards, protective equipment, monitoring devices, or warning systems should be provided.

6. Where accident prevention efforts should be applied.

FMECA is a powerful TQM tool and has important benefits in preventing accidents. Workers appreciate the safety efforts of management, and thus FMECAs can boost morale.

Shortcomings of FMEAs

FMEAs are extremely effective when applied to analysis of single units or single failures, so these methods are often used to complement fault-tree analysis. Fault-tree analysis provides the means for isolating critical failures and then using failure modes to determine the extent of the damage. FMEAs are not very effective when multiple failures are considered, that is, the product fails due to a combination of more than one defect.

The second most important failing of this method is its low attention to human error. Since most products and processes involve people, the effects of human negligence in causing failure cannot be ignored. Finally, the probabilities of environmental conditions causing the failure are rarely addressed in FMEA studies.

Other Tools to Determine Product Reliability

Fault-tree analysis is another method of measuring the reliability of a system. The analysis begins with identifying the failure modes for which the designer must provide some solution. It then looks for possible direct causes that could lead to failure. The failure mode branches out into origins and causes, giving the method its name. Fault-tree analysis leads us through the sequence of steps leading to the failure, and is used in place of FMEAs, which are costlier and more time consuming. This method attempts to evaluate the possibility of occurrence of one event through the complex relationships that can cause it, endeavoring to include all the contributory factors. This method was developed by Bell Laboratories to determine quantitative probabilities, but is used primarily for its qualitative aspects.

The sequence of steps that leads to the development of a fault tree are

1. *Selecting the top event.* This is the event whose probability must be determined, and selecting this event is the first priority.

2. *Building the tree.* Contributory events that could cause this event are determined.

3. *Identifying faults, effects, and conditions.* Each possible event is studied for circumstances under which it will occur and factors that will cause it.

4. *Using the tree.* The tree indicates where corrective action should be taken.

Other techniques used are worst-case analysis and sneak-circuit analysis, among others.

Reliability Tests

There are basically four areas of testing for both product and process:

1. *Environmental stress screening.* This is used primarily to discover weak points in new designs, and failure in the product or process due to weak parts, defects in processing, and other reasons for nonconformance.

2. *Reliability development tests.* This testing is performed prior to releasing the product for production by following the sequential steps in problem solving.

3. *Reliability qualification.* These are the reliability tests conducted to a production part that is representative of the actual production run.

4. *Reliability acceptance tests.* These tests are conducted to evaluate the reliability of the actual production equipment on periodic basis, especially when changes in tooling, processing, or other changes have been made.

Reliability tests are conducted to ensure that the following requirements of reliability are met:

1. Performance environments
2. Environmental conditions during use
3. Time requirements

The performance requirements for each product have to be defined uniquely. During this performance, products are subjected to stresses and strains, and since these cannot be easily duplicated, tests are performed to simulate the actual working conditions. Similarly, the actual operating environmental conditions have to be determined and tests performed under simulated conditions to ensure that the product can withstand the operating conditions.

The final condition for reliability testing requires testing the product to failure, followed by repairing it and then recycling it to failure through several times. This provides useful data on the life expectancy to failure.

Statistical Process Control

Purpose of SPC

In recent years quality has become the focus of companies expecting to compete in the nineties. Such businesses have to have a master plan to implement SPC. The purpose of SPC is to attain a continually improving process. SPC is the most important ingredient in reducing variability, a major goal of TQM. The concept of variability reduction was originally developed by Dr. Shewhart in his research at Bell Laboratories in the 1920s and it has been expanded upon by others, including Deming, Juran, Feigenbaum, and Ishikawa.

A part usually has specified dimensions and a tolerance around this specification. The specified dimension is usually the best value for the product's function, fit, and appearance. This is the value that must be attained to ensure the highest level of quality. The further out from the specified target, the lower the quality of the part, and the higher the cost of the part and further processing.

Before going into the methodologies of statistically controlling a process, we have to define the following terms for clearer understanding of SPC:

Process. The combination of people, equipment, input materials, and production methods that work together to produce a product. The performance of the process depends on the way it has been designed.

Information about a process. information about the process is gained by studying the outputs, which also include the intermediate outputs.

Action on a process. Changes in the operations (operator training, materials, and so on) or changes to the process elements; such changes need to be future-oriented.

Action on the outputs. This is future-oriented, based on detecting problems on the outputs already produced.

SPC gives us a method to measure variation, predicts the occurrence of variation, and helps us hold variation within acceptable limits. When a process is producing parts within control limits and it is operating in a random manner with no special disruptions present, the process is then stable or in statistical control, and it is possible to sample from it and draw valid conclusions about how the process is performing and capable of performing in the future. The result of a random process acting over time with only random variability contributing to the differences from part to part gives a distribution of results that approximates a normal distribution. This is shown in Fig. 7.1. This type of curve is very important in most industrial applications because it is the kind of distribution that will result in a process that is in statistical control. Figure 7.2 shows a set of sample data gathered on the journal diameter of the camshaft. Figure 7.3 shows the distribution of the diameter data on the finished ground journals. If these data are taken and plotted on a chart, we see a distribution as shown in Fig. 7.4. The stable bell shaped curve implies that there is no special cause of variation, and the variation is caused by the common causes. The differences can be in location, spread, shape, or any combination of these. Histograms are basic tools for analysis of raw data, and together with a measure of central tendency and a statistic that measures variability helps us determine whether the process will produce parts within specification. The various forms of the histograms that may result are shown in Fig. 7.5.

Variation: Common and Special Causes

To understand the use of process control, it is important to understand variation and how it affects the process. To begin, it is necessary to

Pieces vary from each other:

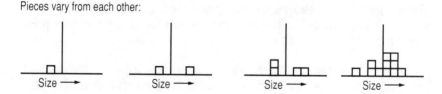

But they form a pattern that, if stable, is called a distribution:

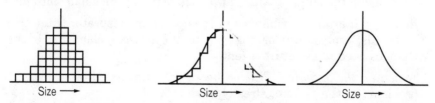

Figure 7.1 Variation—individual pieces may vary but many pieces form a stable pattern.

| LSL = -0.00250 | | USL = 0.00250 | |
Part no.	Journal diameter	Part no.	Journal diameter
1	-0.00170	33	0.00031
2	-0.00180	34	0.00045
3	-0.00130	35	0.00035
4	-0.00140	36	0.00023
5	-0.00120	37	0.00011
6	-0.00140	38	0.00045
7	-0.00052	39	0.00039
8	-0.00062	40	0.00034
9	-0.00056	41	0.00045
10	-0.00077	42	0.00034
11	-0.00067	43	0.00021
12	-0.00076	44	0.00009
13	-0.00086	45	0.00042
14	-0.00075	46	0.00041
15	-0.00054	47	0.00008
16	-0.00059	48	0.00053
17	-0.00052	49	0.00062
18	-0.00032	50	0.00053
19	-0.00047	51	0.00073
20	-0.00036	52	0.00065
21	-0.00023	53	0.00072
22	-0.00011	54	0.00083
23	-0.00047	55	0.00073
24	-0.00043	56	0.00054
25	-0.00032	57	0.00057
26	-0.00045	58	0.00051
27	-0.00036	59	0.00130
28	-0.00023	60	0.00140
29	-0.00011	61	0.00120
30	-0.00047	62	0.00140
31	-0.00043	63	0.00170
32	-0.00007	64	0.00190

Mean = -4.7E-06   Max = 0.0019   Min = -0.0018
Range = 0.0037   Sd = 0.000786

Figure 7.2   Data from camshaft manufacturing system.

understand that no two products are alike. This is because a process contains an inherent source of variability. In machining a camshaft, the variations arise from clearances, bearing wear, tool wear, material hardness, maintenance, operator accuracy, environmental conditions, and so on. Some of these sources of variation such as backlash occur rapidly and affect performance of the fixtures. Other factors such as tool wear cause gradual variation over longer periods of time. Changes in environmental conditions such as a power surge may cause an irregular change in part size. To attain our goal of reducing variation, it is necessary to distinguish between special and common causes of variation.

−.0025/−.0020	0
−.0020/−.0015	2
−.0015/−.0010	4
−.0010/−.0005	11
−.0005/.0000	15
.0000/.0005	15
.0005/.0010	11
.0010/.0015	4
.0015/.0020	2
.0020/.0025	0

Figure 7.3 Frequency distribution of journal diameters.

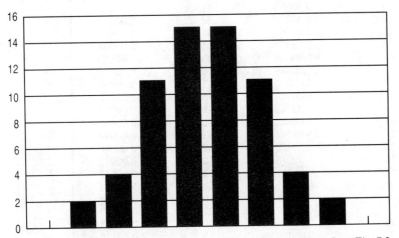

Figure 7.4 Histogram of frequency distribution of journal diameters from Fig. 7.3.

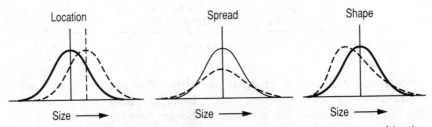

Figure 7.5 Distributions can differ in location, spread, and shape or in any combination of these.

Common causes refer to the many sources of variation in a process that is in statistical control. While individual values are different, they tend to form a pattern that can be described by location, spread, and shape. The common causes can be indicated by simple statistical techniques, but a detailed analysis is needed to isolate them. Identification and correction of the common causes of variation require action on the system. Management has to perform the necessary changes to the system that result in reduction or elimination of these causes.

Special causes, on the other hand, refer to factors that cannot be adequately explained by any single distribution of the process output, as would be the case if the process were in a state of statistical control. These special causes can also be identified by simple statistical techniques and are not common to all the operations. This is functionally the responsibility of the operators to identify and eliminate these causes of variation once the operator has been trained to look for them. Therefore, special causes of variation require local action to eliminate.

It is imperative to talk about the two factors to be considered:

1. Process capability

2. Process control

Process capability should be addressed only after process control has been established, because capability calculations are valid only after the process is in statistical control. Process control establishes that a stable distribution of variation exists. The control chart indicates how a process is behaving over time and gives information about the stability of the process, but does not indicate conformance to specifications, that is, it does not tell us whether the process is capable. The four possible conditions that a process can generate with respect to "stability" or control and capability are shown in Fig. 7.6.

Case 1. The process is in control and capable. These are the desired conditions. *X*-bar and *R* charts from this process demonstrate "stability," that is, no out-of-control points and no runs.

Capability \ Control	"Stable" Process In Control	"Unstable" Process Out of Control
Acceptable Process	Case 1	Case 3
Not Acceptable Process	Case 2	Case 4

Figure 7.6 Combinations of capability and control.

Case 2. The process is in control but not capable. This means we have to center the process. *X*-bar and *R* charts from this process show stability.

Case 3. The *X*-bar and *R* charts show that the process is not in control, but it is capable. Instability in the process implies that no long-term assumptions about the process can be made.

Case 4. Process is neither centered nor in control.

Data, the basis tool for analysis, may either be of the variable type or the attribute type. Variable data are measured, while attribute data are qualitative. SPC is the method used to measure the variability of the process and the capability of the process to produce the part to the required specification.

Any process capable of producing parts within three standard deviations of the norm for those parts is considered to be in a state of statistical control, and the special causes of variation have been removed. The variation in the system results entirely from common causes, such as the insert wearing during the metalcutting process. A special cause, on the other hand, would be the case of insert breaking during the metalcutting process. This cause can be eliminated by using different types of inserts or by changing the feeds, speeds, and so on, in the process.

Looking at Fig. 7.7 we see a situation where the process is in a state of control but can produce acceptable parts only 60 percent of the time. This is because the inherent process variation causes the product to fall outside the specification limits. The measure to determine

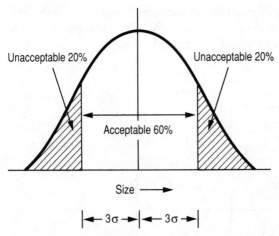

Figure 7.7 Normal probability distribution with 60 percent acceptable parts.

whether a process can produce parts consistently inside the specification limits is termed as the process capability or Cp. Cp is a measure of variation of the process with respect to the acceptable tolerance spread, that is,

$$Cp = \frac{tolerance}{6\sigma}$$

The higher the value of Cp, the lower the variation within the tolerance spread. As a general rule, Cp > 1.33 is considered acceptable, although theoretically this will still continue to produce 66 defects per million parts.

The problem with the Cp index is that it does not take into account the process average. The average of the process may be shifted to one side of the specification limit. This means that although Cp is greater than 1.33, we may have a greater number of parts lost because the average is closer to the high or the low limit. To deal with this situation, another index, termed the Cpk index, is available. Cpk measures the process in relation to the target value and the specification limits. Cpk is calculated as the lower of

$$\frac{USL - process\ average}{3\sigma} \quad or \quad \frac{Process\ average - LSL}{3\sigma}$$

The general rule is to consider a process capable if the Cpk index is greater than 1.33. The higher the Cpk value, the lower the inherent variation in the process. Special causes of variation result in the parts being produced outside the specification limit. As stated earlier, it is our task to minimize the common causes of variation. If the common causes are eliminated or minimized, then the quality automatically improves and the cost is automatically reduced.

Strategic Routing of Parts

One of the most important outputs of the system of measuring machine and process capabilities is the resulting database. This database is indispensable, since it gives us the opportunity for ensuring that the parts for a given run are 100 percent good parts. Of course, many times other constraints may prevent us from achieving this, but if an unacceptable part is produced by a capable machine, then we know that it is due to a controllable factor.

Suppose you know the tolerance on a given part is ±.005 in, and we have two machines that are capable for a tolerance of ±.004 in and ±.006 in, then for the given manufacturing process, it is necessary to use the first machine. If, however, the tolerance is ±.007 in, then we can use either machine to manufacture the part. This means that the machine that is less costly to run can be used in the manufacturing process depending on availability of the machine. Should there be a need for changeover, then it can be easily accomplished without reducing the quality of the end product.

Another competitive advantage of using statistical methods results when a part requires several separate chucking or fixturing operations. For a part that requires a tolerance of, say, ±.008 in, it may appear that either machines can do the job adequately, but if subsequent operations on the part requires workholding of the surfaces machined in the previous operations, then the stack can easily add up to .012 in for the second machine in two setups. Decisions for routing the job can be easily made depending on the machine or process capabilities and the stacking factor.

The process capability data also provide information for how new jobs will run. This information can also determine when you have to be conservative with feeds and speeds and when a policy of wide-open runs can be used. Machining jobs that look good on paper won't end up losing money for the company, resulting in continual changes in the manufacturing process. Quantifying process capability can result in accepting certain jobs while passing up others, based on the capabilities of the machines available in the shop.

Nonnormal Distributions

The calculations of process capability are no longer valid when the distribution is nonnormal. When this situation occurs, it becomes necessary to use what is known as the *Johnson transformation,* which is a system of frequency curves. This transformation was originally discovered by Edgeworth, who called it the method of translation. His ideas were extended by Johnson in later papers through 1949, who proposed two-bounded systems of frequency distributions based on the variate transformation type:

$$z = \gamma + \delta f\left\{\frac{X - \zeta}{\lambda}\right\}$$

where z is a unit normal variable; γ, δ, ζ, and λ are constants; and f is some convenient function.

The S_B distributions use the function $\log [(X - \zeta)/(\zeta + \lambda - X)]$. The S_U family uses the function $\sinh^{-1}[(X - \zeta)/\lambda]$. ($S_B$ is the distribution function that is fit when distribution lies between the upper and lower specification limits. S_U is the distribution function that is fit when data exceed the upper and lower specification limits.) Based on these computations, the process Cp and Cpk are determined for nonnormal distributions.

Descriptive Statistics

The two types of statistics that are most important in SPC are measures of central tendency and measures of variation.

Measures of central tendency

Arithmetic mean. This is the sum of the observations divided by the number of observations:

$$\overline{X} = \left[\sum_{i=1}^{N} X \right] / N$$

Other measures of central tendency are the *median* and *mode,* which will not be used in this book. The difference between the mean and the median is that the mean is a measure of skewness and can thus be used as a measure of central tendency.

Measures of variation

Range. Range is a measure of variation obtained by calculating the difference from the smallest and largest value in the given set of data.

Standard deviation. This is the measure of spread from the mean. This takes all the components of the data set to determine the variation in the process and is computed by the following formula:

$$S = \sqrt{\sum_{i=1}^{N} (X_i - \overline{X})^2 / (N - 1)}$$

Variable Charts

X-bar and R chart (or the mean and range chart)

This is the most commonly used chart, as it is simple to use and measures of central tendency and variability are both charted. A set of data tables and a standard X-bar and R chart are shown in Fig. 7.8. The various calculations involved in the plotting of X-bar and R charts, including the control limits, are average of sample size, n (where n varies from 3 to 6 usually)

$$\overline{X} = \frac{X_1 + X_2 + \cdots + X_n}{n}$$

and average of a group of samples,

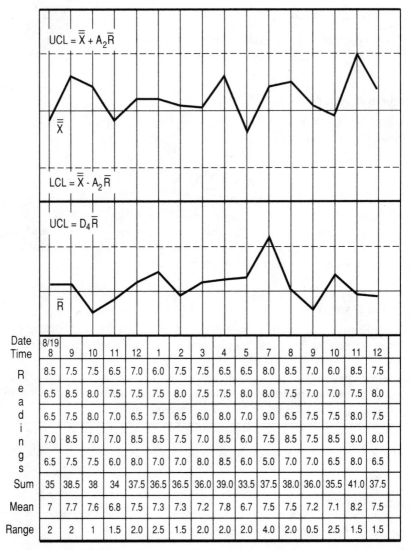

Figure 7.8 X-bar and R chart.

Date/Time columns and data:

Date	8/19															
Time	8	9	10	11	12	1	2	3	4	5	7	8	9	10	11	12
R e a d i n g s	8.5	7.5	7.5	6.5	7.0	6.0	7.5	7.5	6.5	6.5	8.0	8.5	7.0	6.0	8.5	7.5
	6.5	8.5	8.0	7.5	7.5	7.5	8.0	7.5	7.5	8.0	8.0	7.5	7.0	7.0	7.5	8.0
	6.5	7.5	8.0	7.0	6.5	7.5	6.5	6.0	8.0	7.0	9.0	6.5	7.5	7.5	8.0	7.5
	7.0	8.5	7.0	7.0	8.5	8.5	7.5	7.0	8.5	6.0	7.5	8.5	7.5	8.5	9.0	8.0
	6.5	7.5	7.5	6.0	8.0	7.0	7.0	8.0	8.5	6.0	5.0	7.0	7.0	6.5	8.0	6.5
Sum	35	38.5	38	34	37.5	36.5	36.5	36.0	39.0	33.5	37.5	38.0	36.0	35.5	41.0	37.5
Mean	7	7.7	7.6	6.8	7.5	7.3	7.3	7.2	7.8	6.7	7.5	7.5	7.2	7.1	8.2	7.5
Range	2	2	1	1.5	2.0	2.5	1.5	2.0	2.0	2.0	4.0	2.0	0.5	2.5	1.5	1.5

$$\overline{\overline{X}} = \frac{\overline{X}_1 + \overline{X}_2 + \cdots + \overline{X}_n}{n}$$

Upper (UCL) and lower (LCL) control limits are calculated on the basis of the following equations:

$$\mathrm{UCL}_{\overline{X}} = \overline{\overline{X}} + A_2\overline{R}$$

$$\text{LCL}_{\overline{X}} = \overline{\overline{X}} + A_2\overline{R}$$

where A_2 is the factor used to compute control limits of averages, and its value depends on the sample size. The values of this factor are available in standard tables. The average of the ranges ($\overline{R}$) is calculated from

$$\overline{R} = \frac{R}{\text{number of ranges}}$$

The control limit of the ranges is determined from

$$\text{UCL}_R = D_4\overline{R}$$

$$\text{LCL}_R = D_3\overline{R}$$

where D_3 and D_4 are factors used to compute control limits for ranges, and their values depend on the sample size. These values are available in the form of standard tables.

Process standard deviation

Long term. This can be used where it is necessary to estimate the population standard deviation from any set of sampling data and gives a precise estimate of the standard deviation:

$$s_x = \sqrt{[\Sigma X_i^2 - (\Sigma X)^2/n]/(n - 1)}$$

Short term. This method is convenient when the range of each sample has been calculated. This method is less precise than the long-term method:

$$s_x = \frac{\overline{R}}{d_2}$$

Control limits are calculated on the basis of standard deviation:

$$\text{UCL}_X = \overline{\overline{X}} + 3(\overline{R}/d_2) \qquad \text{or} \qquad \overline{\overline{X}} + 3s_x$$

$$\text{LCL}_X = \overline{\overline{X}} - 3(\overline{R}/d_2) \qquad \text{or} \qquad \overline{\overline{X}} - 3s_x$$

Here it is necessary to define $\overline{R}_{\text{max}}$, which is the maximum permissible range for a given tolerance. $\overline{R}_{\text{max}}$ can form a reliable guide for determining the acceptability of the material, but using this parameter requires the process average be at the mean or very near it.

$\overline{R}_{\text{max}}$ is computed by the following formula:

$$\overline{R}_{\max} = \frac{d_2(\text{tolerance})}{6}$$

assuming that the process is in control and the spread is less than the specification. These are the first reject lines calculated, and since these can be calculated prior to any data being accumulated, are termed *reject lines I*.

Another term used in conjunction with X-bar and R charts is R-bar. This is an arbitrary average range used with reject lines II and must be less than $\overline{R}_{\max}$. This term is only used when the past performance of the process indicates that it is stable with the variation substantially lower than the allowable maximum $\overline{R}_{\max}$. The value is determined by looking at the maximum range in the past charts.

Once all these parameters have been determined, we look for any kind of patterns in our charts. The various types of patterns that may exist are discussed later in the chapter.

X-bar and *S* chart (or mean and standard deviation chart)

Standard deviation, while a more consistent measure of the variability of the process, is harder to compute than X-bar and R charts, making this a much less used tool in process control. However, computers should result in use of these charts more often, since the data provided are more reliable than those generated by X-bar and R charts. Once data have been gathered, the X-bar and S are calculated for each subgroup. A chart is shown in Fig. 7.9. The standard deviation S is calculated using the following formula:

$$S = \sqrt{[\Sigma(X_i - \overline{X})^2/(n - 1)]}$$

The next step in the process is to calculate the upper and lower control limits for the X-bar and S charts using the following relationships:

$$\text{UCL}_S = B_4\overline{S}$$

$$\text{LCL}_S = B_3\overline{S}$$

$$\text{UCL}_{\overline{X}} = \overline{\overline{X}} + A_3\overline{S}$$

$$\text{LCL}_{\overline{X}} = \overline{\overline{X}} - A_3\overline{S}$$

where S is the average of the individual subgroup sample standard de-

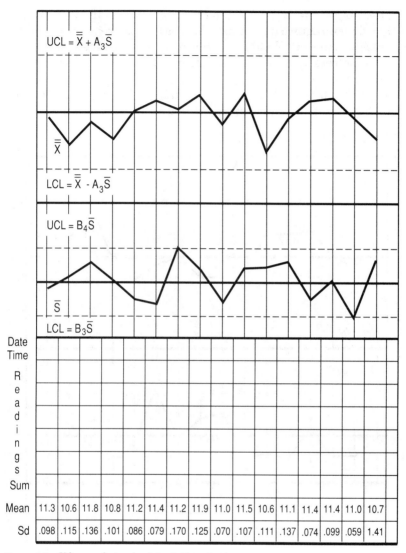

Figure 7.9 X-bar and standard deviation chart.

viations, and B_4, B_3, and A_3 are the constants that depend on sample sizes. These values are available in standard tables.

Median chart and range chart

The median is much easier to calculate but is a less consistent measure of central tendency and therefore is not commonly used. The main advantages offered by median charts are ease of use and the fact that they do not require day-to-day calculations, increasing shop-floor acceptance of the control chart approach. It provides an ongoing picture of the process variation. A sample set of data and the charts are shown in Fig. 7.10.

These charts are used with sample sizes of 10 or less with odd-numbered sizes being more convenient to use. To calculate the control

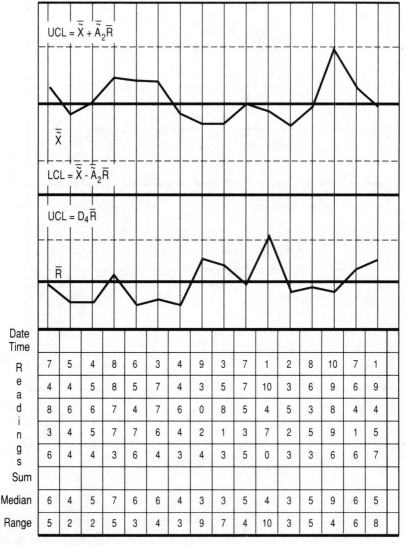

Date Time																
R e a d i n g s	7	5	4	8	6	3	4	9	3	7	1	2	8	10	7	1
	4	4	5	8	5	7	4	3	5	7	10	3	6	9	6	9
	8	6	6	7	4	7	6	0	8	5	4	5	3	8	4	4
	3	4	5	7	7	6	4	2	1	3	7	2	5	9	1	5
	6	4	4	3	6	4	3	4	3	5	0	3	3	6	6	7
Sum																
Median	6	4	5	7	6	6	4	3	3	5	4	3	5	9	6	5
Range	5	2	2	5	3	4	3	9	7	4	10	3	5	4	6	8

Figure 7.10   Median and range chart.

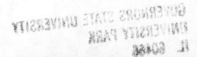

limits, find the average of the subgroup medians, $\overline{\tilde{X}}$, and the average of the ranges, $\overline{R}$. To calculate the control limits for the ranges and medians:

$$UCL_R = D_4\overline{R}$$

$$LCL_R = D_3\overline{R}$$

$$UCL_{\tilde{X}} = \overline{\tilde{X}} + \overline{A}_2\overline{R}$$

$$LCL_{\tilde{X}} = \overline{\tilde{X}} - \overline{A}_2\overline{R}$$

where D_4, D_3, and A_2 are constants varying by sample size and are available as standard sample sizes, and where a tilde means "median."

Individual charts

These charts are used when the use of subgroups is not possible or is not required. Classically, destructive tests, such as tensile testing, are expensive tests and subgroups are typically not used. Testing of pH of a homogeneous liquid would be regarded as a test for which subgroups are not required. These charts plot the individual values on an x chart and the difference from the previous reading on a range chart. These charts are typically not as sensitive as the X-bar and R charts. The other caution to observe in using individual charts is in their interpretation, especially if the distribution is not symmetrical. These charts do not attempt to isolate piece-by-piece repeatability of the process. Even for an extremely stable process, the variability of the process may not be detected.

The individual readings are recorded, and the moving range of these individual readings is calculated. These values are charted on individual charts, as shown in Fig. 7.11. The control limits are calculated on the basis of the following relationships:

$$UCL_R = D_4\overline{R}$$

$$LCL_R = D_3\overline{R}$$

$$UCL_X = \overline{\overline{X}} + E_2\overline{R}$$

$$LCL_X = \overline{\overline{X}} - E_2\overline{R}$$

where R is the moving range; X is the process average; and D_4, D_3,

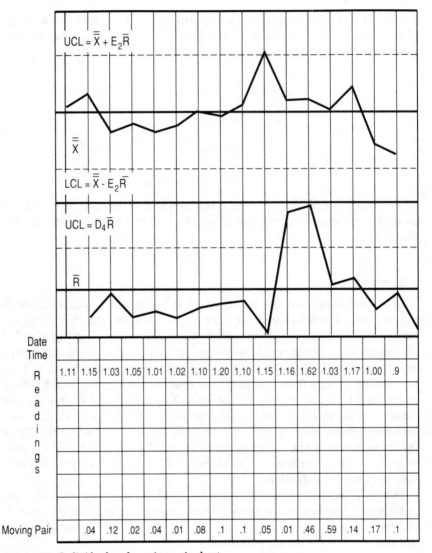

Figure 7.11   Individual and moving pair chart.

and E_2 are the constants that vary according to the sample size used in grouping the moving ranges.

Attribute Charts

p chart

This is the percent-defective chart and is used when you want to indicate a long-term trend in quality. An example is shown in Fig. 7.12.

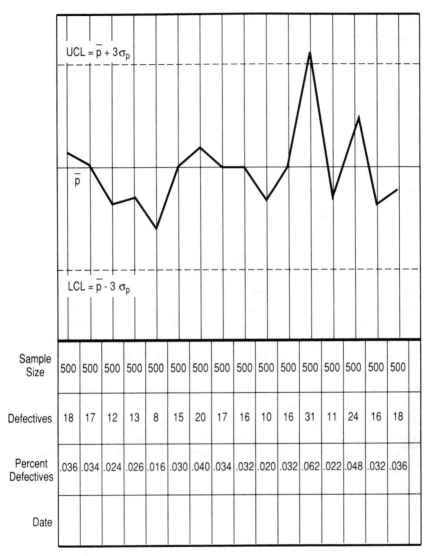

Sample Size	500	500	500	500	500	500	500	500	500	500	500	500	500	500	500	500
Defectives	18	17	12	13	8	15	20	17	16	10	16	31	11	24	16	18
Percent Defectives	.036	.034	.024	.026	.016	.030	.040	.034	.032	.020	.032	.062	.022	.048	.032	.036
Date																

Figure 7.12 p chart.

We begin by computing the value of $\bar{p}$:

$$\bar{p} = \frac{\text{No. of defective pieces} \times 100}{\text{No. of pieces inspected}}$$

The standard deviation of the percent defective is calculated by

$$\sigma_p = \sqrt{\bar{p}(100 - \bar{p})/n}$$

Based on these data, we can compute the control limits for the percent defectives:

$$\text{UCL}_p = \bar{p} + 3\sigma_p$$

$$\text{LCL}_p = \bar{p} - 3\sigma_p$$

The inspection classifications can range from rigid to normal to reduced, based on our knowledge of

1. Production difficulties do not provide for a reliable process to continually produce a good part.
2. Following operation is affected by the presence of the defect.
3. Assembly problems created by that defect.
4. Field performance affected.

Once it is decided to use p charts, then all the inspection should normally be on the basis of the most critical characteristics for which the most rigid inspections are set up. Once the stability of the process is established, then we may reduce the inspection to a normal inspection. Certain operations may even permit reduced inspection, since the possibility of producing a defective part, once the operation is properly set up, is remote, but increased inspection should be reinstituted the moment product quality is found to be deteriorating. The size of the subgroup used should depend on the rate of production, facilities to accumulate and maintain subgroup size, ease of selecting a random sample, quality requirements on a particular part, and utilization of available labor. The parameters for detecting instability in the process and thus more defective parts than allowable, is discussed later in the chapter.

np chart

This is the number-defective chart. It is used when you want to indicate the number of defective items per sample and the sample size is constant. This method uses fewer calculations than a p chart. Here the inspection sample sizes must be equal and the period of subgrouping should make sense in terms of production intervals and feedback systems, with the samples large enough to allow several nonconforming items to appear in each subgroup. An example chart and a sample set of data are shown in Fig. 7.13.

To calculate the process average number (np),

$$n\bar{p} = \frac{np_1 + np_2 + \cdots + np_k}{k}$$

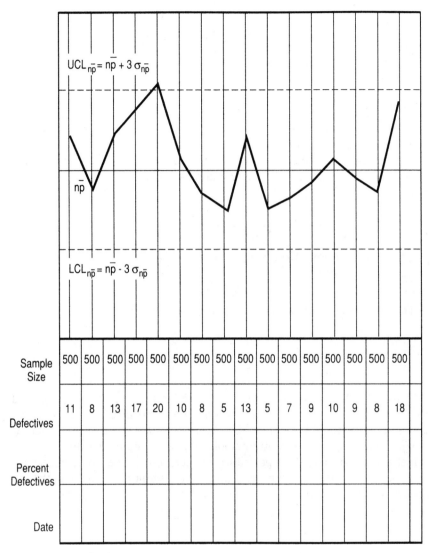

Figure 7.13 np chart.

where np_1, np_2,..., are the number nonconforming in each of the k subgroups.

The upper and lower control limits are calculated according to the following equations:

$$\text{UCL}_{np} = n\overline{p} + 3\sqrt{n\overline{p}\left(1 - \frac{n\overline{p}}{n}\right)}$$

$$\text{LCL}_{np} = n\bar{p} - 3\sqrt{n\bar{p}\left(1 - \frac{n\bar{p}}{n}\right)}$$

where n is the subgroup sample size.

c chart

This tracks the number of defectives per unit and is used when you are concerned with one or more kinds of defects. This chart tracks the total number of defects observed in each sampled lot. The sample sizes used must be equal. An example chart is shown in Fig. 7.14.

To find $\bar{c}$,

$$\bar{c} = \frac{\text{No. of defects}}{\text{No. of pieces observed}}$$

The standard deviation is calculated by

$$\sigma_c = \sqrt{c}$$

To find the control limits for the number of defects per unit,

$$\text{UCL}_c = \bar{c} + 3\sqrt{\bar{c}}$$

$$\text{LCL}_c = \bar{c} - 3\sqrt{\bar{c}}$$

These charts are used when the quality of the product is measured in number of defects per unit rather than the number of defective units. The average value $\bar{c}$ should be set on the basis of past experience, where the average number of defects in consideration does not affect the consumer. If no past data are available, then it is necessary to set a limit based on the best guesses of the supervisor and the inspection and other interested departments.

u chart

This charts the average number of defects per unit and is used when subgroup sizes cannot be equal. This chart is similar to the c chart except that the number of nonconformities is expressed on a per-unit basis. Sample sizes do not have to be constant from subgroup to subgroup, although maintaining them within 25 percent above or below the average simplifies calculation of the control limits. A sample set of data and a typical chart are shown in Fig. 7.15. The number of nonconformities per unit is recorded and plotted. u is calculated from

$$u = \frac{c}{n}$$

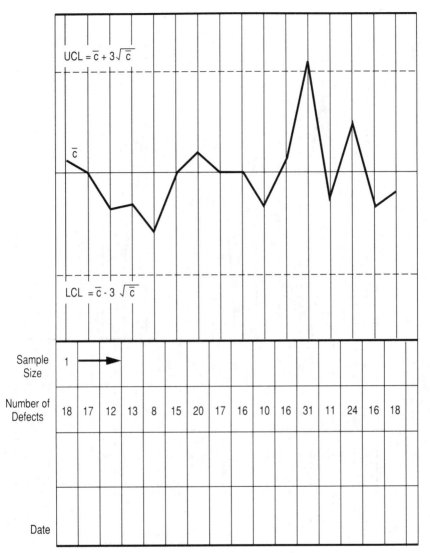

Figure 7.14 *c* chart.

where c is the number of nonconformities found and n is the sample size.

For calculating the control limits, we first calculate the process average of nonconformities per unit:

$$\bar{u} = (c_1 + c_2 + \cdots + c_k)/(n_1 + n_2 + \cdots + n_k)$$

where $c_1, c_2, \ldots$, and $n_1, n_2, \ldots$, are the number of nonconformities and the sample size of each subgroup, respectively.

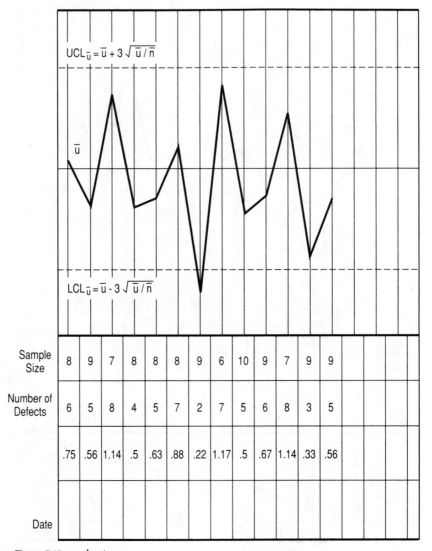

Figure 7.15 u chart.

The upper and lower control limits are calculated according to the following relationship:

$$\mathrm{UCL}_u = \overline{u} + 3\sqrt{\overline{u}/\overline{n}}$$

$$\mathrm{LCL}_u = \overline{u} - 3\sqrt{\overline{u}/\overline{n}}$$

where $\overline{n}$ is the average sample size.

Key Product and Control Characteristics

The first step in establishing a control chart is to determine the need for using an X-bar and R chart for monitoring a characteristic. This can be determined on the basis of whether the feature under consideration is a key product characteristic or if it is a key control characteristic. A feature is termed a key product characteristic if variation in that feature would affect product safety in use, be unable to meet the minimum governmental regulations, or may not fit or perform to the customer's expectation. On the camshaft, failure to meet the diameter or runout specification on the pilot may result in the sprocket not fitting and we would have an extremely dissatisfied customer. A key product characteristic requires machine capability studies and continuous control during the manufacturing and assembly process. For a product characteristic to be key also means that the effects of variation are significant. Usually, reducing variation of a key product characteristic improves the overall quality of the product, reduces cost, and increases customer satisfaction. Key characteristics are usually those features that affect the design and the performance.

Key control characteristics, on the other hand, are determined by the processing method and must be differentiated from key product characteristics, which are determined by product design. Key control characteristics are those features whose variation must be controlled around some target value to ensure that the key product characteristics are maintained around their target values. The control characteristics provide the method for adjusting the key product characteristics to the target value. Reduction in variation of the key control characteristics results in the reduction in variation of key product characteristics. These features are usually not found on the part drawing or related documentation.

Finding Patterns on X-bar and R Charts and p Charts

The most commonly used charts in industry today are X-bar and R charts for variable data and p charts for attribute data. The other charts such as X-bar and σ charts, c charts, and np charts are used less frequently. There are also other types of charts such as CUSUM charts which have important applications but are not dealt with in this book. What we look for when examining these charts are patterns. The existence of any kind of pattern indicates the possibility of problems with the process. Based on extensive studies, 15 characteristic patterns have been identified. These patterns can be more generally classified as

Natural patterns

Shifts in level patterns (sudden shift and gradual shift in levels and trends)

Cycles

Wild patterns (freaks and grouping or bunching)

Multiuniverse patterns (mixtures, stable mixtures, systematic variables, unstable forms of mixture, and stratification)

Instability patterns (interaction, tendency of one chart to follow another)

Based on the above classification the various types of control charts and the reasons for the variation are explained below:

Natural patterns

These patterns do not indicate any unnaturalness over a long series of plotted points and do not indicate evidence of trends, sudden shifts, and so on. The presence of a natural pattern does not necessarily indicate a normal distribution; natural patterns may be fairly smooth, unimodal, not extremely flat, and not extremely skewed. The charts associated with these types of patterns and their distributions are shown in Fig. 7.16.

X-bar and R charts showing natural patterns indicate that the average did not change during the charted period. When both are in control, then reliable comparisons can be made between processes and specified limits.

R charts showing natural patterns indicate process uniformity, meaning that there is a constant fraction of defective parts in the

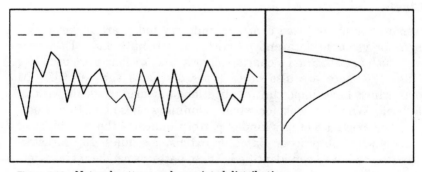

Figure 7.16   Natural pattern and associated distribution.

product. If the chart covers machine dimensions, it shows the capability of the machine.

Sudden shifts in level

The time-series plots of the data and the distributions associated with the sudden shift in level are shown together in Fig. 7.17. These sudden shifts in level occur because of certain special causes and is one of the easiest patterns to detect. The various reasons such a situation may occur are described below.

The X-bar chart being out of control while the R chart is in control may be due to either a change in material, operator, test set, machine, setting, or setup method. This situation can be corrected by changing the parameter that has changed to its original value. R charts may show the same effects whether they are due to a change in operator(s), material, or equipment. The following factors will make R chart levels rise: operator carelessness, inadequate maintenance, or machines not capable of holding required tolerance. The R pattern will drop because of better-trained operators, or more capable machines. R charts exhibit the same characteristics because of different material, change in machine or operator, change in calibration/method. The following will make the p-chart level rise: worse material; poorer machines, tools, or fixtures, and so on; less-experienced operators, and general tightening of requirements. p-chart patterns will decrease due to better-trained operators, better machines and materials, or opening the tolerances.

Gradual change in level

A gradual change in level and the related distribution are shown in Fig. 7.18. A gradual change in level indicates that some portion of the

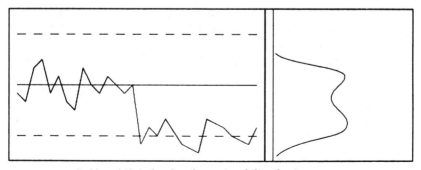

Figure 7.17   Sudden shift in level and associated distribution.

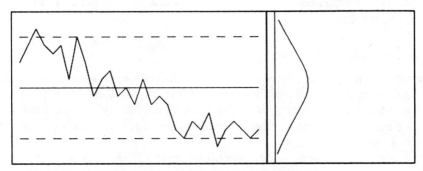

Figure 7.18   Gradual change in level and associated distribution.

process has been changed and that the effect of this change is a gradual shift in the average level of output from the process. These types of pattern are often seen in the early stages of manufacturing, when the operators are learning to operate a new machine or when maintenance procedures are put into action.

If the X-bar chart shows a gradual change in level while the R chart is in control, then the cause is due to a gradual introduction of new material, better supervision, greater skill on the part of the operator, change in maintenance program, operator waiting until the process goes out of control to offset, or introduction of process controls in this or other areas.

R charts show a gradual change to lower level because of better fixtures, better methods, better skills, and so on. Poorer fixtures, methods, and skills will raise the level of the R chart.

p charts exhibit gradual change in level because of addition or removal of product requirements or relaxation or tightening of tolerances.

Trends

Some charts start below the lower control limit and go past the upper control limit. These charts do not have tendency to settle down. The various cases are shown in Fig. 7.19.

If the X-bar chart is not in control while the R chart is, the reasons are tool wear, workholding device wear, seasonal effect, operator fatigue, inadequate maintenance of test set, gradual change in standards, poor housekeeping (for example, dirt clogging up fixtures or holes).

R charts may exhibit increasing trends due to something wearing or gradually loosening, dulling of tools, poor maintenance, or poor process controls in other areas. R charts may exhibit a decreasing trend

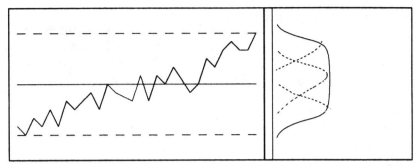

Figure 7.19 Trend and associated distribution.

due to a gradual improvement in operator technique due to learning, improved maintenance, or improved control of prior processes.

p charts exhibit increasing trends due to poorer materials, untrained or careless operators, excessive tool wearing, or tightening of requirements. p charts may show a downward trend due to better-trained operators, better materials, or lowering of requirements.

Cycles

Cycles are repeating waves of periodic low and high points on a control chart caused by special disturbances, and the resulting charts and the distribution are shown in Fig. 7.20. The cyclic pattern is caused by special disturbances that appear and disappear with some regularity.

The reasons for such cyclic patterns appearing on the X-bar chart while the R chart is in control are because of seasonal effects such as temperature and humidity, worn positions or threads on locking devices, roller eccentricity, operator fatigue, rotation of inspectors on the

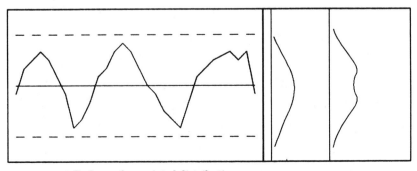

Figure 7.20 Cycles and associated distributions.

job, difference between gages used, voltage fluctuation, or regular difference between day and night shifts.

R charts show a cyclic pattern due to changes in maintenance schedules, operator fatigue, rotation of fixtures and gages, regular difference between night and day shifts, tool or die wear causing excessive play, or tools in need of resharpening (causing burrs, which affect measurements).

p charts exhibit cyclic patterns because of changes in sorting or sampling practices or regular differences between suppliers.

Mixtures

Mixture patterns indicate the presence of two or more distributions for a quality characteristic. For example, two distributions of a part supplied by two or more suppliers. These become more apparent the greater the difference between the component distributions. The charts generated by this and the related distribution are shown in Fig. 7.21.

Stable forms of mixture

There are very few points near the centerline and the chart and the distribution pattern associated with the mixture is shown in the Fig. 7.22. These patterns occur due to two or more distributions of a quality characteristic which does not change over time with respect to the proportion of items coming from each distribution and/or the average for each distribution.

X-bar charts show this pattern when there are consistent differences in material; operators are mixed; differences exist in test sets or gages; and different lots are mixed, such as parts coming from two production lines making the same product.

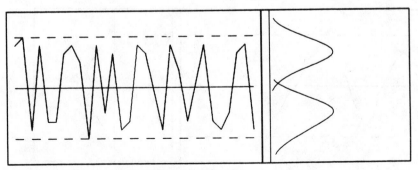

Figure 7.21 Mixture and associated distribution.

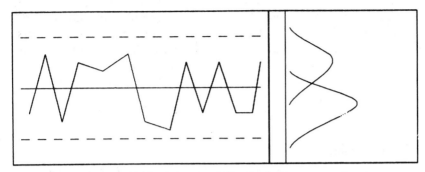

Figure 7.22 Stable pattern and associated distribution.

R charts show this pattern when different lots are mixed, there are frequent drifts in automatic controls, or differences exist in test sets or gages.

p charts exhibit these patterns when a nonrandom sampling pattern is used, lots come from two or more sources, screening some lots are screened at prior operation, or there are differences in test sets or gages.

Unstable forms of mixture

The charts and the distributions associated with unstable forms of mixtures are shown in Fig. 7.23. The most common reasons are described below.

The X-bar chart is out of control but the R chart is in control because of differences in material, operators, or test sets; automatic control failure; overadjustment of the process; wrong sampling procedures; changes in method of measurements; errors in plotting; or if setup parts are used in calculations.

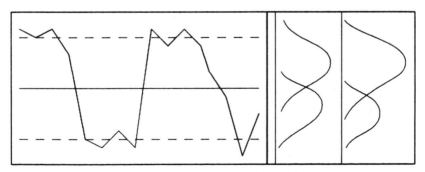

Figure 7.23 Unstable forms of mixture and associated distributions.

R charts show such unstable mixture patterns because of differences in material, operators, test sets, and so on; play in fixtures; unreliable locking devices; chuck moving; inadequate maintenance; tools need resharpening; equipment misaligned; incomplete operation; or setup or experimental pieces are used in calculations.

p charts show such patterns due to unreliable gaging methods, variations in sample size, characteristics that tend to be all good or all bad, or nonrandom sampling.

Systematic variables

The charts associated with this situation are shown in Fig. 7.24. Systematic variables occur due to samples from widely varying distributions, such as two products from different shifts; then a stable mixture pattern will exist. The *X*-bar chart shows a classic sawtoothed pattern leading to the unusually high presence of control chart points beyond the control limits. *X*-bar charts may exhibit this situation due to differences between shifts, differences between test sets, differences between assembly lines, or a systematic manner of dividing data.

R charts exhibit this type of pattern when data are divided systematically (that is, data from two shifts are mixed within a subgroup), or large differences in spread exist between two production lines making the same product.

p charts show this situation when samples are drawn systematically from different sources.

Stratification

The stratification charts and the distribution pattern are shown in Fig. 7.25. If samples drawn from two or more lots have been combined, then the stable mixture pattern can create an extremely small difference

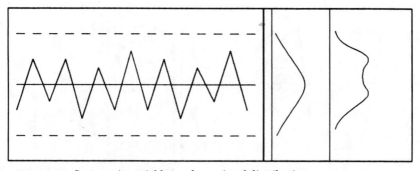

Figure 7.24 Systematic variables and associated distributions.

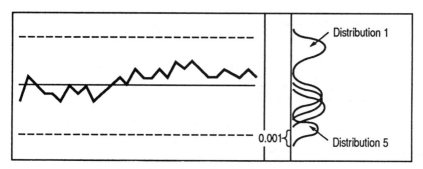

Figure 7.25   Stratification and associated distributions.

among statistics on an X-bar, R, or p chart. These charts will show an unusually high presence of control points near the centerline. The small differences on the X-bar, R, or p charts are frequently interpreted as unusually good control, but nothing could be farther than the truth. The reasons for such a situation occurring are explained below.

X-bar charts are out of control due to anything capable of causing a mixture or incorrect calculations.

An R chart may show the effects of stratification more readily than an X-bar chart. This may be due to different lots of material, large quantities of piece parts mixed on the line, frequent drift in automatic controls, differences in test sets or gages.

p charts may show stratification due to a nonrandom sampling technique, lots coming from two or more sources, screening of some lots at a prior station, difference in the people checking, differences in test sets, gages, and so on.

Freaks

The nature of unstable mixture patterns indicates that the multiple component distributions that make up the distribution of a quality characteristic are sporadically affected by special disturbances. This will cause a systematic variable effect which will occur unevenly, generating unusually high numbers of chart points near or beyond the control limits. The charts and distribution associated with freaks are shown in Fig. 7.26. Freaks do not show up on an X-bar chart without a corresponding indication on the R chart. The exception to this rule may be when a sudden abnormal condition in the process may affect all or most of the units in the sample.

X-bar charts show freaks due to wrong setting that was corrected immediately, error in measurement or plotting, an incomplete or

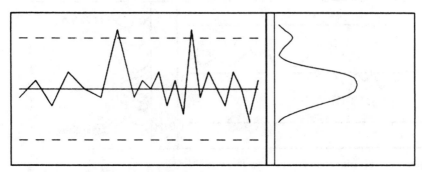

Figure 7.26   Freaks and associated distribution.

omitted operation, a breakdown of facilities, or accidental inclusion of experimental units.

R charts show freaks due to accidental damage in handling, incomplete or omitted operation, breakdown of facilities, experimental units, measured setup parts, calculation, measurement, or plotting error, occasional part from end of rod or strip.

p charts show freaks due to variations in sample size, sampling from distinctly different distributions, or occasional good or bad lots.

Grouping or bunching

The charts and distributions associated with grouping or bunching are shown in Fig. 7.27. The various types of bunching are described below.

X-bar chart shows bunching while the R chart is in control. This may be due to measurement difficulties, change in calibration of a test set or measuring instrument, or a shift in distribution for a limited period.

R chart shows grouping or bunching due to freaks in the data or mixture of distributions.

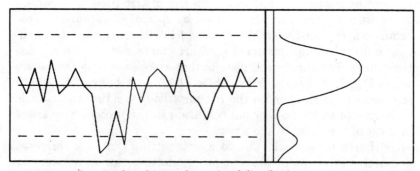

Figure 7.27   Grouping/bunching and associated distribution.

p chart shows grouping or bunching due to change in technique of classification, shift in one of the underlying distributions of the product, or changes in assortment of the product.

Instability

The process tends to run within the control limits with occasional outliers. This is shown, along with the distribution, in Fig. 7.28. X-bar charts show this pattern due to overadjustment of the machine, fixtures that are not repeatable and so do not hold the part correctly, mixed lots, differences in test sets or gages, or many process variables acting together to affect process. This may involve the use of design of experiments to determine which causes have any effect on the process, experimental work data used in calculations, effect of various sorting operations.

R charts are invariably thrown out of control by instability resulting from overadjustment, nonrepeatable fixtures, and so forth. In such a case the X-bar chart may appear to have erratic ups and downs even when the center of the distribution is actually stable. There are many reasons R charts are unstable. If unstable on the high side, the reasons may be play in fixture, untrained or careless operator, unstable testing equipment, assemblies off center, or defective piece parts. Instability may occur on the low side due to better-trained operators, better process control in previous operation, and so on.

p charts show instability on the high side due to untrained or careless operators, poor maintenance, or defective pieces. Instability on the low side could be a result of operator training, better process control in previous operations, lowering of standards, or incorrect checking.

Interactions

These patterns occur when one variable affects the behavior of another variable, or when two or more variables affect each other's be-

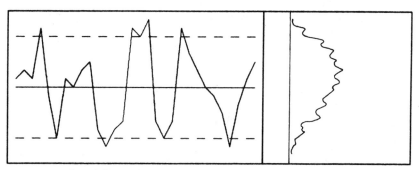

Figure 7.28   Instability and associated distribution.

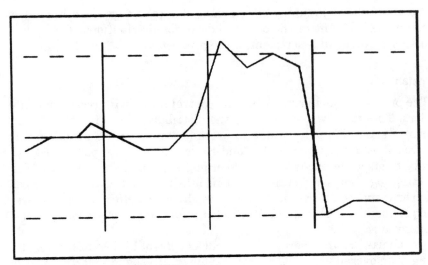

Figure 7.29 Interactions on an X-bar chart.

havior and create an effect that would not have been caused by either variable alone. These interactions between variables can be better understood by the use of experimental design or through the studies of process capabilities. These interactions can be detected by changing the rational subgrouping of the data. For example, the interactions in Fig. 7.29 can be detected by breaking up the charts into shifts.

Tendency of one chart to follow another

Control charts tend to follow one another if they have been constructed from the same samples. In the case of X-bar and R charts, it is natural that corresponding points from the same samples tend to follow one another. However, if the samples were drawn from a normal distribution, there is no relationship between the corresponding points on X-bar and R charts. If the samples were drawn from a skewed distribution, there is a corresponding point on X-bar and R charts, and the greater the skewness of the distribution, the greater the relationship between the corresponding points. Point-to-point correspondence indicates skewness in the starting population, and is shown in Fig. 7.30.

Typical Mistakes and Miscalculations When Using SPC

Machine capability study. This study usually involves using between 30 and 50 consecutive pieces, with a lower limit for Cp and Cpk set as

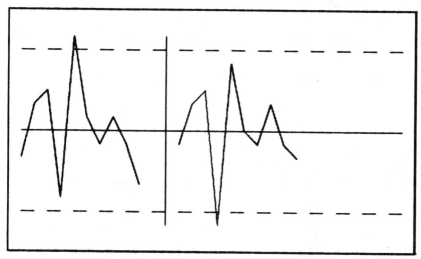

Figure 7.30 Tendency of one chart to follow another (point-to-point correlation; level-to-level correlation may also exist).

the acceptance criteria with one or two dimensions under study. The main sources of error are as follows:

1. A nonnormal frequency distribution. The calculation of Cp and Cpk for nonnormal distributions is performed by many software packages available, but the standard formulas are not valid.

2. One or two dimensions do not represent the variations of the other dimensions.

3. We cannot draw inferences about the potential variability by using consecutive pieces. This means that when, say, 50 pieces are used for determining capability, many factors are not considered, such as a tool presetter, which may not be functioning correctly.

4. No inferences can be drawn about the process stability, which may be more stable, less stable, or unknown.

5. If the gage used does not have a repeatability study performed on it, then the study is not valid, since we do not know the measurement error.

Process capability. This study typically uses 20 subgroups, with 5 pieces in each subgroup. Here again, Cp and Cpk are used to determine the acceptance parameter. The common sources of error are

1. If process shows variation when the sample size is greater than 5, that is, the process is unstable in runs over five pieces.

2. Process mean is not the same as the mean specified by the customer.

3. Measurements are not taken in a situation when, say, the insert breaks during the cutting operation.

4. Subgroups are not taken at regular intervals and there are not five consecutive pieces, then the study is invalid.

5. No attempt made to find out the root cause of the problem.

Statistical process control. This uses a subgroup of five consecutive pieces, and the parameters for acceptability are the control limits on the X-bar and R charts. The use of SPC techniques are not valid if:

1. Control limits are not valid if no capability studies are performed for a given production run.

2. Control limits are calculated such that they signal the effects of special causes of variation.

3. Sample size and sampling frequency do not represent the true product variation.

4. Target for the mean is not the specified nominal.

5. As the tool wears, the sampling frequency must increase. As the tool is used continually, the rate of wear does not remain linear and the rate increases and this means the sampling frequency must be adjusted for this eventuality.

Control Chart Procedures for Short Runs

Although the product used in this book, the camshaft, does not require the use of short run control charting procedure, the importance of the procedure makes it imperative that the methods be discussed, since many products have short runs, and special techniques are required to compensate for the uncertainties involved with small amounts of data. The control charting can be executed in three stages.

The first step is to collect an initial sample of subgroups. Depending on the number of subgroups, the multiplying factor is determined. Once all the data are in control, the overall average of the in-control groups can be compared with the nominal value. If the difference is large, the setup is on target. Calculate the range control chart using the equation $\text{UCL}_R = (D_{4F})R$. Compare the subgroup ranges with the UCL_R and drop any out-of-control groups and repeat the process until all remaining subgroups are smaller than UCL_R. Based on the above calculations, the control limits can be found by adding and subtracting

$(A_{2F})R$ from the overall average. Drop all remaining subgroups that are out of control and recalculate the average. Continue until all remaining subgroups are within control.

The next step is to set up limits for the remainder of the run where the A_{2S} is used for the X-bar chart and D_{2S} for the range chart, and g is the number of subgroups used to compute control limits.

Based on the above analysis, combine the data from the entire run and go through the process described in the first step. When more than 25 subgroups are available, then the standard table of control chart constants can be used, assuming there are no special causes for variation between runs. If special causes exist, then the first two steps have to be repeated for each of the runs, or the special causes of variation between the two runs must be eliminated. Keeping in mind these common sources of errors when using statistical methods avoids considerable disappointment that could lead to a loss of confidence in the use of SPC techniques.

Quality Circles

One of the first notions that must be removed from one's mind when dealing with quality circles is "Taylorism," which works on the premise that the jobs are designed by technical experts and workers simply follow the instructions. Taylor's intentions when he described the principles of scientific management were different from today's managers, who have reduced Taylor's method to focusing on numbers, mostly financial, and narrowly defining the function of workers. The basic principles of scientific management as originally stated by Fredrick Winslow Taylor can be summarized as:

- Scientific management is a science and must not be based on rules of thumb.
- Harmony should exist in the working environment, not discord.
- Cooperation between individuals, not individualism.
- Maximum output instead of restricted output.
- Development of each worker to his or her greatest efficiency and prosperity.

These principles, as stated originally, were designed to create an optimal manufacturing environment, but were reduced to output and productivity numbers, through control of the workers and their functions. It is often difficult to rid American management of this focus on numbers, since they often feel a loss of control. Many managers try to maximize output through cajoling and exhortation rather than evaluation of the system's capabilities. But with the implementation of TQM methods must come the ability for the on-line worker to make decisions about the process, which will remedy the process and get the process in control.

To this end, once the SPC system has been successfully implemented, the next step in the quality improvement process is establishing quality circles. This effectively moves the responsibility of the process and the control to the machine operator. Quality circles involve the use of worker teams to offer suggestions to improve the performance of the manufacturing system. The results of implementation of the suggestions can be quantified by management and members of the quality circles by the process control measures. SPC provides rigorous and reliable feedback of the effects of implemented suggestions. The primary result of quality circles is providing the methodology for building quality and productivity into the same system, thus fulfilling the needs for quality and productivity while making workers an important part in the achievement of organizational goals.

The methodology for operating a quality circle must be clearly established, and usually the team members consist of a group from 3 to 25 members. But usually, teams are 10 strong, since the concept is to get everyone's input into the quality process, and membership should be on a voluntary basis. Meetings should be scheduled for an hour every month, or any other interval deemed necessary. The rewards for participation in a quality circle are not necessarily financial, but are in the form of praise and recognition. The projects undertaken by the quality circle members must fall outside the realm of direct labor cost reduction. The steps prior to forming a quality circle would involve training the operators in basic statistical techniques, cause-and-effect diagrams, and brainstorming methods to organize the problem and improve communication. Another important asset would be to train the operators in the use of Pareto charts to determine the critical problem to be attacked. The process of setting up quality circles involves the following training programs:

1. Introduction to quality circles

2. Brainstorming

3. Fishbone diagrams

4. Histograms

5. Checklists and data recording

6. Graphing the data

7. Interpreting SPC charts

Moreover, the circle leader should be trained in interpersonal skills.

Supplier Quality Management

Managing Supplier Quality

Traditionally, managing the supplier has meant developing an acceptance sampling plan. Statistically valid acceptance sampling methods are described later in Chap. 11. But using only inspection of the parts supplied may prove extremely costly in the long run. Moreover, as awareness of statistical methods of managing quality develops and more and more suppliers adopt these methods for managing quality and improving processes on a continual basis, the use of acceptance sampling becomes less and less necessary. The parameter for judging the quality becomes the ability of the suppliers to provide "zero defects" and implementing statistical methods to these ends.

When managing supplier quality it often becomes necessary to deal with numerous aspects of your supplier's business. More often than not, the person responsible for supplier development has the role of a firefighter, implementing corrective action when a problem arises. Suppliers usually are scared when they receive a call from their customer, assuming that a quality problem exists. When considering supplier development, numerous criteria are used. In this chapter, I will try to highlight the rating criteria when assessing a supplier by quality management standards. Before doing that, we have to examine the role of the buyer in ensuring a defect-free product.

The Role of the Buyer

One of the chief responsibilities for ensuring that the products purchased by your company are defect-free lies with the buyer. Buying nonconforming products and returning or reworking the product adds to the cost of the end product. One of the means to achieve defect-free materials is to reduce the number of suppliers. This does not mean the total number of suppliers for a product should be reduced to one, where you are left to the mercy of the sole supplier. It is better to have 2 or 3 suppliers dedicated to manufacturing a defect-free product than have 10 separate sources who are not committed to the goal of zero defects. In the process of reducing your supplier base, take care to ensure that the suppliers who are retained have a commitment to continuous quality improvement. These days most manufacturing organizations have some form of quality improvement process in place. For the organizations that do not, it might be worthwhile to provide education. Letting your important suppliers' representatives go through your training process helps them understand why process control information is required. Finally, the most important task of the buyer is to expect and demand a defect-free product.

Reducing Your Supplier Base

The main benefits obtained by reducing your supplier base are

1. It gives buyers considerably more spending clout, ensuring supplier willingness to provide a better-product quality.
2. Only suppliers who are committed to the goal of zero defects are retained, and it is easier to train them in the concept of zero defects.
3. It is possible to convey detailed requirements to a smaller supplier base, and since the supplier has a larger share of the business is prepared to better understand the customer requirements.

The buyer is responsible for ensuring that the requirements of every purchase order are fully understood and should try to involve suppliers early on in the design process, so they can make suggestions about the problems they may face in manufacturing the product and incorporate necessary changes to the design. The buyer is also responsible for making sure that the process of two-way communication between the buyer and the supplier are ensured. For this reason, buyers should try to develop a long-term relationship with suppliers with whom they intend to place repeat orders. The buyer must take great care in matching the right product with the right supplier, and for this the buyer must have precise knowledge of the supplier's capabilities, equipment, personnel, pricing strategies, and quality policies. Mismatched relations will place a great strain on your quality improvement process. The need for deviations, waivers, material reviews, and charge-backs can be completely eliminated, since the emphasis is on prevention by the supplier.

Selecting Your Suppliers

The main overall criteria to be followed when selecting your supplier are discussed below. It is important to develop a questionnaire for the supplier to fill out. This initially helps the supplier to meet the quality standards expected of them. Once the supplier is convinced that he or she has met all the requirements for manufacturing a quality product, the customer must visit the supplier and determine if the supplier has met the requirements specified in the questionnaire. It is usually advisable to award a supplier meeting the quality requirements with an award of recognition as a preferred supplier. Once the supplier is recognized as a preferred supplier, then that supplier is given preferential treatment for future supplies or services that may be required. The categories for measuring performance are listed below. Depending on special needs, certain other features may be added to this list or certain features may be removed from the list.

General

This aspect of evaluating suppliers looks at the overall business of the company involved; the following features are examined.

Business position. This involves a comparative study in the performance of the supplier in question as related to other suppliers of similar products. Business position should also attempt to determine the financial ability of the company to continue supplying goods and services to you.

Growth prospects. Growth of a company is one of the better indicators of its health. Care should be taken to ensure that the fast-growing company is not out of control and may go into a tailspin at any moment.

Cost-reduction efforts. A system for reduction of costs while ensuring the quality of the product should be in place. Some major customers are even demanding that suppliers decrease the price of products they supply after adjustment for inflation over a given period of time.

Cooperation. When buyers and suppliers can interact fairly comfortably, then an environment is conducive for quality improvement. Inputs from the customer are solved by the supplier and there is a constant feedback of actions taken.

Location. This may not be an important criterion, except for certain critical items. With most companies adopting a worldwide supplier base, the location may not be as important a criterion as in the past.

Control

This is the most important criterion in evaluating a supplier. It involves the following.

Quality control. This covers the entire gamut of the TQM tools described in this book and the application of these methods to the management of quality. Documentation of these methods in the TQM process should be part of the supplier evaluation.

Process control. This could essentially be covered by the quality, since the manufacturing process and the TQM system cover every aspect of the business. Of special importance is the use of SPC methods for managing the manufacturing process. Many suppliers do tend to pay lip-service to the use of SPC methods, but it is important to evaluate whether the commitment to SPC is real or not.

Material control. Use of just-in-time techniques should be adopted as far as possible by the customers to ensure optimal production conditions. The quality control techniques applied to ensuring that the subsuppliers meet the quality standards should be an important parameter for evaluation of the supplier.

Technology

This is the measure of the technical abilities of personnel within the company and is an important part of the TQM process. The features to look for are as follows:

Technical problem solving. This is another aspect covered by the TQM system and includes the various problem-solving techniques described in this book, including design of experiments, Taguchi methods, Pareto analysis, histograms, and so on. Attempts must be made to evaluate the technical personnel for performing the problem-solving process.

Test equipment. The availability and accessibility of the supplier to various test equipment and the ability to perform tests on this equipment should be determined.

Research and development activities. The supplier should perform adequate research activities to improve the process or the product.

Production

The management of production, using modern quality control techniques, determines the ability of the supplier to supply adequate parts to the supplier.

Equipment. The supplier should have adequate, modern, and sufficiently automated equipment to be a satisfactory supplier.

Layout. The plant layout should optimize production and reduce material handling.

Rate of operation. The rate of operation should meet the requirements of the customer.

Employee attitude. This is an important factor in the evaluation of the supplier. Many suppliers do not pay market wage rates, leading to a high turnover among employees and as a result the supplier cannot meet the quality requirements. Another factor to examine is the motivational tools used by the supplier such as training and teamwork to improve the morale and increase productivity.

System flow

The ability of management to fit all these aspects of their business together and meet the quality commitment should be measured.

A system for evaluating each of the above criteria so that they fit together has to be developed. You could use a scale from 1 to 5, where 5 represents an outstanding performance in a particular criterion and 1 point is awarded for the worst performance. A score of 2 would be regarded as bad, 3 as marginal, and 4 as good.

Supplier Evaluation for Quality

Now let us consider a system of evaluating a smaller segment of the supplier quality management function, where quality is the only basis for evaluating the supplier. There are certain conditions that have to be met prior to implementing a supplier quality management program, including top management support and informing your supplier of the basis you are using for evaluating them. Usually implementing an award to recognize the supplier is beneficial, though care should be taken not to alienate the suppliers that do not meet your requirements. The suppliers that do not meet the criteria should be encouraged to meet the required criteria at an early date. The chief bases for consideration for evaluating the supplier should be the following.

Material quality

If the process or machine capabilities of the supplier are not established, incoming inspection may be required. Any supplier that does not have its machine capabilities established would be automatically disqualified from the evaluation. The supplier should have established Cpk's greater than 1.33. Material quality is then established for the acceptable suppliers on the basis of the formula

$$MQ = \frac{TQR - MR}{TQR} \times 100$$

where MQ = the material quality
TQR = the total quantity received
MR = material rejected

Another measure of the performance of a particular supplier is the number of parts that fails to meet the minimum life expectancy. This count would take the place of the material rejected. This would be particularly true for inserts, drills, and so on, used in the metal-cutting process. The process of selecting the correct tooling is dealt with in detail later in the chapter.

Delivery performance

Here again, the basis for evaluation would be the formula

$$DP = \left(\frac{QP - SQ}{QP} \times 100\right) - PD$$

where DP = the delivery performance
QP = the quantity purchased
SQ = the shipment quantity early or late
PD = the penalty for delivering too early or too late

Delivery performance can often be a function of the location of the supplier, though shrinking global distances have allowed much quicker delivery.

Manufacturing and quality processes

The quality and manufacturing processes require evaluation on different bases than above two criteria, including how scrap and rework are handled by the supplier. Ascertaining that systems to ensure that none of the defective parts reach the customer are implemented should form the basis for evaluating the supplier. Existence of SPC methods for monitoring and controlling processes becomes an important criterion.

Supplier responsiveness

Here the criterion is to evaluate how fast a supplier responds to a quality problem, including documented solutions to the problem. Using continuous and systematic problem-solving methods is an important measure of the performance of the supplier.

Quality improvement and training

Systems established by the supplier to improve quality on a continuous basis and to train employees should be evaluated. As stated earlier, suppliers who have systems for training their operators have better prospects for surviving the intensely competitive, quality-conscious manufacturing environment of the future.

The last three criteria are mostly of a qualitative nature and the customer should use numerous representatives to evaluate the performance of the supplier. Based on all the above criteria, we will use a numerical method termed TOPSIS, or the technique for order preference by similarity to the ideal solution, for ranking a supplier. This method is based on the concept that the chosen solution should have the shortest distance from the ideal solution and the farthest distance from the most negative solution and will give you a basis for ranking your suppliers based on various criteria chosen above.

Method for Evaluating Your Top Suppliers

Assume you have three suppliers, A, B, and C, for a particular product. The five criteria listed above form the basis for ranking your supplier and for our convenience are termed C1, C2, C3, C4, and C5. The decision matrix for evaluating your supplier looks like this:

	C1	C2	C3	C4	C5
A	x_{11}	x_{12}	x_{13}	x_{14}	x_{15}
B	x_{21}	x_{22}	x_{23}	x_{24}	x_{25}
C	x_{31}	x_{32}	x_{33}	x_{34}	x_{35}

where C1, C2, and so on, are the criteria for comparing your suppliers A, B, and C.

Now calculate the square root of the sum of squares of each column. For column 1 the calculation is

$$SQ = (x_{11}^2 + x_{21}^2 + x_{31}^2)^{1/2}$$

Now divide each element in the decision matrix by the square root for that column.

Our normalized decision matrix looks like this:

	C1	C2	C3	C4	C5
A	x_{11}/SQ_1	x_{12}/SQ_2	x_{13}/SQ_3	x_{14}/SQ_4	x_{15}/SQ_5
B	x_{21}/SQ_1	x_{22}/SQ_2	x_{23}/SQ_3	x_{24}/SQ_4	x_{25}/SQ_5
C	x_{31}/SQ_1	x_{32}/SQ_2	x_{33}/SQ_3	x_{34}/SQ_4	x_{35}/SQ_5

Each of these attributes must be assigned a weight. For example, the criterion C1 determines the percentage accepted by the customer and may therefore have higher weight than criterion C5 involving implementation of training systems by the customer. Assume the weights assigned are

$$(C1,C2,C3,C4,C5) = (.3,.3,.2,.1,.1)$$

Multiply each of the columns by the weights to determine the weighted decision matrix:

	C1	C2	C3	C4	C5			C1	C2	C3	C4	C5
A	$.3x_{11}/SQ_1$	$.3x_{12}/SQ_2,$	..., etc.				A	v_{11}	...	...	...	...
B	$.3x_{21}/SQ_1$					=	B	...	...	v_{ij}	...	...
C							C	...	...	...	...	v_{mn}

Determine the ideal and negative ideal solutions:

$$A^* = \frac{\max}{i}\, v_{ij} \qquad \text{for each column}$$

$$A^- = \frac{\min}{i}\, v_{ij} \qquad \text{for each column}$$

It must be remembered here that if the criterion under consideration is a negative criterion, then the positive ideal solution will use the minimum value, for example, price, where the lowest price is considered the best.

Calculate the separation measures:

$$S_{i*} = \sqrt{\sum_{j=1}^{n}(v_{ij} - v_j^*)^2} \qquad S_{i-} = \sqrt{\sum_{j=1}^{n}(v_{ij} - v_j^-)^2} \qquad i = 1, 2, \ldots, m$$

Calculate the relative closeness to ideal solution:

$$C_{i*} = \frac{S_{i-}}{(S_{i*} + S_{i-})} \qquad 0 < C_i < 1, \text{ where } i = 1, 2, \ldots, m$$

Rank your suppliers in descending order of preference.

A sample test and the ranking of the various suppliers as a result of the test is shown in Fig. 8.1. The preferred suppliers are determined from the order of preference as determined by the test. A separate measure of which of the suppliers are acceptable for the job must be made.

Method for Evaluating Tooling Manufacturers

Since selecting cutting tools that consistently perform at acceptable levels is one of the most important requirements in the metal-cutting environment, let us go through the process we developed to select our cutting tool supplier(s). The tools selected should be such that they do not affect manufacturing efficiencies or lead to parts that do not conform to specifications. Let me take you through the process of selecting the tool for milling the keyway in the camshaft.

One of the essentials of purchasing quality is listing the complete list of requirements or specifications to ensure that those requirements are being met. The tool's geometry and tolerance requirements for reconditioning should be specified prior to purchase. Selecting tooling suppliers can be somewhat different than other supplies. A number of factors have to be taken into account prior to making a decision as to which tool manufacturer to go with. The following factors should be considered prior to selecting a tooling manufacturer.

The first step in the process of selecting the tooling manufacturer is determining the material to be machined. The geometry and composition should be such that it is compatible with the workpiece material. Tool geometries and tool materials that work well with one material may not work well with another material. Numerous factors, including hardness, machinability, and work-hardening tendencies, have to be considered prior to selecting a tool. Machinability comparisons with other known materials form an important basis for selecting the tools.

The second step in the process is to determine the tooling material. The cost of tooling is finally determined by the material. If a carbide tool is used where a high-speed steel tool can be used, your tooling costs can go through the ceiling. Special materials should be selected so that the tool can be reground. The most important criteria for selecting the tooling would be the abrasion resistance and impact strength at the given cutting conditions so that the life of the tool is optimized.

The third step in the process is determining the tool procurement specifications or the tool characteristics required. This may involve

Decision matrix:

	C1	C2	C3	C4	C5
A	95	95	100	4	1
B	98	92	95	4	4
C	90	100	100	3	4

C1, C2, ... are criteria for comparing suppliers A, B, and C.

Square root of sum of squares of each column:
        163.4901   165.7981   170.3673   6.403124   5.744563

Normalized decision matrix:

	C1	C2	C3	C4	C5
A	0.581	0.573	0.587	0.625	0.174
B	0.599	0.555	0.558	0.625	0.696
C	0.550	0.603	0.587	0.469	0.696

Calculate the weighted decision matrix:

Weights: 0.3   0.3   0.2   0.1   0.1

	C1	C2	C3	C4	C5
A	0.174	0.172	0.117	0.062	0.017
B	0.180	0.166	0.112	0.062	0.070
C	0.165	0.181	0.117	0.047	0.070

Ideal solution:
        $A^* = 0.180$ 0.181   0.117   0.062   0.070

Ideal negative solution:
        $A^- = 0.165$ 0.166   0.112   0.047   0.017

Calculate the separation measures:

        $S1^* = 0.053$ $S1^- = 0.020$ $C1^* = 0.270903$
        $S2^* = 0.016$ $S2^- = 0.056$ $C2^* = 0.783266$
        $S3^* = 0.021$ $S3^- = 0.055$ $C3^* = 0.717767$

The preferred supplier is supplier B, followed by supplier C, and finally supplier A.

Figure 8.1   TOPSIS calculations.

specifying the heat-treatment and hardness requirement. Various other parameters, such as the material, diameter, cut length, and radius must also be specified. Also, the tool's function and reconditioning instructions, if any, must be specified. Once these specifications are decided upon, it may be helpful to talk to the cutting tool manufacturer to determine if there are any complications involved with manufacturing the tools to the required specifications. If required, changes are made to the specifications. There are several advantages to specifying the buying requirements. First and foremost would be that unacceptable tools do not reach the shop floor and disrupt production. Second, quotations are to your specifications and you avoid irrelevant quotations and improve your inventory control and reconditioning results. Third, implementing any improvements as a result of the improvements becomes much easier. Finally, all the manufacturers can conform to one set of requirements.

The fourth step in the process of determining your tooling supplier is to test the tools' performance under actual working conditions. Here, we do not give any importance to the other factors to be considered in selecting the supplier, such as delivery and cost. The only consideration is the performance of the various tools under the test conditions. For obtaining valid results, all the tools should be tested under identical conditions. Once the results of the tests are obtained, the toolmakers should be informed of the problems faced with the tooling supplied by them and given a chance to respond to them. The variables should be controlled as closely as possible and tests should be conducted on a representative sample. The variables to test are the machine tool's condition, rigidity, horsepower, speeds, feeds, material being cut, and so on. Process variables such as fixturing, clamping, coolants, chucks, and collets must also be noted. Other factors, such as cutter geometries, tool positioning, and set lengths are also noted.

Once all the above conditions are met, the fifth step is to make the trial run under the predetermined parameters. The test may require modifications to allow for studying the tools' required characteristics. These trials determine whether the tools can run under the given conditions and tool geometries can be studied along with signs of failure. The accuracy of the part produced is checked. Metallurgical analysis of the tools and the workpiece materials may be used to determine if there are any variations in the tools.

Once the trial run is over, the next step is the actual testing where each tool is run up to a predetermined test point or until it fails, and data are recorded to determine the high- and low-performing tools. These test results become the basis of determining any changes required to the tool geometries or materials. The tooling manufacturer is ranked according to the performance of the tool. If any changes are

Tool	Number of Pieces Made by Tool																			
Drill 17/32"																				
Drill 29/64"																				
Tap																				
Center Drill (P)																				
Center Drill (J)																				
Insert (P)																				
Insert (J)																				
Insert (JR)																				
Date																				
Shift																				

Indicate with a vertical line when shift changes.

Figure 8.2 Chart for monitoring tool life.

effected as a result of the studies, then the tools must be retested to determine if the performance goals as a result of the new geometries have been met.

Based on the above tests, all the suppliers whose tools meet the minimum requirements are asked to quote for the job. Based on the various criteria specified, the suppliers are ranked. TOPSIS or any other ranking methods may form the basis of ranking the order of preference. The ranking would be based on quality, delivery, price, and other criteria as determined necessary.

Each of the vendors vary in manufacturing capabilities, facilities, equipment, personnel, and quality control, and a detailed analysis has to be made prior to selecting the vendor.

Once all of these tests are complete, the final step is to place a trial order with all the acceptable suppliers whose product performed to the minimum quality specifications. This trial order helps the tooling manufacturer to develop the necessary procedures, cost data, and operational techniques necessary to meet production demands. It also helps determine the ability of the acceptable suppliers to meet the specifications. Using t tests or ANOVA as described in Chap. 10, it is possible to determine whether there is a significant difference in average tool life, and using F tests or Bartlett's tests, also described in Chap. 10, it is possible to determine whether there is a significant difference in the standard deviations of the performances of the various tools.

Based on the results obtained, we now continually monitor the performance of the various tools selected. We use a chart as shown in Fig. 8.2 to monitor the performance of the tool or insert to ensure that the variances between the individual tools are satisfactory. A high level of variance or a high level of breakage may require us to reevaluate either the process or the tools. If the process parameters, such as speeds and feeds, are not set at the correct levels, then we would expect considerable variance in performance of the tools.

Chapter

9

Problem-Solving and Continuous Improvement Techniques

The Need for Structured Problem Solving

The next step in developing your TQM system is implementing a problem-solving approach. The reason for using a systematic approach is to create a mind set for problem solving, setting up a system to prevent similar problems from recurring, and systematizing continuous improvement. This systematic approach to problem solving forms the basis for improving the reliability of the manufacturing process. The main benefits attained by using this system are providing a structured and common environment for problem solving, basing the problem solving on facts. This structured approach helps create a database for understanding processes which can be used at a later date by extrapolation or interpolation. A key step in systematic problem solving is to develop a communication process allowing information to flow to the person responsible for solving the problem, while keeping the person responsible for initiating awareness of the problem aware of the action being taken on the problem. A sample flowchart to ensure adequate communication leading to finally solving the problem is shown in Fig. 9.1. Figure 9.2 shows the chart used for documenting problems and the results of the actions taken in the camshaft process. Documenting problems and the solutions to the problems is an important part of the TQM strategy, since we may be able to apply the results for one study to another problem either directly or by extrapolating the results.

Structure in the problem-solving method provides for a systematic search for the root cause. It provides a system that is internally consistent and flexible, and also forms the basis for communication be-

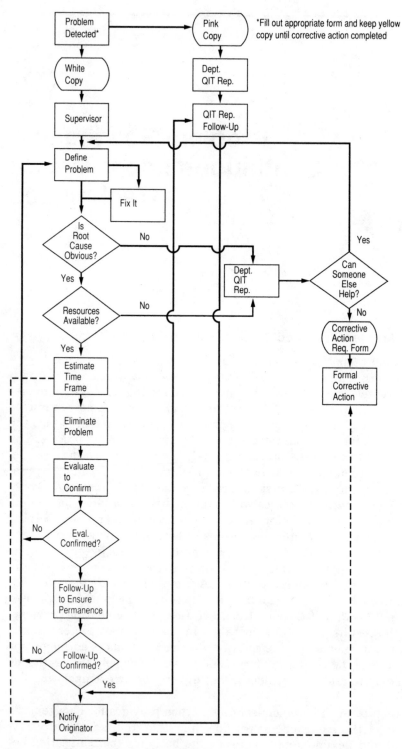

Figure 9.1 Flowchart for problem solving.

ERROR CAUSE REMOVAL FORM

Error cause removal is not a suggestion system. It is a method of communicating to management the situations that make it difficult for employees to meet the pledge to improve. Its purpose is to remove all current and possible opportunities for error and hassle and any other items that keep people from doing the job right the first time. All problems identified through ECR must be taken seriously. Often, simply communicating the problem will eliminate the nonconformance.

Reported by: _____ Date: _____ To: _____

Problem description: _____
_____
_____
_____
_____
_____
_____
_____

Corrective Action Taken

1. Quick fix: _____
_____
_____
_____

2. Responsibility: _____
3. Time required: _____ (notify originator at this point)
4. Root cause: _____
_____
_____
_____

5. Problem elimination: _____
_____
_____
_____
_____
_____
_____
_____
_____
_____
_____
_____
_____
_____
_____
_____
_____

6. Date completed: _____
7. Verified by: _____
8. Originator notified: _____

Figure 9.2 Error cause removal form.

tween the various groups involved in solving a particular problem. Most problems arising in companies transcend the borders of manufacturing, design, quality engineering, and even financial and personnel disciplines. Using a common approach aids management evaluation and control. The sequence of steps in problem solving is based on objective fact-finding and evaluation before a problem is attacked and conclusions drawn. The methods described will provide a documented solution which can be extrapolated or interpolated to solve similar problems.

Prior to setting out to solve any problem, the priority associated with that particular problem should be identified. The technical support to tackle all the problems arising in the system is generally not available, and the problem which affects the process the most must be tackled first. One of the tools available for the prioritization of problems is a Pareto chart. This tool is used in the design of quality improvement programs to identify and separate the "critical few" projects which will justify the effort for improvement. The Pareto chart is constructed by listing the defects on the X axis, starting on the left with problems in decreasing order of magnitude. This type of chart is shown in Fig. 9.3. The left side of the Y axis shows the number of defective items, while the right side of the Y axis shows the percentage of defectives. The number of defective parts is represented by bar charts and the cumulative percentage is shown by the line chart. These charts help establish the relative criticality of the problem as well as to determine the most serious problem existing in the system. The criticality of the problem could be affected by any customer complaints, which take a higher priority over any

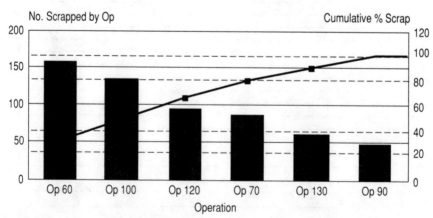

Figure 9.3 Pareto chart: scrap by operation and cumulative percentage.

problems determined critical by the Pareto chart. For example, the center out-of-roundness became a critical problem after the customer complained about it, although the Pareto charts did not show it as a critical problem.

Steps in Problem Solving

The various steps involved in problem solving are as follows.

Problem description

The problem has to be described as succinctly as possible. Usually a description of the effects of the problem helps to determine the significance of the problem. While describing the problem it is necessary to realize that we have to get a written set of specific objectives to be attained, and this should include the long-term objective and the immediate problem to be solved. It is also important to include all charts which demonstrate the significance of the problem. All the potential causes of variability should be identified. The knowledge required to quantify the problem must also be defined, and a suitable experiment outlining necessary data collection requirements must be designed. All data collection check sheets should be constructed. We also need to define the data analysis plan and the measurement system needed to identify the problem. A timetable of the elements listed should be made so that all concerned can perform accordingly. All of these steps required for defining the problem can be summarized by asking and answering the following questions:

Who is complaining? Identify the customer.

What is the problem? Describe the problem.

Where is the problem? Location of the problem.

When did the problem start? Time.

Why did the problem start? Identify the reasons known, remembering that others may exist.

How did the problem occur? Define the existing parameters of operation.

How many parts are affected? Quantify the problem.

It is important to remember here that the complaints could be internal or external. It is especially important to explain the problem to the external customer, since misunderstanding may result in effort wasted in solving the wrong problem. Internal problems should be understood clearly; this may be accomplished as easily as walking over to the next department to determine what the problem is.

Quantify the problem

Once the problem has been identified, it may be necessary to analyze it further to determine whether the problem occurs on all shifts, all spindles, all fixtures, and so on. This questioning strategy helps identify the various factors that could result in the problem defined above. If any past experience with the problem exists, then the need for researching the problem for root cause may not exist and the past solution may be applied to solve the problem. This demonstrates the importance of documenting the information gathered in the problem-solving process. At this stage it is necessary to quantify the problem and answer questions concerning how many defective parts have been produced, the causes for the problem, and the extent of the problem, that is, if a length dimension is off, then by how much is it off?

Depending on the situation, many manufacturers may assess a problem's severity prior to defining it, especially when tools such as Pareto charts are used to quantify the severity of the problem. Based on the measure of severity, an attempt is made to define the problem and follow through the sequence of steps leading to its solution and setting up systems to prevent recurrence. Quantification in terms of dollar values is perhaps a primary consideration in selecting the problem to be solved. The problem with the highest associated dollar loss is tackled on a priority basis. The only situation in which a problem that does not exhibit high costs is tackled first is when the solution to the problem is simpler and immediate savings can be effected by solving the problem.

Root causes

Once a problem has been identified, the steps needed to contain the problem to prevent the customer (internal or external) from being affected by the problem while the root cause is being corrected need to be taken. These steps may involve the following:

100 percent inspection

Changing tooling more frequently

Introducing an intermediate processing step to prevent the problem from reaching the customer

The next step is to identify the reasons for the problem occurring. For identifying the root cause(s), one of the primary tools available is brainstorming. Brainstorming is a process of gathering information from all employees, resulting in identification of the possible cause(s). It is important to remember here that brainstorming should not be allowed to turn into a gripe session, which may result in no new ideas being generated. If an unproductive situation develops, then it is important to immediately stop the session and bring the group together later. Another important factor to remember is that the best-sounding solution to the problem may not be the most cost-effective solution. It is also important to decide who should attend a brainstorming session. The following criteria should be observed when conducting a brainstorming session:

1. Make sure all those involved attend at least one of the sessions.

2. Only one problem should be discussed at a time. Multiple goals or problem-solving attempts may lead to considerable confusion.

Plotting the course of action based on the various suggestions should be part of the brainstorming session, along with assignments to the participants or those outside the group. These sessions may have to be repeated numerous times before the problem is solved. Each brainstorming session should have a follow-up session during which you are essentially looking for solutions and not more problems.

Another important tool available for identifying the root cause of a problem is the cause-and-effect diagram, which is also called a *fish-bone diagram* in common parlance. An example of a fish-bone diagram is shown in Fig. 9.4. This was developed for analyzing the causes for a high number of broken center drills that resulted in a large number of cams being scrapped. The fish-bone diagrams are a graphic display of theories of potential causes for a problem or a nonconformance by identifying the potential sources of variation. It is based on systematic testing of theories to affirm or disprove a cause as the most significant contributor to a problem or nonconformance. These theories can be tested by analyzing the past or current data or can form the basis for the design of an experiment. The cause-and-effect diagrams build branches that continually build from potential cause until a more specific cause is determined.

Developing a successful cause-and-effect diagram requires that you

1. Be specific.

2. Compare procedure with actual process flow diagram. The problem may be arising due to failure to follow the requirements of the process flow.

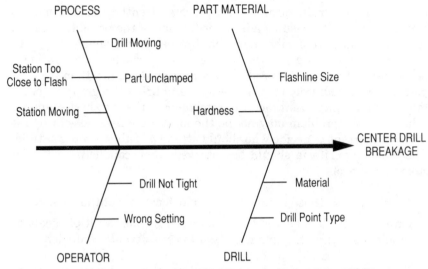

Figure 9.4   Fish-bone diagram showing possible causes for breakage of drills.

3. Ask the question, "What cause of variability could contribute to the problem?"

4. Ensure all methods, procedures, and standards are clearly defined and are adequate, including setup and adjustment.

5. Make sure of the following: Are the gages and machines involved capable? Is preventive maintenance adequate? Does material used meet the specifications? Do any environmental conditions exist that prevent the correct processing?

Once all the above questions are satisfactorily answered, then attempts to determine the causes of variability should be determined. In fact the end result of the brainstorming process can be the development of a fish-bone diagram. Fish-bone diagrams can also form effective tools for anticipating problems by focusing on the sources of variability. The entire process is looked at for the source of the problem. All the above processes described help us establish a plan for investigation, obtain related data, initiate process control, develop a communication system, and correct the products already produced.

One of the primary advantages to using the brainstorming and fish-bone diagram methods is that these methods also provide a method for solving the problem. Many of these brainstorming sessions will lead to a suitable course of action, provided the members of the brainstorming group are closely associated with the problem.

Once the possible root causes have been identified, it is necessary to identify the actual root causes of the problem. Whenever possible, the identification of the root causes should use design-of-experiment methods. These methods provide the basis for evaluating the effects of each of the possible root causes and the interactions between the various root causes. Only when identifying the root cause(s) is fairly simple and can be performed without using design of experiments should these methods be avoided.

Corrective actions

The actions taken may be of an interim or a permanent nature depending on the root causes identified. The other action that may be taken is to get the problem-causing equipment or part serviced. This is also the time to start systematic investigation, conduct special studies and statistical experiments, and review experience and data with current trends to understand more about the problem. A design test on data collection can be used to evaluate the effectiveness of the actions. Based on the data gathered, the next step is implementing corrective action based on the data gathered. The questions to ask at this stage are: have all the sources of variation been identified and have all the sources of information been used to define the cause of the problem? It is also necessary to establish the relationship between the problem and the process. Why the problem was not experienced before and what changed in the process that led the problem to arise must be answered so that the problem can be satisfactorily resolved. All actions should be based on answering what changed in the process, including questions such as change in tooling, change in suppliers, change in operators, change in measurement systems, and change in raw materials. Even seemingly trivial questions such as a change in the weather must be considered for its effect on the quality of the product.

Verification

It is necessary to verify the results obtained for the study. There are three elements to verification:

- Common sense
- Cause and effect
- Statistical theory

Ultimately the verification that counts is whether the customer likes the product or not, but data collected from customers may often be unusable since they are too late. So customer-oriented measures of SPC help to verify the measures of customer satisfaction. These measures should be rated against a baseline. This emphasizes the importance of having data-gathering mechanisms in place for key items. Ideally the measures should be based on design of experiments, a rigorous methodology based on statistical theory that helps the engineer understand the impact of a number of design and manufacturing decisions by changing them in a specific organized manner. A "robust" design performs consistently in the face of widely varying "noise" variables which the engineer cannot control.

Prevention

To ensure that the problem does not recur, the method used is to establish machine capabilities for the problem under consideration or any other measure to ensure the problem is detected. SPC methods should be established to make sure that the problem does not recur. Once all of the above steps are implemented, it becomes necessary to go back through the steps of identifying root causes, taking corrective action, verification, and prevention until the problem is completely corrected. The end result of using this method is that the problem may have to be redefined and we may have to go through the problem-solving process once again.

Using Teams for Problem Solving

America has traditionally been an individualistic society, with the basic attitude of each for him- or herself. With the advent of high technology, it is often impossible for an individual to have the knowledge base to solve every problem that may arise. This means that in order to look at the whole problem in perspective, it is necessary to get all possible input into the problem-solving process. This brings us to the delicate question of building teams to effect problem solving. Team building, while in theory a simple process of throwing the people with necessary input into the problem-solving process and getting them to work together for a solution, is in reality much more complex. The members of a team must be willing to work together, and this requires the members of the team to perform their share of the task, with the related issue of who gets credit for solving the problem. Management must take special care to ensure that the contributions of each member of the team are recognized and due credit is given to the individual members of the team. When forming teams, many questions need to be answered, including why the team approach is used. The primary reason for using the team approach is to tackle a problem that cannot be solved easily and quickly by an individual, or when the nature of the problem transcends the boundaries of expertise of a single individual. The team approach is then used to investigate the problem and resolve it. In modern manufacturing environments a team approach is the overriding framework for decision making.

When forming a team it is necessary to consider the team size, which most people prefer to restrict to 4 to 10. Any team that is larger than 10 results in an ineffective team, with extremely low commitment to the problem-solving process. It is also important to note here that the team should consist of members that have sufficient decision-making skills and association with the problem to be able to come up with a solution. Other important considerations in the team management process are the frequency of the team meetings and whether the setting is formal or informal. Interaction among team members is extremely important to the successful functioning of the team.

The team should be formed with a clear goal in sight. Usually when a problem is identified it becomes necessary to define the problem as a clear-cut goal before assigning team members to the task. The goal should then be put down in writing so that the possibility of each team member following his or her own separate agenda is eliminated.

In forming a team it is necessary to identify a leader who has the authority to assign responsibilities for resolving the problem. Another person who has the highest knowledge about the problem should be identified for the actual problem-solving process and would be responsible for implementing the final decision and the corrective actions. Usually it helps if the individual responsible for ensuring the implementation of the corrective action keeps a record of the minutes of the meeting. Often for teams that involve 8 to 10 members it is also necessary to appoint a facilitator whose primary responsibility is to ensure that all the members of the team do not lose track of the original problem. The other participants must see themselves as members of the team, keeping an open mind and being a part of the consensus-building process which is a necessary part of effective team functioning. Each participant must understand his or her assignment and contribute effectively.

To promote effective functioning, it is necessary to use a predetermined agenda, with meetings held regularly and minutes distributed within an appropriate period of time. Team members should be receptive to ideas generated in these meetings. Certain interpersonal skills are required for effective team functioning, including leadership, communications, conflict resolution, recognition and feedback, and consensus-building skills. Commitment has to be developed so that team building does not become a process in itself. In the process it also becomes necessary to determine the power structure, including the process of settling disputes, how issues are decided, and who leads the group.

Other Considerations for Problem Solving

When using the problem-solving techniques described above there are some important considerations:

- Write clearly, so even the uninitiated may understand, avoiding acronyms, jargon, and so on. Many larger organizations tend to use acronyms as a part of their reporting system, and this is more often than not confusing for suppliers who don't understand them.

- Explain clearly what you are talking about, be it part, concern, root cause, or so on. Any reader should be able to understand the thought process that went into the problem-solving methodology.

- Document the information gathered. This documentation may save considerable grief later in case of any legal implications, or the same problem recurring at a later date. Other problems may be solved by extrapolation of the data and analysis.

- Provide a structure so that there will be ongoing control so that the problem does not recur after the team stops working on the problem. Simply stated, create systems to monitor the recurrence of the problem.

- Remember that the important question is *why* the problem occurred, and not *who* caused the problem. This is important to bring about participation at all levels in the company in the problem-solving process. If any particular individual is blamed for the problem, then it leads to resentment and the person concerned is not mobilized to become a part of the solution.

- Do not let the report become an end in itself. There is a tendency among larger corporations to make the generation of reports more important than implementation. To this end the person or team charged with solving the problem should be responsible for implementing the solution and documenting the results.

- Use internal data instead of customer complaints as the basis for evaluating whether a problem exists; that is, do not assume there is no problem if no customer complaints exist.

- Use design of experiments as the basis for selecting the best possible course of actions.

Example Problem

Based on the methodologies studied, let me describe a problem and the sequence of steps resulting in the resolution of the problem.

Problem description.   A customer reports extremely high numbers of parts being rejected due to journals showing out-of-round conditions during grinding. This problem does not exist with the parts being shipped by the other customer.

Root cause.   The problem was determined to be due to the difference in the centers between the cams supplied by us and the other supplier.

Examination of the process control chart of the center reveals the process to be in control. This is shown in Fig. 9.5.

The next step was to plot the center out-of-roundness. The chart

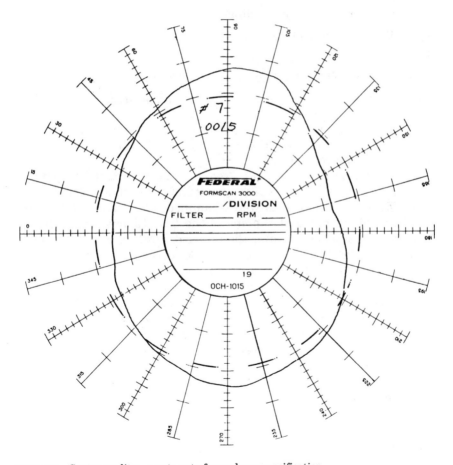

Figure 9.5   Center ovality—meets out-of-roundness specification.

showed the shape shown in Fig. 9.5. This showed that the centers were egg-shaped and that this was affecting the grinding of the journals.

Interim action.   Lapping all the centers using a diamond lap to make the centers round.

Identifying the possible causes.   Brainstorming led to identification of various possible causes for the egg-shaped centers. The various possible causes for the problem were identified as

1. Facing and center drilling in the same operation. This was almost immediately identified as the most important reason for the problem, since the other supplier did the center drilling and facing in two separate steps. This was the only significant processing difference between the two suppliers.

2. Runout on the center drill.

3. Part moving in fixture holding part.

4. Drill and facing station moving.

5. Dwell time not adequate.

6. Feed rate too slow leading to work-hardening of part.

7. Difference between various stations in the process.

After setting up numerous experiments and examining all related data, it was determined that the problem was due to facing and drilling in the same operation.

Permanent corrective action.   Tooling was redesigned to perform the operations in two steps. The new tooling was implemented.

Verification.   The charts were examined after this operation and charts were examined at the end of the line. Charts reveal that no egg-shaped centers exist after the center-drilling operation, as shown in Fig. 9.6. But the parts, when checked at the end of all the operations, reveal the centers to be egg-shaped.

Interim action.   Continue lapping centers.

Identifying the possible causes.   The problem at the center-drilling operation was corrected, but out-of-roundness was being caused somewhere else in the process. Cams were checked after each operation to see where the centers become egg-shaped. Cams exhibited egg-shaped centers after the spacing operation.

The following factors were checked to determine if they were the possible causes for the out-of-round conditions on the spacer:

1. Steady rest not adjusted properly. This was checked and found to be properly adjusted.

2. Clamping grippers may be loose. Grippers were all in place.

3. Collet broken. This was checked and not found to be broken.

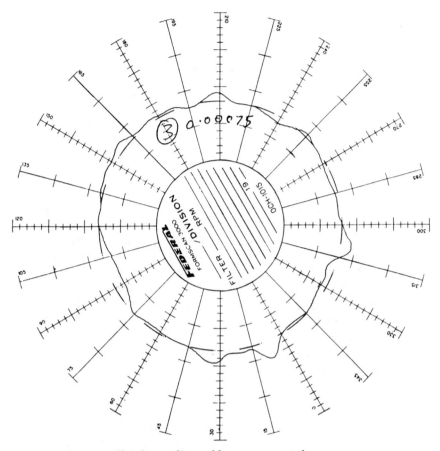

Figure 9.6 Center profile after ovality problem was corrected.

4. The clamping pressure on the camshaft during the spacing process. Inadequate clamping pressure caused the cam to move away from the center during the spacing operation. The center was being brinelled into an egg shape. Immediately, clamping pressure was adjusted to the levels recommended by the machinery maker.

Verification. Centers were checked for egg-shape condition after each operation in the process to ensure the problem did not reappear. Once this system was installed, the problem was deemed satisfactorily resolved.

Manufacturing Improvement Process

The manufacturing improvement process is also known as the continuous improvement process, which it is called throughout this book. It is important to remember that a continuous improvement process has the key focus of customer satisfaction with quality of the product, improving profitability, and delivery and increasing efficiencies by using better technologies. These continuous improvement systems can be effected by creating conditions conducive to these ends. The chief requirements for a continuous improvement process are as follows.

The leadership system

The leadership system includes the overall management system, including human resources management and effective management of suppliers and subcontractors. These systems must result in the development by top management of a comprehensive business plan covering all aspects of the business, including business strategies related to marketing, financial planning, growth projections, plant facilities management, cost objectives, human resources development, R&D, quality objectives, competitive comparisons, and continuous improvement systems and the interaction of all of these systems to create a TQM system. To this end the organization must create systems leading to effective management and development of human resources and ultimate job satisfaction, with a concern for health, safety, and the environment. Proper concern for the development of subcontractors and suppliers must be addressed. This aspect is dealt with under supplier development methods.

Quality management systems

Quality management systems cover all aspects of TQM systems. This book has attempted to cover various aspects of the TQM systems. Most major corporations do provide guidelines of expectations with regard to quality of products purchased from suppliers. These quality systems deal with quality improvement planning and processes; procedures describing the quality function; process control techniques; in-process controls; final inspection; control of measurement systems; material control systems; drawing and specifications control; record retention systems; internal audits; process corrective action, problem reporting, and resolution; and purchased material and supplier control. All these aspects are dealt with at appropriate locations throughout the book.

Costing systems

Costing systems are an important part of the overall improvement strategy for most major corporations, especially when dealing with their suppliers, since the existence of these cost-monitoring systems leads to manufacturing efficiencies. While modern manufacturing systems will eventually have to adopt a time-based system for monitoring costs, existing systems use standard cost and actual cost-based systems with certain cost-reduction systems for competitive product development. Systematic efforts must be made to pricing the products based on normal capacity and standard, actual, and other administrative costs.

Delivery systems

Another aspect of the continuous improvement process is the ability to meet the customer's delivery needs. Any improvement leading to better delivery is an important factor in the continuous improvement process. At this time, it is necessary to understand a just-in-time delivery system, keeping in mind the external constraints such as packaging, labeling, handling, and shipping systems. Delivery systems are also dependent on the utilization of capacity, production scheduling, and inventory management and become an important part of TQM systems and the continuous improvement process. At the end of this chapter there is a discussion on how TQM systems form an important part of the strategy to effect just-in-time systems.

Technology systems

These refer to the ability to design and develop new products and processes and developing manufacturing capacities. These include the computer-aided design, engineering, and manufacturing systems, and the adoption of automation systems to effect greater manufacturing efficiencies. Tool design capabilities, operating instructions, and existence of preventive maintenance schedules are an important part of the TQM systems and the continuous improvement process. Efforts leading to productivity and operating efficiency improvement are an important part of the strategy.

How to Effect Manufacturing Improvement Systems

The system of improving the process is as critical to remaining competitive as solving critical problems. Set correct management guidelines for a continuous improvement program using a capable study team. The beginning of the process to establish a system of continuous improvement is outlining the program objectives, identifying the constraints, and establishing the level of involvement. Continuous improvements have to be made on the basis of knowledge of the manufacturing process, organization, systems, human resource problems, and potential. The person or persons charged with the task of improving the manufacturing process must have the ability to define the problem, develop alternative solutions, and establish and implement an improvement program. This task must be performed such that political factors affecting the improvement of the process can be bypassed, without actually antagonizing the person or persons affected. The process of establishing continuous improvement is a five-step one, involving determining the current status, developing alternative plans for improvement, determining the process that must be adopted, developing systems for implementing the improved systems, implementing them, and evaluating the results. These steps are described below.

Determine the current status

The first step in the continuous improvement process is to determine the current status of the process, which may involve checking the capability of each process to determine the process that needs the greatest attention. The process having the greatest variation would be the process to concentrate on. Cost of the variation may also be used for determining the most important process to target for improvement. Other suitable methods for determining the process that needs improvement, such as Pareto charts, can also be used.

The next step in the process is to audit the systems, procedures, equipment, and controls to determine if they are adequate for the task. A sample chart, showing the audit systems used by us, is shown in Fig. 9.7. This is fairly important information for determining the areas where opportunities exist for improvement.

Although the audits are conducted on a regular basis, it is also necessary to identify improvement potential, including material transfer and handling systems, and design changes. All aspects of the process, including the labor analysis, processing analysis, and material analysis must be done. Any change in process sequence, automation of tasks, or reduction in inventory that would result in better process controls must be considered.

Develop alternative process improvement plans

Based on the analysis above, it becomes necessary to develop alternatives for improving the system. Sometimes there may be more than one alternative for process improvement, achieved through consolidations, eliminations and deferrals, automation, modifying existing equipment, and improved material handling. Here again, the best al-

QUALITY SYSTEMS AUDIT

Date _____   Time _____   By _____

	House-keeping	Gaging Calibration	Daily Reports Properly Used	Tags Used	Spec Used in Control	Process Spec Available	Defectives Tagged
Raw Stock							
Rework							
Op 60							
Op 70							
Op 80							
Op 90 - 1							
Op 90 - 2							
Op 90 - 3							
Op 90 - 4							
Op 100 - 1							
Op 100 - 2							
Op 110							
Op 120							

Systems Rating

1. In use and functional
2. Not operating
3. Calibration/adjustment needed
4. C/A needed, Q.C.
5. Immediate C/A needed

Figure 9.7 Quality systems audit.

ternative based on cost savings must be developed. Once all these tasks have been accomplished, the next step is to convince management of the importance of implementing the identified improvements.

Develop systems for implementation of new processes

The next step in the process is developing a system for implementation of the improved process. The time required for implementation of the process improvement must be determined. Time required to implement design changes to fixtures, tooling changes, and so on, must be allowed. Availability of the resources for implementation of the improved process must be determined. Depending on the size of the task, various project management tools such as PERT (project evaluation review technique) or CPM (critical path method) must be used to manage the project. Based on the decisions made, the process improvement plans must be implemented.

Implement the new process

The next step in the process of continuous improvement is implementing the improved process, either through automation, combining operations, changing order of processing, changing material-handling methods, or any other improvements that may come about.

Evaluate the results

Once all of the process improvement plans have been implemented, an evaluation of the cost savings and improved process controls must be made. This can be performed by auditing the results of the improved process.

All these improvement steps can be attained using the knowledge base available within the company, because the employees often have the best awareness where better process controls can be gained. These process improvements, used in a sequential fashion, may lower the operating costs, improve process controls, increase throughput, improve information flow, and so on. The process improvement must be distinguished from problem-solving techniques where the objective is to solve a particular problem; the continuous improvement process tries to improve performance, which is critical to remaining competitive.

Kaizen

The quality improvement process described above is fairly efficient in achieving its goals. Other experts have their own sequence of steps for effecting quality improvement. In *Kaizen—The Keys to Japan's Competitive Success,* Masaaki Imai describes a sequence of seven steps to create a continuous quality improvement system. The seven steps are

1. Select a theme.
2. Grasp the present situation.
3. Analyze the present situation.

4. Set countermeasures into motion.

5. Determine the effectiveness of the countermeasures.

6. Use standard operating procedures.

7. Plan for future action.

These steps are repeated to create a continuously improving system. Careful analysis shows that the basic sequence of steps is fairly similar whether you want to use Kaizen techniques or Deming's PDCA cycle. Incorporating team efforts to get continuous improvements of the process can get quicker results.

Benchmarking

This is another powerful tool in managing for quality and setting in place the continuous improvement process. Benchmarking attempts to compare similar products manufactured by competitors to gain a competitive advantage. The method used is to measure the process, service, and product to assess current activities compared to the competitor and determine where competitive advantage might be gained. Benchmarking is a five-step process and is described below.

Deciding what to benchmark

This involves gathering and reviewing information that is important to your business and should attempt to answer the following questions:

- What products or services do we produce?
- Where are our growth opportunities?
- What problems do we need to overcome?
- What processes are critical to our success?

Once a potential benchmarking subject has been selected, the subject can be evaluated by asking the following questions:

- Is the subject chosen consistent with the corporate objectives?
- Is this important to the customers?
- Is there an important business need for the subject?
- Are any factors left out of consideration and will any additional information affect the future plans?

Based on the answers to all of these questions, we are now ready to state why the benchmarked subject is important to the business.

Planning the benchmarking project

Here the important steps are

- Designate a leader for the project.
- Determine the range of skills that team members should possess.
- Determine the ground rules for the team, such as when the teams will meet.
- Define "excellence" for the subject being benchmarked. Identifying the competitor with the best similar product in the market could be an important part of the criteria.
- Develop a flowchart of the activities being addressed by the benchmarking topic.
- Refine the scope of the benchmarking project by determining who the customers are, what the boundaries are, and the characteristics that must be measured.
- Gather all existing information about the subject, including a literature survey.
- Based on the above information, develop a project proposal for the sponsor, outlying the customers, purpose, scope, potential characteristics that will be measured, roles and responsibilities for team members, schedule, budget, and logistics.

Understanding your own performance

This requires the team members of the benchmarking project to:

- List the major substeps or subprocesses under each of the activities in the top-level process flowchart.
- Prepare a preliminary cause-and-effect diagram of the factors that influence the performance of the benchmarking project.
- Narrow the list of subprocesses to those that have the most significant bearing on the subject.
- Identify a measurement that assesses the current performance of each of the subprocesses and factors identified.
- Create an operational definition of the characteristics associated with the subprocesses and factors chosen.

- Collect data (both current and historical) and plot them over time.
- Examine the theoretical limits of performance by considering if the activity can be eliminated and determine the physical hindrances to the process, including the possibility of performing the activity correctly all the time.
- Create a list of barriers to attain the theoretical limits for each characteristic of the product under study.
- List the aids that help reach the theoretical limits.
- Modify the flowcharts, cause-and-effect diagrams, and characteristics based on the information generated above.
- Once this is done, develop a list of questions that others must ask.

Studying others

The whole purpose of the benchmarking process is to evaluate performance of our product or service in comparison to the others in the market and attempt to be better than the best existing product or service. This requires us to:

- Identify the characteristics in the target.
- Identify the other products or services that meet the requirements of the customers.
- Develop criteria to narrow the list of competitors to between three and six, preferably comparing organizations of identical stature.
- Prepare a questionnaire that forms the basis for evaluating the competitor's product or service.
- Gather information about the competitor's product or service that is available in the form of open literature.
- Search for other sources of information; regular customers of the competitor may be interviewed if possible.
- If possible contact the competitor organization, keeping the legal and other implications in mind.
- Perform the benchmarking using the other organization's perspective.
- Collect and collate all data gathered from all sources.

Learning and using the data

The reason for all of these studies is to compare our performance with our competitors'. The steps to be taken to do this are

- Compare the objectives of the benchmarking as viewed by the organizations studied.
- Construct flowcharts and cause-and-effect diagrams of the benchmarking subject as seen by each of the competitors studied.
- Compare operational definitions of each of the characteristics with those of the benchmark organizations.
- Plot graphs to clarify this process of comparing operational characteristics.
- Identify the most important factors that contribute to the differences in performance among the benchmarked organizations.
- Extrapolate the information gathered to determine the direction in which this difference will head in the future.
- Identify steps necessary to close the gap.
- Identify actions to surpass the performance of the target competitor.
- Communicate the results to those responsible for implementing corrective action.
- Identify members of the organization that would be affected by the recommendation in the benchmarking analysis.
- Save the information documented above for future reference.

10

Design of Experiments

Introduction to Design of Experiments

Every process capability study may be considered an experiment where the object is to learn what the process is able to do. Design of experiments helps us study the effect of several variables simultaneously and also to study the interrelationships and interactions between them. Designing and conducting a statistically correct experiment helps us determine what the best process would be. Normally, industrial experiments may be categorized into the following methods.

1. *Trial-and-error methods.* These methods introduce a change in the process to see whether an effect shows up in the results. This is perhaps the most commonly used method, although it is the slowest and most erroneous of the methods.

2. *Running special lots.* These methods are usually used when a new product is introduced or a specific change is made and must be tested. Changing the position of the keyway as shown in Fig. 10.1 eases the mounting of the sprocket on the camshaft by removing the burr from the front end of the camshaft. This was verified by using a special run of 400 cams prior to actual production.

3. *Pilot runs.* With pilot runs certain process elements are deliberately set up with the expectation of producing an effect; the results are studied to see how close they come to the anticipated outcome. This method is often used to check for any unanticipated problems when a new product is introduced or any major changes in the design are made.

4. *Comparing two methods.* This is perhaps the simplest method of experimental design encountered in industry. Various methods to analyze the data are used, such as *t* tests for comparing the difference

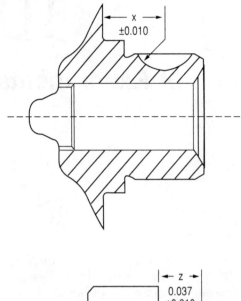

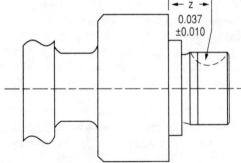

Figure 10.1   Running special lots: moving the keyway 0.037 in.

between the means and F tests to compare differences between the
variances. Other methods such as tests of normality and other statistical methods are described for ease of understanding.

5. *ANOVA methods.*   ANOVA is perhaps the most important statistical tool for a great many of the designs of experiment used in industry.

6. *Other methods of analyzing experiments.*   Other methods for analyzing experiments are briefly described, though the scope of this
book does not permit describing each experimental method in detail.

Experiments are designed using each of the above methods and results obtained from each of them can and must be ultimately verified

by process control charts. We will not discuss the first three method-ologies since they are not of a statistical nature and should be avoided as far as possible. We will begin our discussion with the comparison of two methods.

Comparison of Two Methods

This is usually the simplest experiment conducted in industry, where one experiment is designed in the hope that it is superior to a second experiment. One example of comparison of two methods is comparing two types of drill points for a resharpened drill for the pilot-side spring pocket. The number of pieces made by the operator before changing drills is collected for 20 drills. The data collected at the different feed rates are shown in Table 10.1.

Analysis of this kind of data involves comparing the tool life for the two kinds of drill points. The various methodologies available are dis-cussed below.

Observation of data

The following comparisons may be made without using statistical tests:

Visual comparison. Do parts made using drill point 1 appear better than those of drill point 2 to the eye? A simple chart of the tool life provides a good estimator, and this is shown in Fig. 10.2.

Average of measurements. The measurements made by using method 1 average to 193 part while method 2 averages to 178. Should this dif-ference be considered significant?

TABLE 10.1   Data from Two Methods (Using Two Types of Drills)

Method 1		Method 2	
200	58	296	300
194	212	98	207
98	224	110	302
234	112	129	198
120	129	140	219
296	289	299	149
300	300	167	179
229	287	340	110
100	257	222	268
224	289	119	148

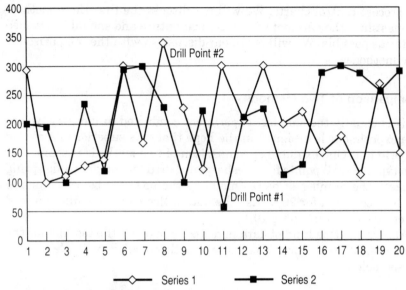

Figure 10.2 Charting the data from two drills.

Observed range of measurements.   Method 1 ranges from 12 to 300, while method 2 ranges from 4 to 340. Should this indicate a significant difference between the two types of drill points under consideration?

Simple observed proportions.   Drill point 1 gives five drills that can be used for fewer than 100 cams, while drill point 2 gives four drills that last less than 100 cams. Should this difference be considered significant?

Distributions

Using the frequency method for two types of drill points:

	Method 1	Method 2
0–49	3	3
50–99	2	1
100–149	1	4
150–199	1	3
200–249	6	3
250–299	5	3
300–350	2	3

The distributions may or may not be statistically significant and no conclusions can be drawn without a statistical test.

Statistical analysis

Tests of normality. For large amounts of data (preferably over 30 sample pieces), it is possible to use the chi-squared goodness-of-fit test for the normality of the observed data. The sample we have used is too small to test for normality, and in fact there is no satisfactory test for normality for a small sample. The samples should therefore be assumed to have come from a normal population.

F test. This is the test for equivalence of variance. It can be used when there are two variances to be compared. This test would not be used if a third type of drill point were being tested. The values calculated for variances and the result of the analysis are shown in Fig. 10.3. To apply the test look up the value for F for degrees of freedom 19 and 19 in the standard F tables.

Variance ratio table. The analysis shows that the F value of .99 is definitely not significant.

	Drill point 1	Drill point 2
	200	296
	194	98
	98	110
	234	129
	120	140
	296	299
	300	197
	228	340
	100	222
	224	119
	58	300
	212	202
	224	302
	112	198
	129	219
	289	149
	300	179
	287	110
	257	268
	289	148
Mean	207.55	201.25
Maximum	300	340
Minimum	58	98
Std dev	76.73361	74.84242
F	1.025269	
SigmaD	23.96814	
t	0.262849	

Figure 10.3 F calculations.

Bartlett's test. This is used for comparing any number of variances. To apply this test look up the value of chi-squared for $(k - 1)$ degrees of freedom in a chi-squared table.

Testing for constancy of cause systems. We assume that the cause did not change provided we kept the conditions constant while collecting data for method 1 and method 2.

Based on the above analysis we may assume that the data have come from a normal population and the variance may be considered equivalent and the two-cause systems may be considered constant. Under these conditions it is possible to test for significant differences between the averages using either the t test or analysis of variance. The calculations are shown in Fig. 10.3. By looking up the value of t for 38 degrees of freedom from the t table and comparing to a value of .25 obtained for 38 degrees of freedom, it can be stated that the averages can be considered equal.

Analysis of Variance

Variation of products or processes is the primary reason why the quality of the product varies. Experiments are primarily designed to find ways to reduce this variation, with the net result that losses are minimized and quality is improved. This can be done by a statistical method termed *analysis of variation,* or ANOVA. It is the primary method for analyzing data generated by the experiments. For understanding ANOVA, we need to build up from extremely simple cases to complex problems.

Zero-way ANOVA

This is the simplest case of analysis of variance. For simplicity, it is necessary to use fictitious data. This is done for your ease in following through the calculations, though the experimental situations described are real. ANOVA tries to break up the data into its components. In case of the zero-way ANOVA, the components are

1. Variation of the mean relative to the individual data points.
2. Variation of the individual points around the mean.

Consider the coolant flow through eight different drills used for center-drilling the camshaft. The rate of coolant flow through the drill, assuming all other conditions are the same, can be observed by using a gage. A simplified data table is shown in Table 10.2. One part of the data can be attributed to the mean. There will be a certain error

TABLE 10.2   Coolant Flow Rate through Drills

Drill number	Flow rate
1	3.2
2	4.1
3	2.8
4	4.6
5	3.1
6	3.6
7	6.1
8	3.9
9	4.9
10	1.8

in the gage used to measure the rate of coolant flow which will constitute one fraction of the error. Even though all the drills are taken from the same production lot, through the variation of the drill-making process there is a difference in the flow rate, and this constitutes another fraction of the error.

Summing the data points gives us the value of 40 and the sum of the error terms is equal to zero. This information does not allow us to draw any significant conclusions. By using an extremely simple operation a much clearer picture emerges. The magnitudes of each value obtained can be squared and then summed to provide a measure of variation present.

This is calculated by using the equation

$$\text{SST} = \sum_{i=1}^{n} y_i^2 = (3.2)^2 + (4.1)^2 + (2.8)^2 + (4.6)^2 + (3.1)^2 + (3.6)^2$$

$$+ (6.1)^2 + (3.9)^2 + (4.9)^2 + (1.8)^2 = 158.29$$

The magnitude of the portion of the line segment due to the mean can be squared and summed:

$$\text{SSM (sum of squares due to the mean)} = \frac{\left(\sum_{i=1}^{n} y_i \right)^2}{n} = \frac{T^2}{N} = \frac{(38.1)^2}{10}$$

$$= 145.16$$

The portion of the magnitude of the line segment due to the error can be squared and summed to provide a measure of the variation around the average value:

$$\text{SSE} = \sum_{i=1}^{n} (y_i - \overline{T})^2 = (3.2 - 3.81)^2 + (4.1 - 3.81)^2 + \cdots + (1.8 - 3.81)^2$$

$$= 13.13$$

Calculating SSE was not necessary since the ANOVA method states that

$$SSM = SSA + SSE$$

This leaves one more element to be considered, which is degrees of freedom. The degrees of freedom are computed by allowing 1 degree of freedom for each independent comparison that can be made for the data. Only one independent comparison can be made for the mean of all the data.

For the error in this example, one independent comparison can be made between observation 1 and 2 and one between 2 and 3. Comparison between 1 and 3 would not be independent. This means that for the given 10 pieces of data, 9 degrees of freedom are associated with the error. Similar to the summation for the sum of squares, a summation for the degrees of freedom can be made:

$$v_T = v_m + v_e$$

where v_T = the total degrees of freedom.

This leads us to the computation of the variance due to the error, which is SSE divided by the degrees of freedom for the error:

$$V_e = \frac{SSE}{v_e}$$

Computing the square of the standard deviation for the sample, we have the relationship

$$S = \left[\frac{\sum_{i=1}^{N}(Y_i - \bar{y})^2}{n-1} \right]^{1/2} = \left(\frac{13.13}{9} \right)^{1/2} = 1.208$$

This means that the variation due to the error is the square of the standard deviation, which is fairly easy to compute for the simple example shown. This is not so easy to do as the experiment gets more complex.

The information can be tabulated as shown in Table 10.3.

TABLE 10.3   Zero-Way ANOVA

Source	SS	df
Mean	145.16	1
Error	13.13	9
Total	158.29	10

ANOVA is based on the least-square approach, with the error variance being equal to the minimum of the sum of the squares about some reference value divided by the degrees of freedom for the error.

One-way ANOVA

The discussion brings us to the next stage of ANOVA, where one parameter is controlled. Consider the case of the coolant through drills considered in the previous example. Once again, three different sizes of coolant holes are considered to optimize the diameter. Ten drills with each size of coolant hole were used in the experiment. The parameter measured was the tool life using each drill. For simplicity of calculation, small numbers representing the coolant flow through each drill are used. The data are shown in Table 10.4.

There are two methods for decomposing the variation into the appropriate components. Both the methods are described below.

Method 1: including the mean. The components are

1. Variation with reference to the zero.
2. Variation of the mean under each factor around the overall mean.
3. Variation of each observation around the mean of each factor level.

The calculations are similar to zero-way ANOVA except for the component due to differences in size of the coolant hole:

$$\text{SST} = \sum_{i=1}^{n} y_i^2 = 124.7$$

$$\text{SSM} = \frac{T^2}{N} = 112.067$$

These calculations are identical to the calculations shown in zero-way ANOVA. The variations due to the size of coolant hole can be calculated by the following relationship:

TABLE 10.4 Rate of Coolant Flow through Drills with Three Levels of Through-Hole Diameters

Level	Velocity, ft/s					A_i	n_{A_i}	$\overline{A}_i$
a_1	3.2	1.8	3.9	4.1	4.6	17.6	5	3.52
a_2	2.1	1.9	3.1	2.1	3.3	12.5	5	2.5
a_3	1.9	1.6	1.8	2.7	2.9	10.9	5	2.18
						$T = 41.0$	$N = 15$	$\overline{T} = 2.73$

$$SSA = n_{A_i}(\overline{A}_1 - \overline{T})^2 + n_{A_2}(\overline{A}_2 - T^2)^2 + n_{A_2}(\overline{A}_3 - T)^2$$

$$= \left[\sum_{i=1}^{k_A} \left(\frac{A_i^2}{n_{A_i}} \right) \right] - \frac{T^2}{N} = \frac{(17.6)^2}{5} + \frac{(12.5)^2}{5} + \frac{(10.9)^2}{5} - 112.067$$

$$= 4.894$$

Finally, the error portion of the calculation is computed from the variation of each level about its mean from the relationship

$$SSE = \sum_{j=1}^{k_A} \sum_{i=1}^{n_{A_i}} (y_i - \overline{A}_j)^2 = 7.739$$

This leaves us with calculations for the degrees of freedom for each component of variation. For this we have the relationship

$$v_T = v_m + v_A + v_e$$

where

$$v_T = N = 15$$

$$v_m = 1$$

$$v_A = k_A - 1 = 3 - 1 = 2$$

$$v_e = 15 - 1 - 2 = 12$$

Based on these results an ANOVA summary table can be made (Table 10.5).

Method 2: excluding the mean. From the above calculations it can be seen that the variation due to the mean does not affect the variation due to the error, nor the calculations for the factor effects. In most situations, with the possible exception of cases where lower is better, such as runout and surface finish, the variation due to the mean has no practical significance. In the lower-is-better situation we try to establish how the factors can be set to reduce the average to zero.

Now the factors consist of the following:

TABLE 10.5   One-Way ANOVA Including the Mean

Source	SS	v	V
m	112.067	1	112.067
A	4.894	2	2.447
e	7.739	12	0.645
T	114.700	15	

1. Variation of the mean of observations of each level around the overall mean.
2. Variation of the individual observations around the mean of each factor level.

Therefore the following calculations have to be made:

$$SST = \left[\sum_{i=1}^{N} y_i^2 \right] - \frac{T^2}{N} = 112.067$$

$$SSA = \left[\sum_{i=1}^{k_A} \left(\frac{A_i^2}{n_{A_i}} \right) \right] - \frac{T^2}{N} = 4.894$$

$$SSE = \sum_{j=1}^{k_A} \sum_{i=1}^{n_{A_j}} (y_i - \overline{A}_j)^2 = 7.739$$

The calculations for SSA and SSE do not change in the second method.

Once again the degrees of freedom associated with the sum of squares have to be calculated:

$$v_T = v_A + v_e$$

where

$$v_T = N - 1 = 14$$

$$v_A = k_A - 1 = 2$$

$$v_e = 14 - 2 = 12$$

The results can now be summarized as shown in Table 10.6.

Assuming a confidence level of 90 percent, the risk factor is .10 and at this risk level from the F tables,

$$F_{.1;2;9} = 3.01$$

This means that from a practical point of view the individual variance based on variation of averages is inordinately high when com-

TABLE 10.6   One-Way ANOVA Excluding the Mean

Source	SS	v	V	F
A	4.894	2	2.447	3.794
e	7.739	12	0.645	
T	12.633	14		

pared to the actual individual variance. Since the F ratio is greater than the values obtained from the tables, the factors have an influence on the average value of the population, that is, there is a significant difference between the flow rates of coolant through the three types of drills at a 90 percent confidence level.

Two-way ANOVA

This is the next-higher order of ANOVA, where two controlled parameters are used in an experimental situation. Consider the case of two operators using their own verniers to measure a part. From the observations of the X-bar and R charts we find that there is a significant difference between the averages, though there does not appear to be a significant difference between the ranges. Since each operator has his or her own vernier, it is possible that the error in readings is due to the differences between the verniers or a difference in the method used by each operator.

This calls for a two-way analysis of variance. Let the two verniers be called a1 and a2 and the operators used be called b1 and b2. The experiment would be arranged in a table (Table 10.7).

TABLE 10.7   Arrangement of Experiment for Two-Way ANOVA

	a1	a2
b1		
b2		

Consider again that two parts are selected to be measured. This means that each operator uses both verniers and measures both the parts. The results of the test, once again simplified for ease of calculations, are tabulated in Table 10.8.

$$n_{a1} = 4n_{a2} = 4n_{b1} = 4n_{b2} = 4$$

The total variation for the problem at hand can be decomposed into the following factors:

1. Variation due to A
2. Variation due to B
3. Variation due to interaction of A and B
4. Variation due to error

This can be put down as the mathematical equation

$$SST = SSA + SSB + SSA \times B + SSE$$

TABLE 10.8   Data for Two-Way ANOVA Comparing
Two Operators Using Two Verniers in Their
Respective Shifts*

	a1	a2	
b1	2.5,3.0	3.4,2.9	11.8
b2	1.8,2.8	3.4,3.1	11.1
Total	10.1	12.8	22.9

*Shown with two parts even though actual experi-
ment was performed with 50 parts.

Each element can be calculated from the following equations:

$$SST = \left[\sum_{i=1}^{N} y_i^2 \right] - \frac{T^2}{N} = 67.47 - 65.55 = 1.92$$

$$SSA = \left[\sum_{i=1}^{k_A} \left(\frac{A_i^2}{n_{A_i}} \right) \right] - \frac{T^2}{N} = \frac{A_1^2}{n_{A_1}} + \frac{A_2^2}{n_{A_2}} - \frac{T^2}{N} = \frac{(A_1 - A_2)^2}{N} = 0.9113$$

$$SSB = \frac{(B_1 - B_2)^2}{N} = 0.0613$$

$$SSA \times B = \left[\sum_{i=1}^{c} \left(\frac{(A \times B)_i^2}{n_{A \times B_i}} \right) \right] - \frac{T^2}{N} - SSA - SSB$$

$$= \frac{(A \times B_1 - A \times B_2)^2}{N} = 0.1513$$

$$SSE = SST - SSA - SSB - SSA \times B$$

$$= 1.92 - 0.9113 - 0.0613 - 0.1513 = 0.7961$$

Similarly, calculating the degrees of freedom for all items is similar,
except the case of the interaction:

$$v_T = N - 1 = 8 - 1 = 7$$

$$V_T = v_A + v_B + v_{ax} + v_e$$

$$v_A = k_A - 1 = 2 - 1 = 1$$

$$v_B = k_B - 1 = 2 - 1 = 1$$

$$v_{A \times B} = v_A \times v_B = 1 \times 1 = 1$$

$$v_e = 7 - 1 - 1 - 1 = 4$$

The results can be tabulated as shown in Table 10.9. The F column

TABLE 10.9   Two-Way ANOVA, Summary of
Results

Source	SS	v	V	F
A	0.9113	1	0.9113	4.5793
B	0.0613	1	0.0613	0.3080
$A \times B$	0.1513	1	0.1513	0.7603
e	0.7961	4	0.199	
T	1.920	7		

is calculated by dividing the variance of that element by the variance of the error. From the F tables we get the values

$$F_{.1;1,4} = 4.54 \qquad F_{.05;1,4} = 7.71 \qquad F_{.01;1,4} = 21.2$$

The results indicate that there is a significant effect of the second factor on the measurements taken, that is, one of the two verniers is defective and must be repaired or replaced. There is no significant interaction between the vernier used and the operator using the vernier. This indicates the possibility that the operator owning the defective vernier has developed a better method of measuring the part as a result of practice.

Three-way ANOVA

This is used when there are three controlled factors in an experiment with one of the factors having three levels and the other two factors having three levels. The experimental layout will be as shown in Table 10.10. This time the total variation can be written as

$$SST = SSA + SSB + SSC + SSA \times B + SSA \times C$$
$$+ SSB \times C + SSA \times B \times C + SSE$$

TABLE 10.10   Three-Way ANOVA, with One Factor
at Three Levels and the Other Two Factors at
Two Levels

	A1	A2	
B1	$\begin{cases} 1,4 \\ 1,1 \end{cases}$	2,3 2,1	C1 C2
B2	$\begin{cases} 2,2 \\ 1,4 \end{cases}$	3,1 4,2	C1 C2
B3	$\begin{cases} 2,3 \\ 3,2 \end{cases}$	1,2 4,1	C1 C2

The total variation can be calculated as before:

$$SST = \left[\sum_{i=1}^{N}(y_i^2)\right] - \frac{T^2}{N} = \frac{140}{112.67} = 27.33$$

$$SSA = \frac{(A_1 - A_2)^2}{N} = \frac{(26 - 26)^2}{24} = 0$$

$$SSB = \frac{B_1^2}{n_{A_1}} + \frac{B_2^2}{n_{B_2}} + \frac{B_3^2}{n_{B_3}} - \frac{T^2}{N} = \frac{15^2}{8} + \frac{19^2}{8} + \frac{18^2}{8} - 112.67 = 1.08$$

$$SSC = \frac{(C_1 - C_2)^2}{N} = \frac{(26 - 26)^2}{24} = 0$$

$$SSA \times B = \sum_{i=1}^{c}\left(\frac{(A \times B)_i}{n_{A \times B_i}}\right) - \frac{T^2}{N} - SSA - SSB$$

$$= \frac{7^2 + 9^2 + 10^2 + 8^2 + 10^2 + 8^2}{4} - 112.67 - 0 - 1.08 = .75$$

$$SSA \times C = \frac{[(A \times C)_1 - (A \times C)_2]^2}{N} = \frac{(24 - 28)^2}{24} = 0.67$$

$$SSB \times C = \left[\sum_{i=1}^{c}\left(\frac{(B \times C)_i}{n_{A \times B_i}}\right)\right] - \frac{T^2}{N} - SSB - SSC$$

$$= \frac{10^2 + 5^2 + 8^2 + 11^2 + 8^2 + 10^2}{4} - 112.67 - 1.08 = 4.75$$

$$SSA \times B \times C = \left[\sum_{i=1}^{c}\left(\frac{(A \times B \times C)_i^2}{n_{A \times B \times C_i}}\right)\right] - \frac{T^2}{N}$$

$$- SSA - SSB - SSC - SSA \times B - SSB \times C - SSA \times C$$

$$= \frac{5^2 + 5^2 + 2^2 + 3^2 + 4^2 + 4^2 + 5^2 + 3^2 + 5^2 + 5^2 + 6^2 + 5^2}{2} - 112.67$$

$$- 1.08 - 1.83 - 4.75 - 0.67 = 0.08$$

$$SSE = SST - SSA - SSB - SSC - SSA \times B - SSA \times C$$
$$- SSB \times C - SSA \times B \times C = 27.33 - 0 - 1.08 - 0 - .75$$
$$- .67 - 4.75 - .08 = 20.00$$

Similarly, the values of the degrees of freedom of the various factors and interactions can be determined as follows:

$$v_T = v_A + v_B + v_C + v_{A \times B} + v_{A \times C} + v_{B \times C} + v_{A \times B \times C} + v_e$$

$$= 24 - 1 = 23$$

TABLE 10.11   Three-Way ANOVA, Summary of Results

Source	SS	v	V	F
A	0	1	0.00	0.000
B	1.08	2	0.540	0.323
C	0	1	0.000	0.000
$A \times B$	0.75	2	0.875	0.523
$A \times C$	0.67	1	0.670	0.401
$B \times C$	4.75	2	2.375	1.422
$A \times B \times C$	0.08	2	0.040	0.024
e	20.00	12	1.670	
T	27.33	23		

$$v_A = k_A - 1 = 2 - 1$$

$$v_B = 3 - 1 = 2$$

$$v_C = 2 - 1 = 1$$

$$v_{A \times B} = v_A \times v_B = 1 \times 2 = 2$$

$$v_{A \times C} = 1 \times 1 = 1$$

$$v_{B \times C} = 2 \times 1 = 2$$

$$v_{A \times B \times C} = v_A \times v_B \times v_C = 1 \times 2 \times 1 = 2$$

$$v_e = 23 - 1 - 2 - 1 - 2 - 1 - 2 - 2 = 12$$

These results can be summarized in an ANOVA table (Table 10.11).

Each of the factors does not have a significant effect of the averages at a 99 percent confidence level. The interactions are not significant. Some other factors have to be considered to evaluate the causes for the variation.

Four-factor ANOVA experiment using two levels

Extending the methods involved in three-way ANOVA and considering the situation of four factors at two levels, we shall now attempt to design and implement a solution. The experiment to be studied involves the effects of the various factors affecting the phrase angle of the camshaft from lobe 1 to lobe 3. During the process of forging, a flash line is also made and this has to be trimmed. The problem with trimming the cam is that the operation has to be carried out while the forging is still hot. The angle between lobes 1 and 3 is 112°, which means the trim die tries to twist the lobe while the flash is removed. The trimming is such that it is difficult to support the lobes whose noses are not parallel to lobe 1. This means we have to determine the conditions under which the twisting effect is minimized. Fifty consecutive pieces showed a Cpk value of $-.876$ for lobe 3. This meant that over the 8-hour period the wear and tear on the die had some effect on the phase angle or it was the effect of operator tiredness that affected the temperature of the part placed into the trim die. We felt that there was the possibility that the operator waited too long after the part comes out of the forging die, thus causing a decrease in temperature at the time the parts are trimmed.

The variables that can be controlled are the size of the forging in relation to the trim die, pressure of the trimming die, temperature of forging at which it is trimmed, and thickness of the flashline. Two levels for each of the variables will be considered for the purposes of conducting this experiment. For changing the size of the die a new forging die and a used forging die will be used. The temperature will be controlled by trimming the forging immediately after it comes out of the press and after waiting for a certain interval to determine the effect of temperature. Two levels of pressure, including the current level and a lower level that can also be used to get an effective trim will be used. The arrangement of a four-way ANOVA is shown in Table 10.12 with each factor at two levels.

Conventionally, these experiments would be studied one variable at a time keeping the others constant. These tests fail to determine the effects of any of the interactions each of the factors may have on the other and numerous experiments have to be used to determine the effect of each of the possible combinations.

By proper planning and using a balanced block factorial experiment design arranged in the form of a square, as shown in Table 10.12, the problem can be analyzed. This is done by reserving half the squares for characteristic $A1$ while the other half is reserved for characteristic $A2$. At the same time half the squares are reserved for characteristic $B1$

TABLE 10.12   Data for Four-Way ANOVA at Two Levels

		a1		a2	
		b1	b2	b1	b2
c1	d1	2.5	4.1	0	5.4
	d2	-0.2	4.6	-1.5	3.9
c2	d1	3.1	-3.8	4.2	-1.2
	d2	5.2	0.2	2.9	1.8

$C = T^2/16 = 60.8.$

while the other half is reserved for $B2$. By dividing the space horizontally instead of vertically, it is possible to reserve half the squares for $C1$ and the other half for $C2$. Similarly, horizontally half of the squares are reserved for $D1$ and half for $D2$. Based on these charts it is now possible to study the following variables and the following combination of variables:

A alone

B alone

C alone

D alone

A combined with B

A combined with C

A combined with D

B combined with C

B combined with D

C combined with D

A combined with B and C

A combined with B and D

A combined with C and D

B combined with C and D

Certain effects not attributable to any combination of these variables will exist and these will be termed *residuals*. In running this experiment one drill was used with each combination of these variables and the number of parts prior to failure was recorded. These combinations were tried out in a random manner until all the boxes were filled. The randomness can be ensured by filling out the various combinations possible on a slip of paper and putting them into a hat, and the combination that is pulled is tried. Other methods for completely randomizing the sequence are available but this is one of the simplest. Once the experiment is set up and the data collected, the next step in the process is to analyze the data. This can be done by using the ANOVA method described earlier. This method involves the use of many complicated calculations and reference to various statistical tables. The calculations are shown in Table 10.13; they are a natural extension of the methods for zero-way, one-way, two-way, and three-way ANOVA described prior to this. The explanation for each of the columns is described below:

TABLE 10.13 Calculations and ANOVA Table

(1) Source of variation	(2) i	(3) Number of levels or combinations	(4) Numbers to be squared	(5) Sum of data in (4)	(6) Sum of squares	(7) (6)/(2)	(8) (7) − C	(9) Corrections	(10) df	(11) Mean squares
	1	16	2.5 4.1 0 5.4 −0.2 4.6 −1.5 3.9 ; 3.1 −3.8 4.2 −1.2 5.2 0.2 2.9 1.8	31.2	172.74	111.9	111.9	15	1	—
A	8	2	15.7 15.5 ; 16.2 15	31.2	486.74	60.843	0.0025	0.0025	1	0.0025
B	8	2	16.2 15	31.2	487.44	60.93	0.09	0.09	1	0.09
C	8	2	18.8 12.4	31.2	507.2	63.4	2.56	2.56	1	2.56
D	8	2	4.3 16.9	31.2	490.1	61.263	0.4225	0.4225	1	0.4225
AB	4	4	10.6 5.1 5.6 9.9	31.2	267.74	66.935	6.095	6.0025	1	6.0025
AC	4	4	11 4.7 7.8 7.7	31.2	263.22	65.805	4.965	2.4025	1	2.4025
AD	4	4	5.9 9.8 8.4 7.1	31.2	251.82	62.955	2.115	1.69	1	1.69
BC	4	4	0.8 18 15.4 −3	31.2	570.8	142.7	81.86	79.21	1	79.21
BD	4	4	9.8 6.4 4.5 10.5	31.2	267.5	66.875	6.035	5.5225	1	5.5225
CD	4	4	12 6.8 2.3 10.1	31.2	297.54	74.385	13.545	10.562	1	10.5625
ABC	2	8	2.3 8.3 8.7 −3.6 −1.5 7.1 9.3 0.6	31.2	302.34	151.17	90.33	0.0625	1	0.0625
ABD	2	8	5.65 4.2 1.4 0.3 4.8 4.2 5.7	31.2	149.22	74.61	13.77	0.04	1	0.04
ACD	2	8	6.6 4.4 −0.7 5.4 5.4 2.4 3 4.7	31.2	158.58	79.29	18.45	0.81	1	0.81
BCD	2	8	2.5 9.5 −1.7 8.5 7.3 −5 8.1 2	31.2	319.54	159.77	98.93	0.5625	1	0.5625
								109.94		
Residual							1.96	1.96	1	1.96

203

Total number of observations = n = 16

Sum of all observations = T

Correction factor = $C = T^2/n$

Column 1. This lists the individual effects, the main effects, first-order interactions, and second-order interactions.

Column 2. Lists the number of individual measurements in each level or combinations associated with the source listed in column 1.

Column 3. Number of levels or combinations associated with each source.

Column 4. Lists the totals separately for each level of combination.

Column 5. Sum of data in column 4.

Column 6. Sum of squares associated with each source of variation.

Column 7. Column 6 divided by column 2.

Column 8. Column 7 − C.

Column 9. Subtract other corrections. This means that when considering the effects of A and B together, the individual effect of A and B separately must be subtracted. Similarly, when considering the effect of A, B, and C, the corrections would be subtracting the individual effects of A, B, and C and the effects of A and B together, A and C together, and B and C together.

Column 10. List the degrees of freedom. In case of individuals, the degrees of freedom are $n − 1$. For main effects the degrees of freedom are column 3 − 1. For the first-order interaction the degrees of freedom is the product of the degrees of freedom of the main effects involved. Similarly, the second-order interactions would be the product of the degrees of freedom of the variables involved.

Column 11. Column 9 divided by column 10.

To find the significance of the difference sources of variation, use the F test as follows: Form a ratio of mean square to be tested divided by the residual. Start by testing the second-order interactions. If these interactions are found to be insignificant, then pool them with the residual and obtain a new residual to test the first-order interactions. Similarly, pool the nonsignificant of the first-order interactions to obtain a new residual. When a first-order interaction is significant, do not test the main effects associated with that interaction.

Analysis of Means

Before going on to a discussion of analysis of means, we should note that ANOVA techniques can be used to compare several treatments, variables, or averages for equality. The application of ANOVA techniques is limited only by the imagination of the experimenter. The biggest obstacle to the use of ANOVA is its complexity. Analysis of means is another powerful technique to utilize the statistical power of a designed experiment. This method has power of discrimination identical to the ANOVA methods.

The basic steps involved in the use of analysis of means are illustrated using the following example. Consider the case where four methods are available for manufacturing a part. Each method produces parts of differing tensile strength, and the resulting tensile strength obtained for each method is recorded. Each method is repeated four times for convenience of calculations, though in an actual experiment more repetitions may be required. The method assumes the highest tensile strength is best. The results are shown in Fig. 10.4 followed by a set of calculations following the sequence of steps for conducting the analysis of means.

Step I.   Calculate the average and ranges for each of the methods used.

Step II.   Test the hypothesis:

H_0: All variances are equal.

H_A: All variances are not equal.

The hypothesis is tested by comparing the calculated range of decision values to a set of control limits:

$$\text{UDL}_R = D_4 \overline{R}$$

$$\text{LDL}_R = D_4 \overline{R}$$

where R-bar is the average of the ranges of the different methods of treatment. The values of D_3 and D_4 for a given number of samples can be obtained from standard tables. If any of the ranges fall outside the UDL_R and LDL_R, then the null hypothesis is rejected and all the variances are not equal. If, however, all the variances are equal, then proceed as follows.

Step III.   If all the ranges are within the decision limits, then the estimated standard deviation is calculated as follows:

Five different temperatures were used to heat-treat forgings to determine if there was a significant difference in the hardness of the parts obtained. Five samples of each type were drawn.

Test no.	Production temperature				
	1	2	3	4	5
1	33	33	36	30	29
2	32	32	37	30	30
3	32	33	37	30	28
4	31	34	36	34	29
5	34	31	35	33	31
Total	162	163	181	157	147
Average	32.4	32.6	36.2	31.4	29.4
Range	3	3	2	4	3

$$H_0 = \text{all variances are equal}$$
$$H_A = \text{all variances are not equal}$$

$\text{UDL}_R = D_4 \overline{R} = 2.282(3) = 6.846$ (D_4 values are from standard tables)
$\text{LDL}_R = D_3 \overline{R} = 0(3) = 0$ (D_3 values are from standard tables)

All the ranges are within the decision limits 0 and 6.846.

Calculate the standard deviation: $\hat{\sigma} = R/d_{2*} = 3/2.12 = 1.415$
Degrees of freedom: $\nu = .9K(n - 1) = .9(5)(5 - 1) = 18$
Grand average: $\overline{\overline{X}} = (32.4 + 32.6 + 36.2 + 31.4 + 29.4)/5 = 32.4$

Test the hypothesis that all averages are equal:

$$H_0 = \text{all treatments are equal}$$
$$H_A = \text{all treatment averages are not equal}$$

$\text{UDL}_{\overline{X}} = \overline{\overline{X}} + H_\alpha(\sigma/\sqrt{n}) = 32.4 + 3.23(1.415) = 36.970$
$\text{LDL}_{\overline{X}} = \overline{\overline{X}} - H_\alpha(\sigma/\sqrt{n}) = 32.4 - 3.23(1.415) = 27.830$

The decisions are based on the upper and lower control limits. All the averages lie between the limits, so the differences between the averages are not statistically significant.

[Refer to *Process Quality Control* by Ott and Shilling (2d ed., McGraw-Hill, 1990) for values of H_α at the 0.01 and 0.05 levels.]

Figure 10.4 Analysis of means calculations.

$$\hat{\sigma} = \frac{\overline{R}}{d_{2*}}$$

where the values of d_{2*} can be once again obtained from the standard-ized table.

Step IV. Calculate the degrees of freedom:

$$\nu = .9K(n - 1)$$

where K is the number of treatments and n is the sample size using the average sample size in case of unequal sample sizes.

Step V. Calculate the average of the averages.

Step VI. Calculate the upper and lower decision limits to test the hypothesis that all treatment averages are equal:

H_0: All treatment averages are equal.

H_A: All treatment averages are not equal.

Calculate the upper and lower decision limits based on the equations

$$UDL_{\bar{X}} = \bar{X} + H_\alpha\left(\frac{\hat{\sigma}}{\sqrt{n}}\right)$$

$$LDL_{\bar{X}} = \bar{X} - H_\alpha\left(\frac{\hat{\sigma}}{\sqrt{n}}\right)$$

where $\bar{X}$ is the grand average and n the sample size, and H_α can be obtained from standard confidence tables.

Step VII. Plot the averages on a chart showing the upper decision limits and the lower decision limits and determine which of the methods provides the best results for the required properties, and if there is a statistically significant difference between the means. This method requires us to use a larger sample than required by ANOVA, but the end results are much easier to explain. It should be noted here that analysis of means methods are effective when used with fractional factorial experiments, since fractional factorial experiments can be performed with fewer experiments.

Other Types of Experiments

While the experiments described above are some of the major types of experiments conducted and used in industry, it should by no means be assumed that these are the only types of experiments available to the statistician. There are numerous other types of experiments and some of the others are listed below along with their applications to different types of experiments.

1. *Completely randomized.* When only one experimental factor is being investigated.

2. *Factorial.* When several factors are to be investigated at two or

more levels and interaction of the factors may be important. These methods for full factorial experimentation have been discussed above.

3. *Blocked factorial.*   When it is difficult to maintain the homogeneity of the experiment for the number of runs required.

4. *Fractional factorial.*   When there are many factors and levels and it is impractical to run all combinations.

5. *Randomized block.*   When one factor is being investigated and experimental material or environment can be divided into homogeneous blocks.

6. *Balanced incomplete block.*   When the treatments cannot be accommodated into a block.

7. *Latin square.*   When one primary factor is being investigated and the results may be affected by two other variables and it is assumed that no interactions exist.

8. *Youden square.*   Same as Latin square but number of rows, columns, and treatments need not be the same.

9. *Nested.*   When the primary objective is to study relative variability instead of main effect of the sources of variation. An example of this would be when we consider the variance of tests on the same sample and variance of different samples.

While the list of possible designs is not exhaustive, this does describe the scope of the various experimental methods available for the user. The most commonly used method besides randomized design and full-factorial design is the fractional-factorial experiments, which is used extensively in off-line design of Taguchi experiments.

Taguchi Methods

The Taguchi methods for design of experiments are a tool used for reducing the inherent variability in a product or a process. It combines engineering and statistics to directly address the process variability problem. The Taguchi methods are employed primarily in product and process engineering to identify and optimize conflicting inputs to enable improved quality at reduced cost. In short, Taguchi methods provide a system to develop specifications, design those specifications into the product, and create products that continually surpass the specifications. These methods described were developed by Dr. Genichi Taguchi of Japan. The factors in product and process design are defined by Dr. Taguchi as controllable and uncontrollable. The interaction of these factors has a direct impact on the performance variation inherent in the product. By concentrating on the controllable factors, and their resultant effect on variation, the engineer can design a product or process that minimizes variation, which in turn improves quality and reduces cost.

Aspects addressed by the Taguchi methods

There are seven aspects addressed by these methods:

1. The quality of a product is measured by the total loss created by the product to society.

2. Continuous quality improvement and cost reduction are necessary for an organization's health in a competitive economy.

3. Quality improvement requires the neverending reduction of variation in product and process performance around the nominal values.

4. Society's loss due to performance variation is proportional to the square of the deviation of the performance characteristic from its nominal value.

5. Product and process design have a significant impact on the product's quality and cost.

6. Performance variation can be reduced by exploiting the nonlinear effects between a product's and process's parameters and the product's desired performance characteristics.

7. Product and process parameter settings that reduce performance variation can be identified with statistically designed experiments.

The Taguchi philosophy is based on the premise that cost can be improved by increasing quality, which in turn is attained by reducing variation. This is in wide contrast to the "goalpost syndrome" pervading quality concepts taught in America. The goalpost syndrome refers to the mentality that regards a part within the given specification as good. The important factor to remember here is the fact that customers want a product to be as close to nominal as possible. Suppose we went out to buy a battery to light a bulb, and the manufacturer uses a voltage tolerance for the battery of 3 V ± .5 V; the batteries generating voltages close to 3.5 V will burn out the bulb quickly, while the batteries with voltages close to 2.5 V will result in the bulb glowing dimmer. So it is important to realize that the batteries with voltages closer to 3 V will be preferred by the customer. The goalpost syndrome neglects the most important aspect of quality—*satisfy the customer*.

Tolerance limits are usually defined to cover up problems in design of the product or process. Minimal variation around the target value is the only true way to attain high levels of quality. Usually, for machined part which is barely within specifications and a part that is just out of specification may be a few tenths of an inch but one is considered good and the other is considered bad. After grinding, the out-of-roundness allowed on the journal is a maximum of .0002 in, but a part with an out-of-roundness of .00021 is automatically scrapped. Following this philosophy, Taguchi defines quality as, "the loss a product causes to society after being shipped, other than any losses caused by its intrinsic functions." Any product that varies from its intended value causes a loss to society and hence has poor quality.

To quantify this definition of quality, Taguchi has developed the Taguchi loss function. The Taguchi loss function recognizes the customer's desire to have a product that is more consistent part to part, and the producer's desire to have a low-cost part. In case of the camshaft example we have been using throughout this book, the envelope for machining on the forging used in the manufacture of the camshaft is a classic example. If the envelope is too small, then the number of cams with no cleanup needed on the lobes increases, while an increase in machining envelope means the cost of producing the forging goes up while the number of cams with no cleanup needed decreases. This, along with the loss to society as a result of the changes in envelope thickness, is shown in Fig. 10.5.

So it is necessary to design a product that is close to the nominal, and insensitive to noise (the noise factors involved in manufacturing do not affect the quality of the product). This will enable the final product to be of consistent quality, and thereby reduce the need for using inspection as the means for achieving quality. Here it is necessary to define controllable and uncontrollable factors. *Controllable factors* are those that can be easily controlled during the production of a product, such as the increase in part size as the tool wears; this can be controlled by giving the appropriate offsets. On the other hand, *uncontrollable factors* are defined as factors that are impossible to control or too expensive to control. There are three types of noise factors including

- External (environment)
- Internal (shrinkage)
- Product to product (part-to-part variation)

The objective of Taguchi methods is to reduce the effect of the noise factors on variation by concentrating on their interaction with controllable factors, since they are the only factors that can be controlled.

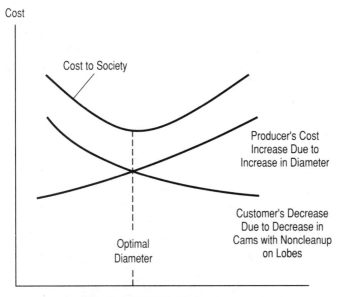

Cost

Cost to Society

Producer's Cost
Increase Due to
Increase in Diameter

Optimal
Diameter

Customer's Decrease
Due to Decrease in
Cams with Noncleanup
on Lobes

Base Circle Diameter of Lobes

Figure 10.5 Cost to society curve with increase and decrease in journal diameters as process variation for forging the lobes decreases.
The base circle diameter of the lobes reaches the finish machined diameter of the lobes, thus lowering the cost of production.

The Design Process

Improvements in process or product design can be attained by concentrating on the process itself. Taguchi formalized the design process by
defining three distinct stages for all products and processes.

System design

Determine the product's intended function and build the prototype to
accomplish objectives. Tentative parameters are specified to construct
the prototype. The parameter settings are defined by a set of nominal
values; their respective tolerances are based on the results of quality-
of-design-redesign and quality-of-performance studies. These parameter settings create a product prototype that considers the needs of the
customer and also satisfies the requirements of manufacturability.

System design concepts are used when we wish to provide our customers with improved products. One of the most important tools for remaining competitive is the use of advanced technology. But if a competitor is
able to copy the technology quickly and produce a more uniform product,
then the technological advantage is lost. So parameter design has to be
used to make the process less sensitive to the causes of variation.

Parameter design

Determine the factors affecting product design and distinguish between controllable and uncontrollable factors. The objective of the experiment is to determine the combination of factors least sensitive to changes in the uncontrollable factors through the design of experiments. The chief sources of product variation which are usually chronically present and affect the product performance are classified into three categories.

1. *Outer noise.* Conditions that exist in the environment in which the product will be used by the customer, including the human variations in using the product. These include environmental factors such as ambient temperature, humidity, pressure, people, and different batches of material.

2. *Inner noise.* This includes variation from inside the product or the process and wear and tear on the product or process during its lifecycle.

3. *Product noise.* This refers to manufacturing conditions that lead to deviations from the nominal value and includes such factors such as part-to-part variation.

Tolerance design

Tolerance design has to be used when the parameter design methods have not yielded satisfactory results. Here the loss function is used to substantiate the increased costs of higher-quality components by the lower loss to society. The existence of tolerance design is not contradictory to the philosophy of neverending improvement because engineers will continuously endeavor to produce a better design, and production personnel will continuously strive to reduce variation around the nominal values established in the parameter design. If the reduced variation determined through parameter design is not acceptable, design changes are made to attempt to achieve objectives. This usually involves increasing manufacturing costs and purchase costs, that is, improved grades of material, tighter tolerances, and so on.

Signal-to-Noise Ratio

The effect of a specific noise factor on the quality of the design is defined by its signal-to-noise (S/N) ratio. The S/N ratio refers to the statistical measurement of the stability of a quality characteristic's performance. The S/N ratio is determined by the Taguchi loss function and is the target for the parameter design stage. The control factors that may contribute to reduced variation can be easily identified by looking at the amount of variation present as response. There are several S/N ratios depending on the type of characteristics: lower is better (LB), nominal is best (NB), and higher is better (HB). The S/N ratio which condenses the multiple data points depends on the type of characteristics being evaluated. The equations for calculating LB, NB, and HB are

$$S/N_{LB} = -10 \log\left(\frac{1}{r}\sum_{i=1}^{r} y_i^2\right) \quad \text{where } r \text{ is the number of tests in a trial}$$

$$S/N_{NB} = -10 \log v_e \quad \text{variance only}$$

$$S/N_{NB} = +10 \log\left(\frac{v_m - v_e}{r\,v_e}\right) \quad \text{mean and variance}$$

$$S/N_{HB} = -10 \log\frac{1}{r}\left[\sum_{i=1}^{r}\left(\frac{1}{y_i^2}\right)\right]$$

Performing an analysis of variance on the raw data identifies factors which affect the average and the S/N data identify the control factors that affect variation. Once these tests are done, the control factors may be classified into factors that affect both average and variation, factors that affect variation alone, factors that affect average only, and factors that affect nothing. Parameter design tries to select the proper values of the factors that affect the average, the variation, and both to adjust the average to the target value. Factors that affect nothing may be set at the most economical level since they do not affect the parameter design.

The larger the S/N ratio the more robust the design, that is, the less-sensitive performance will be to noise. If the S/N ratio is less than the target value, then tolerance design needs to be performed. Orthogonal arrays can be used to simulate the results of different factor combinations to greatly reduce the number of experiments to complete the design. Statistical analysis utilizing the arrays quickly aids the engineer in eliminating the factors that will not affect design.

The process of making a product or process robust against noise by using correct levels of the various parameters is the lowest-cost way of designing quality into a system. Once a satisfactory set of parameters has been developed, then it is necessary to use the process control techniques to ensure that the performance requirements are met and the process is being continually improved by identifying and reducing or eliminating causes of variation.

Inspection, Audit, and Poka-Yoke Systems

Inspection Systems

This chapter deals with the inspection systems as applied to the activities of the inspection department and the process sorting performed by the operating organization. While most books on quality control recommend the use of a formal inspection organization, the proper use of all the process control steps described in the earlier chapters may lead to minimal inspection. So instead of having a formal operating organization, rotating operating personnel through the inspection function has definite advantages. The argument in favor of a separate inspection organization is that it represents the customer and thus ensures that the operating organization has performed its functions properly and provides adequate safeguards against shipment of defective products. Since in these days of intense competition no one wants to ship a defective product, moving the operators through the inspection function helps make individual operators aware of the possible problems created by the operation he or she regularly performs on the part. This helps the operator become aware of any possible problems that may be caused by his or her operation.

Inspection, while being a powerful tool in providing checks on the satisfactory performance of the process controls, is disadvantageous because it is after the fact and basically consists of examining a specific quantity of the product to provide a basis for action. Acceptance inspection is a means for checking the adequacy of the process controls. If the process is in control, the product should slip past acceptance inspection without delays. But if the process controls fail, then the inspectors step in and screen the process effectively, keeping the bad product. The criticality of the use of inspection as a tool for quality control becomes greater in case of life-and-limb components that go into automobiles, drugs used by people, and other important components that could result in injury or death.

Operational Sorting and Corrective Sorting

Operational sorting may have to be used when the process capability shows that the process is not capable of performing the task. If the Cp's and Cpk's are lower than required for establishing a stable process, then the use of operational sorting may be unavoidable until steps are taken to improve the process capability parameters. The other kind of sorting used is corrective sorting, which occurs when the process fails to perform normally or when workmanship is poor. An example of corrective sorting would be if the tap broke in the middle of the process without the operator being aware of it. The operator may go on producing parts until he or she actually checks one. Then the operator has to go back through the process to find the defective parts until all the defectives are removed from the system. If the same problem had occurred due to poor workmanship, the parts would have been found throughout the system and all the parts would have to be checked to determine which are defective. When they handle sorting the tendency of operating chapters is to reduce the levels of sorting to much lower levels than the 100 percent that may often be required of the inspection department.

The next step in the process of developing an inspection system is an understanding of acceptance sampling. Acceptance sampling is used on the assumption that it provides greater cost savings over 100 percent inspection since it offers greater speed of handling, minimizes handling, reduces errors due to monotony, and can be implemented faster. The process of sampling should be such that all the items in the population have an equal probability of being selected. This is termed as random sampling and is based on the assumption that, when a sufficient quantity of items is chosen, then it reflects all the characteristics of the whole population. Acceptance sampling plans lead to producer's risk, which refers to the probability that a good lot will be rejected by the sampling plan and a buyer's risk, which is the risk that a bad lot will be accepted by the buyer. These can be quantified by using the operating characteristic (OC) curves. The OC curve is the plot of the percent defective in a lot versus the probability that the sampling plan will accept the lot. These curves help us develop a sampling plan that will reduce the probability that a good lot will be rejected and a bad lot will be accepted.

Some of the basic rules for an acceptance sampling plan are

1. Do not mix products from different sources.

2. Do not mix products over different time periods.

3. Use large lot sizes so sample size has no effect on the OC curves.

4. Use the sampling plan in conjunction with a fully implemented statistical process control plan.

Classification of sampling plans

There are three basic types of sampling plans:

Acceptable quality levels.   This refers to the maximum number of percent defectives which can be considered a satisfactory process average. These plans favor the manufacturer since they provide high assurance of probable acceptance and do not take into account the customer's risk.

Lot tolerance percent defective.   This tries to determine the quality level or percent defective which can be tolerated in small percentage of the product. These plans tend to favor the customer since they decrease the risk of accepting a lot equal to or below the lower-quality limits. LTPD plans do not tell us anything about the product that will be accepted.

Average outgoing quality limit.   As soon as the percentage of defectives exceeds a given limit, a 100 percent inspection policy is adopted. Here, the rejected lots are accepted after 100 percent inspection and replacing the defective parts.

One of the important rules for using an acceptance sampling plan is that the sampling plan must be statistically valid. If a maximum or a minimum acceptance level is specified, then it is termed a *one-sided specification*. If both a minimum and a maximum are specified then it is termed a *two-sided specification*. The formulas for acceptance sampling plans are

$$L_U = S_U - k\sigma_x$$

$$L_L = S_U - k\sigma_x$$

$$n = \left(\frac{t_a + t_b}{t_{p1} - t_{p2}} \right)^2$$

$$k = t_{p1} - \frac{t_a}{n}$$

where L_U = the upper acceptance level based on the specification and
the standard deviation of the product

L_L = the lower acceptance level

S_U = the upper specification limit

S_L = the lower specification limit

k = factor for acceptance sampling by variables

σ_x = the standard deviation of the product

t_a = point on the curve beyond which lies the areas represented by the producer's risk

t_b = consumer's risk

t_{p1} = point on the curve beyond which is the area represented by the AQL value

t_{p2} = LTPD values

The curve referred to above is the OC curve and is the percentage of lots that is expected to be accepted for all possible submitted lot or process qualities for a given acceptance sampling plan.

This terminology of AQL, LTPD, and AOQL are used extensively, even though most buyers are becoming more aware of the immense possibilities created by TQM systems and statistical methods, leading to zero defects. Most buyers are extremely reluctant to accept any levels of defects in the supplies received. Inspection is definitely not the answer to providing the customer with zero defects, and acceptance sampling with acceptable levels of defects is not the answer. Automation in inspection using vision systems, nondestructive testing methods, and so on, may be more reliable than using people in the inspection process. Moreover, Dr. Deming has mathematically proved that the least-cost method of inspection is either zero inspection or 100 percent inspection. With all these considerations in mind, the use of any acceptance sampling plan may end up being costlier than 100 percent inspection.

Setting Up Inspection Lines

Using inspection as a tool for detecting certain types of defects often becomes necessary to create systems to detect certain surface defects such as noncleanup and subsurface defects. These tests may involve use of nondestructive tests such as eddy current testing, magnafluxing, ultrasonic testing, and magnetic particle inspection. Usually the detection of surface noncleanup, presence of nonfill, and so on, may be done visually. Many organizations prefer to set up a final inspection line to detect the presence of surface defects and subsurface defects using some or all of the techniques described above. Using inspection systems may often be necessary, but all efforts must be made to detect possible causes for the occurrence of the defect in the first place and finding the means to prevent the defects. These techniques should be treated as what they are and should form a shorter pipeline for feedback of the shortcomings of the manufacturing processes. Some of the checks may also reveal the shortcomings of the processes of your suppliers and feedback should be provided to them for correcting their processes. Other steps that are often used in the final inspection is straightening and measuring straightness. These techniques help us prevent customer dissatisfaction.

Audit Systems

After talking about inspection systems, it is necessary to discuss the creation of audit systems to ensure that all the systems are performing the task of ensuring the quality of the end product. Audit systems are the methods used to ensure that the methods established are working correctly. Audits provide for regular monitoring of all aspects of the company and ensures that all controls are in place. Our audit systems are set up to be monitored by the top management on a quarterly basis, with inputs to the audit systems coming almost on a daily basis. A company should establish a quality council with a manager from each end of the business, including manufacturing, engineering, marketing, personnel, sales, and quality control. The members should participate in plant inspections and interviews throughout the company at all levels. A questionnaire should be designed to establish a baseline for improvement, amount of improvement, and verification of improvement. It is important to establish a system of quantifying performance so that subjectivity in evaluation is eliminated.

Audits must be conducted using a written questionnaire, followed with recommendations for corrective actions and an action plan for implementation. These audits must be conducted by personnel independent of the function being audited. The system for these audits must involve procedures for determining who is responsible for conducting the audit, the frequency of the audit, the content of the audit, the action to be taken when deficiencies are found, and verification of the corrective action.

The audit system should cover numerous aspects of the quality process and the aspects to consider when auditing the quality management system are as follows.

Quality improvement planning and implementation

Here the audit team must attempt to determine the quality improvement plans, based on customer expectations and business plans of the company. In a TQM approach, the overriding concern for quality improvement by reduction of variation becomes the business plan and this in turn leads to a reduction of costs. These quality plans, once developed, must not become ends in themselves, but must be communicated throughout the organization for effective implementation. Once implemented, these systems must be evaluated in a quantifiable fashion and progress must be documented. This also leads us to the question of effective management controls for performance evaluation. Based on a management evaluation, systems must exist for revising the plans and the quality objectives. These plans should be based on an organizational commitment to quality with the target to reduce variation and therefore reduce waste. Training plans for all levels of employees must also be evaluated to ensure that each employee has an adequate level of statistical training. The quality plan must also include a system for developing and maintaining an environment for quality improvement. Continuous improvement systems must also be evaluated. An appropriate questionnaire must be designed for the auditors, keeping in perspective the parameters described above.

Describing the quality function

This refers to the various systems that exist, including instructions for operating various machinery and parameters for ensuring that defective parts are not produced. The total maintenance management system procedures should also be documented, as should the systems for assigning responsibility of activities. Characteristics for monitoring continuous improvement must also be determined. We used a pie chart to determine the total quantity of scrap, as shown in Fig. 11.1. These costs are quantified as shown in Fig. 11.2.

Process control systems

The next step in the audit process is evaluation of the satisfactory performance of the SPC systems, including performing short- and long-term capability studies, and related process corrective action. SPC systems must exist for all key dimensions, and documented evidence of the effectiveness of these systems must exist. Corrective action must be implemented for unstable processes, with steps taken to reduce variability. Design of experiments techniques, failure modes and effects analysis techniques, and quality function deployment must be used wherever possible to reduce variability. All of this information must be documented and the records retained for a reasonable period as determined by either the customer or the requirements of the law.

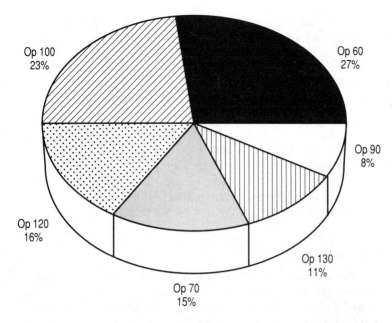

Total pieces manufactured = 20,000

Figure 11.1   Scrap report: actual pieces (= 597).

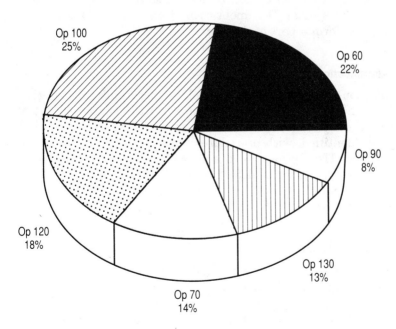

Number of cams produced = 20,000

Figure 11.2   Scrap report, January 1991: total cost = $4731.70.

The audit should determine methods to ensure that these documents are retained for an adequate period of time.

Inspection systems

Inspection systems must form a part of the audit process, and the audit system must ensure that instructions for conducting inspections correctly must exist, with definitions for the characteristics being evaluated, sample size, frequency and acceptance criteria, and methods and tools for implementing the inspection process. The number of defectives found must be documented, along with the inspector who identified them. By properly using statistical techniques, we were virtually able to eliminate the need for in-process inspection.

Control of measurement system

This includes the maintenance of the gaging systems and the capability of the measurement systems used to evaluate key characteristics. Calibration and verification of each gaging system (variable and attribute) must be maintained and must be traceable to recognized standards as applicable. The gage repeatability and reproducibility must also be similarly documented and related data must be checked as a part of the audit system. Documentation of any corrective action on the gages must form a part of the audit.

Material identification and control

The audit should encompass the control on incoming raw material, equipment, and spare parts. But the most critical material control would be in the area of nonconforming material. These materials must be carefully identified, with procedures for segregation, verification, and disposition. Usually, a lockup area with accessibility limited to the inspector to segregate the defectives must exist. This is to prevent mixup of these materials with good parts. Methods to identify the lots after they have been shipped to the customer must be used.

Drawing and specification control

This is another important part of the audit, and written procedures for receipt, review, and distribution of these drawings must exist. Care should be taken to ensure that all active files contain up-to-date drawings and specifications. Methods to handle obsolete specifications and drawings must also exist.

Process corrective action

Systems established to report failures must exist, as also must methods to prevent the occurrence of these defects. If the defective part has reached the customer, then action necessary to inform the customer must be taken and systems must exist for handling such a situation. This is dealt with in greater detail in Chap. 13, Measures of Customer (Dis)Satisfaction. The audit merely tries to determine the existence of such systems and to measure the effectiveness of these systems.

The Concept of Poka-Yoke

Finally, let me explain the concept of Poka-Yoke for mistake-proofing systems by using certain techniques to effect 100 percent inspection. (Poka-Yoke means "mistake-proofing" in Japanese.) This method is espoused by Shigeo Shingo, a Japanese manufacturing consultant, in his book *Zero Quality Control: Source Inspection and the Poka-Yoke System*. Most quality control systems are based on the development and analysis of scrap and rework documents to explain the causes of failure. A lot of working time is spent with equipment, systems, methods of measurement, and data collection and analysis.

A number of large Japanese and American companies have adopted the zero-defects method of manufacturing. Shingo's profound zero-defects system is based on four elements: successive checks, self-checks, source inspections, and Poka-Yoke devices (devices that prevent the defect from occurring in the first place). Successive checks is based on the fact that the product is passed on to the next worker down the line, who inspects the product and returns it to the first worker if a defect is found; that operator then shuts down the line to correct the problem. This compensates for the fact that the worker producing that part may miss defects or may ignore them. Successive checking compensates for the deficiencies of the SPC system, because it makes it possible to conduct 100 percent inspection, perform immediate feedback and action, and have inspections done by someone other than the person responsible for processing. These systems can be all the more effective when Poka-Yoke devices are applied, leading to tremendously reduced rates of defects. To attain the goal of rapid and effective corrective action, it may be necessary for the worker to conduct 100 percent inspection of all possible defects in his or her work. So Poka-Yoke devices can be installed within the process boundaries. This self-check system can cut defects even more than successive checks.

Finally, source inspections are used to detect errors or undesirable abnormalities in process conditions, leading to feedback and action at the error stage and thus avoiding the possibility of defects.

Let me give you an example of Poka-Yoke devices used in the process of milling the keyway on the camshaft. One of the clamps on the lathe is hidden away from the operator's sight. This led to the clamp overshooting the stop, and resulting in broken milling cutters. If the operator did not clamp the part at all, feedback to the machine control prevented the machine from starting. If the operator attempted to clamp the part, but did not realize that the part actually was not clamped (due to the fact that the clamp slipped), then the cutter broke in the process of trying to cut a moving part. This was prevented by installing a stop under the clamp as shown in Fig. 11.3. This resulted in the problem being eliminated and no more cutters are broken because of unclamped parts. Similarly, the fourth journal has a blind hole and a through hole, and our operators were repeatedly locating the blind hole until we made it impossible for the operator to load the part 180° off, thus making the keyslot 180° off and as a result producing a scrap cam. This problem was particularly critical since either operator or final inspector negligence would result in our customers crashing the grinder into the part when they tried to grind the lobes. The bar shown in Fig. 11.4 obstructs the operator from loading the

Figure 11.3 Using Poka-Yoke techniques: putting a stop under the clamp prevented overshooting and thus prevented scrap.

Figure 11.4 Using Poka-Yoke techniques: vertical bar on one side prevents loading the cam in reverse (180° off) and thus prevents scrap.

cam 180° off. Once this was implemented all customer complaints related to the key being located in the cam 180° off were eliminated. It is important to remember that successful use of these methods is an important part of the strategy to effect 100 percent inspection and prevent scrap from being generated. It is important also to remember that the use of such methodologies need not involve expensive devices. In fact, both the techniques used cost less than $100, and in effect eliminated the possibility of ever shipping a defective part to the customer.

12

Computer-Aided Inspection, Data Collection, and Analysis

Computer Systems in Manufacturing

Before dealing with computer-aided data collection and statistical analysis software, let's mention the various aspects of computer-aided manufacturing tools and software. The first and foremost would be computer-aided design (CAD) software, which helps simplify the process of designing the product. Computer-aided process planning software can be used for cost-effective sequencing of the manufacturing, inspection, and testing operations under a given set of conditions. Computer-aided design for manufacturability and assembly systems can help generate designs that are easier to manufacture and assemble and has been dealt with in some detail in an earlier chapter. Inventory control software can help implement just-in-time methods. Computer software can be used for generating computer numerical control (CNC) programs from the designs generated by the CAD systems and may be used in cost estimation of the product manufactured. Finally, there are the computer-aided inspection, data collection, and analysis systems which round out the list of manufacturing systems.

There are numerous software systems available to improve manufacturing efficiencies, but this chapter will attempt to deal with computer-aided inspection systems, computer-aided data collection and statistical analysis systems, and the questions that must be asked prior to procuring such systems.

Criteria for Selecting Data Collection and Analysis Software

Before dealing with the necessary criteria for selecting data collection and statistical analysis software, we must consider why many SPC systems lead to considerable disappointments. There are three primary reasons for the failure of SPC systems, including:

1. The analytical techniques are not designed for real-time and/or zero-defect quality control due to the fact that the methods are designed by statisticians for statisticians. These systems fail to take into account the expectations of the operators.

2. Modern manufacturing systems cannot use a one-fits-all type of charting. Sampling procedures and acceptance criteria for each part of the process must be designed for it.

3. Data collection and control charting, although performed by the operator, does not offer itself to expert analysis until it is too late, that is to say that the operator is not trained in interpreting the data.

These are the primary considerations to keep in mind when selecting any data collection and statistical analysis software.

Computer-aided data collection and statistical analysis is one of the most important factors in the successful management of your TQM system. SPC software associated with dimensional gaging only will be discussed, and there will be no reference to other aspects of using computers and SPC software with other types of gaging. The insights offered in the area of dimensional gaging can easily be extended to other areas of gaging. Before investing in an automated data collection and analysis system, certain questions must be asked before investing in an SPC package. Most of today's software packages are fairly user-friendly and so the users should be involved in the decision-making process instead of depending on the data processing department to come up with a solution. This is really important since someone else's solution may end up being completely different from the solution you are looking for. The main points to consider for such a system are as follows.

Correctness

This refers to the program being able to satisfy your requirements in terms of the method by which the data are collected and whether the software meets all the data analysis needs. Most software has a disclaimer declaring that the author or the company supplying the software is not responsible for any errors that may occur as a result of the use of these programs. This means it is your responsibility to ensure that the correct algorithms are used for processing the data collected. If possible, contact other users of the program to ensure that they have not faced any problems related to correctness of the program.

Reliability

This is the measure of how well the program has been debugged by the author of the program. Programs should not fail if the user accidentally hits a wrong key, and should offer the means for the user to backtrack. I have had numerous experiences with software that dies completely when a wrong key is hit accidentally. This is particularly true of custom software, where many times the programmer has been unable to debug the software completely. Most software suppliers will offer to debug the software if you make the programmer aware of a bug in the program after you have made the purchasing decision.

Efficiency

This is the amount of computing resources required by a program to perform the required task. Most of the PC-based software offered is fairly efficient in the use of computing resources and can perform as standalone units when they have hard disk to store data. It is also important to note if the program lets you know when the database is full. Some software does not tell you when the database for storing data is full. Such software should be avoided.

An important factor in the efficiency of the program may be the speed of the computer system itself. Many DOS-based programs are affected by the limit on the random access memory of 640 kB. This process can be accelerated using expanded or extended memory if the software will permit the use of these features.

Accessibility

Does the program offer a hardware lock or a password lock to prevent unauthorized access to the program or the data? This may be particularly necessary, since operators without adequate knowledge may wipe out the database or program. The operator's access should be limited to data entry, access to the last datum entered, mastering, and the X-bar and R charts. Many other features of the software such as access to the operating system, repeatability and reproducibility, and other areas should be either accessible by a password lock or an external device.

Usability

This is another important criterion for deciding which software to go with. Data collection and the viewing of the process control charts should be controlled by a minimal number of keystrokes. Process control charts accessible in multiple keystrokes are a hindrance to many operators. A one-keystroke access to the X-bar and R charts is preferable. Ease of use is an important factor in determining operator acceptance and in turn the success of your SPC program.

Portability

This is an important criterion for determining the use of a particular software. How easy is it to move the software to another system? If it is not easily portable to another computer then there may be problems with moving the data over to another computer for a more detailed analysis, or you may not be able to use this software with another system.

Reusability

The main question to ask here is, how easy is it to set up a different gage; that is, how easy is it to set up a new gage using the same software? Some programs require you to know the use of programming language, and hence are considerably harder to set up. They may require you to get the software manufacturer to set up the system when you wish to move to a new gage. Other software can be set up with a new gage in a few keystrokes.

Networkability

This has become a very important criterion for determining which software to use for your data collection methods. Accessing the data available on one system from another computer has become very critical, since this allows data to be centrally gathered and analyzed for any problems that may exist with the process. Many companies are offering software with networkability built into it. If the company has a working networked system, then it should be examined closely. Many claims of networking abilities are not reliable, since they do not have any working systems and you may realize that there are many bugs in the program which prevent you from accessing the data easily.

Maintainability

How easy is it to locate a problem and fix the error in the operational program? This may often not be possible without getting the software manufacturer to your plant. One of the problems associated with this function is the ease with which the software manufacturer service department can be obtained at your site. Another factor is the ease of loading the software into the computer system should it be accidentally destroyed on the hard disk drive. Any software that requires the software company to send out its representative should be avoided.

Is the software real-time?

This is an important consideration when selecting a software. What real-time means is simply this: Does the software keep track of the time at which the operator checked the part? For successful implementation it may be necessary for the software to be real-time so that the time at which the problem occurred can be found, based on which other decisions can be made.

Is Cpk valid?

This is another important question when selecting software because the Cpk computation for nonnormal data may require a different computation. In many situations, due to problems in the machine you may end up with a nonnormal data distribution; then Johnson transformation techniques must be used to determine the fit and the Cpk values. Much of the existing software in the market does not offer this feature and thus should be avoided. When checking many characteristics on a part, the ability of the software to show the capabilities of all these characteristics is an important consideration.

Steps in Acquiring Data Collection and SPC Software

When acquiring an SPC package, you will find that there is a large variety of software claiming numerous features. The best way to go about deciding on the best software package is to follow the steps described below:

1. List your present requirements and the application in detail.
2. Survey all the packages available for the job at hand.
3. Examine whether the package has sufficient documentation and user manuals.
4. Check whether the package has sufficient application parameters. This means that if your application requires 20 inputs, then an application package that can handle only 16 inputs would not be usable.
5. Check if the package has adequate maintenance aids. This may include locally available service personnel.

6. Draw up a list of suitable packages, including the list of packages that will let you try their packages in-house for a month or so. This will help highlight any shortcomings the software may have. Avoid any software that involves bringing the software company in for moving the gage over to a new product.

7. Find out what it takes to link the database generated by the software to other corporate database plans.

8. Use the benchmark comparison trials conducted by a number of quality magazines to find out the shortcomings and advantages of the software under consideration so that you will not overlook any of the problems that may exist with the selected software.

We found that most operators adapt more easily to color displays. If the plotted points on the X-bar and R charts are not connected by lines, the harder it gets for the operators to interpret the charts. These charts should be available to the operator at the touch of a keystroke instead of multiple keystrokes. If multiple keystrokes are required, then the operators prefer to use the data from the last gaged part instead of using SPC. Another pitfall to keep in mind is that software calibrated using a mean master is considerably riskier than the programs that work with a min/max master. Mean masters do not check for accuracy of resolution of the gage, so any program that cannot use a min/max master combination for calibrating the gage should be avoided. Another important consideration in selecting the computer system is whether the gaging system in use is an in-process gaging system or if the gaging is external to the gage. This may result in the following four types of options.

1. *In-process gaging, where the part is gaged right in the machine at the end of the processing and the offset is automatically sent to the machine controls.* This takes the human element out of the gaging system because the parts are automatically gaged while in the machine and, depending on the computer system, the offsets are sent directly to the machine. This is useful where dimensions are extremely critical and 100 percent inspection is required. This type of system is available from a limited number of suppliers, and as the prices involved are high, extreme care should be taken before investing in such systems.

2. *External gage with automatic offset input to the controls.* The gage can be set up to input offsets to the controls at predetermined intervals or offsets can be sent to the controls manually. While selecting software for SPC, it is important to consider the ability of the gaging system to link to the machine control. Any software that does not have past experience with linking to the machine controls should be avoided.

3. *External gaging system with manual offsets.* It must be reiterated that any software that does not have the capability to link with the machine control should be avoided. This is an important feature, since at a later date you may decide to link the gaging system to the machine controls to automatically offset the machine.

4. *Software that cannot take direct input from the host gage but performs all the necessary statistical analysis when the data are input manually.* This type of software should not be given preference over the types of software that interface with the gaging system directly. For statistical analysis involving the use of experimental design or some special analysis only should software which allows only manual data entry be used. For standard X-bar and R charts and related analysis of machine capabilities, histograms, kurtosis, skewness, and so on, the inspection system and statistical analysis software should be interfaced.

One more factor affecting a purchase decision is that if the gaging manufacturer offers the whole package, then preference should be given to such suppliers. This helps in getting better overall support than purchasing the gaging from one source and getting the computer system and the software from another source. Gaging manufacturers are better able to understand the mechanical fixturing associated with the computer system as it relates to the SPC software.

While purchasing the SPC software, another important feature to ask for is the ability of the package that is attached to a gaging system to have the gage repeatability and reproducibility software along with the ability to perform SPC. This helps avoid the need for manual data collection and then computing the gage repeatability and reproducibility separately. This is a fairly useful feature. Another added feature could be that the software run a self-check every time it is booted up, so that it would remind the operator when the last R&R was conducted at a date earlier than say six months or the frequency at which this gage R&R must be conducted. Most software does not currently offer this facility, but this could be a useful added feature. Another feature that is important while considering data collection and analysis software is whether the software automatically tells you when the database is full and a new database needs to be created. Much of the software available in the market can tell when this happens, but some cannot. Software that does not tell you when the database is full should also be avoided.

Most of the important parameters necessary for selecting the proper software for data collection and analysis have been described above, and in most cases you will have to compromise on the features.

Using Expert Systems for Interpretation

Before wrapping up the discussion on the use of SPC, one more powerful tool that has become available must be discussed. This software that works alongside the SPC software is the expert system software. The mechanism by which expert systems operate is shown in Fig. 12.1. Expert systems consist of a knowledge base, an inference engine, and a user interface. The knowledge base consists of rules and facts contributed by an expert in a specific area. The inference engine calls on information in a knowledge base to determine what question to ask the user, rules to make, and conclusions to draw.

These systems are designed to adapt to an ever-changing machining process using a variety of functions such as total measurement error, statistical approval of setup, and generating sampling plan. As each dimension shifts out of control, inspection intervals and sample size variation are permitted by expert system software. The expert system can be programmed to make recommendations regarding sample size and the need to compensate for a dimensional drift in process. The ex-

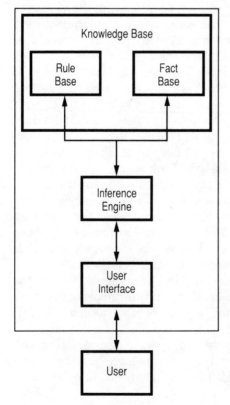

Figure 12.1 Expert system structure.

pert system can be set up for no instructions to the operator if the process is running in control, but as the process drifts out of control, it instructs the operator to inspect sooner. Expert systems can also be set up to use the specification limits to determine the location of the control limits based on statistical calculations. The use of expert systems in the monitoring of process control can make up for inadequacies in the training process for the operators or lack of understanding on the part of the operators. The operational theory for SPC is ever-present in the background without making the operator uncomfortable. Most expert systems may have to be custom-designed for application with the SPC software you are using, but existence of expert system software may be an important consideration in selecting SPC software in the future.

Software of Inspection Systems

Other important uses of computers are the ones associated with inspection systems such as with coordinate measuring machines and vision systems, which usually depend on a computer system to perform the required computation and may or may not be attached with SPC system software. In the case of vision systems, computers are set up for video image processing, auto focus, mass data storage for uninterrupted cycle execution, part and table multiple action, positioning, and inspection of unaligned parts. In the case of a coordinate measuring machine, geometrical tolerance programming, tolerance analysis, data handling and multiple probe calibration, laser calibration, math processing, contouring, operator prompting, editing, feedback, and accept/reject decision making are associated with it. Since any of this equipment is a major investment, it is necessary to evaluate the various features offered by various manufacturers critically before making the purchasing decision.

When purchasing a coordinate measuring machine (CMM), the primary considerations are sufficient accuracy to enable production to use a majority of the tolerances, retention of accuracy of the shop-floor-type environment, universal applicability to the entire spectrum of measuring jobs, flexibility for changing and extending measuring jobs, speed of measuring so machine downtime is reduced, ease of training operators to use the CMM, meeting of the safety requirements, allowance for material flow integration, attachment to a statistical package, and allowance for integration into the standard SPC network. Each of these parameters must be considered when purchasing an automated inspection system for a manufacturing environment. Similar criteria can be developed for other inspection systems such as an optical comparator or a vision system.

13

Measures of Customer (Dis)Satisfaction

The Need to Measure Customer Satisfaction

The primary goal of all the systems described in this book is to create a "market-driven" manufacturing system, where the customer is never dissatisfied with the product received. As more and more manufacturing companies accept the principles of SPC and start making products that are identical in quality, the competitive difference is going to be the kind of service the customer receives when he or she has a complaint. Today, more and more companies are attempting to determine the exact needs of the customer in terms of service and other requirements. Attending to customer complaints, whether real or imagined, is a part of the strategy for establishing TQM systems in the company. In fact, numerous indicators of the quality of service customers receive must be used to ensure that the customers are satisfied.

Before going on with this chapter, it must be reiterated that the goal of this book is to provide you with systems so that all the measures of customer (dis)satisfaction have a value of 0; that is, there are no customer complaints, no failures in the field, no returns, no claims, and no service costs from the customer associated with the product in question. Properly implemented, the TQM system will lead you to the goal of zero defects, and all the information you will need to know from the customer is that the values of the above parameters are zero. The reason for attempting to ensure zero defects reaching the customer and minimizing customer complaints cannot be overemphasized, particularly since quantifying loss in customer goodwill is extremely difficult.

In spite of all the care taken, there can be some system failures that get overlooked or are not prevented in time to keep defective products from reaching the customer. This chapter attempts to deal with situations that result in defective products reaching the customer and satisfying the customer in terms of service once the customer is actually using the product.

Importance of Proper Packaging

There are numerous aspects to the measures of customer satisfaction, and this can be one of the critical aspects of your TQM process. In a product like the camshaft, a number of factors may not be used, but an attempt is made here to consider all aspects of customer satisfaction. Once the product is manufactured it has to be packaged and shipped to the customer, and care must be taken to ensure that no damage to the product occurs due to poor packaging or mishandling during transportation. In a product such as the camshaft, the aspect of packaging design is taken care of by the customer who provides standard packaging to handle the product. If this is not provided by the customer, then it becomes necessary to provide adequate packaging for the product. Care similar to the process of designing the product must be exerted in designing the packaging. Care should be taken not to overpackage or underpackage the product, since overpackaging increases the cost of the product while underpackaging may result in a damaged product.

Another aspect of packaging is the handling of the product from operation to operation within the plant, especially when the product is not sent to the subsequent operation by a conveyor. Usually the forklift operator moves the parts in tubs from station to station. Care should be taken to handle the product so that either the critical operations are performed last or extra care is taken once the critical operations have been performed. The critical operations on the product are usually the features of the product that are most likely to be damaged by unnecessary handling. The customer is unwilling to accept any product that has damage to that particular feature. This means that if a particular feature is damaged, then the product would be regarded as scrap. In the case of the camshaft, we knew that any damage to the keyway would be deemed unacceptable, since the keyslot is used to drive the camshaft once it reaches our customer for all the operations performed by them. So we decided to mill the keyslot at the end of our manufacturing process just prior to packing the product.

Packaging should also protect the product during transportation to the customer and should be able to withstand the handling and transportation. This was not extremely critical in the manufacture of the camshaft, since the packing material was provided by the customer in the form of standard dunnage for holding the camshaft. These were designed specifically for handling the camshaft, and so no problems arose during handling.

One more packaging factor to consider is the method to prevent deterioration during storage. In the case of the camshaft, the major cause of deterioration is rust, and this is usually prevented by applying rust preventive on the product. Most products require protection during storage, and this can be either provided by using protective agents or by packaging the product to prevent deterioration due to storage. Most packaging is usually designed to handle deterioration due to age.

Customer Processing and Installation of the Product

The next aspect to consider is the processing of the product by the customer and/or installation. An independent audit should be conducted to ensure that during the processing or assembly of the product no damage to the product occurs. This may often be a critical aspect for consumer products, where the customer may install the product incorrectly or use in environments never envisioned, or apply stresses never contemplated, or fail to take the necessary precautions for maintaining the product. For a product such as the camshaft, the only care that needs to be exerted is to ensure that products are not being rejected due to processing errors, mishandling during processing, or assembly by the customer. An example of processing error would be the following: if the steady rests have not been adjusted correctly during the journal grinding operation, then the journals may exhibit an out-of-round condition which cannot be corrected during the straightening operation, but the customer may tend to attribute the problem to the supplier, assuming that the camshaft was bent prior to being put in the grinder. Many problems that occur during handling and processing can take place at the customer's location and can be attributed to the supplier. Care should be taken, therefore, to ensure that the customer is meeting the parameters for processing the product.

Dealing with Customer Complaints

Customer complaints may take many forms, and it is important to attend to any customer complaint as fast as possible. Complaints that are not attended to immediately can haunt you in many ways. In case you are an automotive product supplier, it may result in your not being considered for other products or cancellation of the order. Any of the above situations may result in loss of customer confidence at large and may have repercussions on the work with other customers. To prevent dealing with the repercussions of not attending to a problem, it often becomes necessary to have a problem reporting and resolution system.

The problem reporting and resolution system must consist of the following steps:

1. Inform the customer as soon as the manufacturer becomes aware of nonconforming material, including customer locations where the product in question may have been delivered. In case of camshaft problems, as soon as we were aware of the existence of a problem, we reported it to the buyer and the quality control department.

2. Take immediate steps to prevent further shipments. Should such a situation arise, we immediately instituted redundant 100 percent inspection to ensure that the problem in question did not get shipped. This meant checking all the shipments twice for the defective feature prior to shipment.

3. Almost simultaneously, it is necessary to take steps for disposition of the material. This means a determination has to be made about the seriousness of the problem and a decision has to be made whether a representative should be sent to the customer or the material in question called back to the manufacturing location. In the early days of manufacturing the older version of the camshaft, we did have a situation where the entire lot had to be recalled from the customer. With proper implementation of the TQM system for the new camshaft, the problems have never been that major.

4. The customer should also be informed of the date from which the material shipped would conform to specifications. This means that as soon as a system has been instituted to prevent the defective part from being shipped, the customer should be notified.

5. The next step is the problem-solving process. The steps in problem solving must be used to identify the root causes for the occurrence of the problem. Root cause analysis can take the form of design of experiments, failure modes and effects analysis, or any other format deemed suitable for correctly identifying the root cause.

6. Based on the identification of the root cause, it becomes necessary to implement corrective action for preventing the occurrence of the problem and also to institute a monitoring system to detect the problem should it occur again. The monitoring system helps verify that the problem does not recur. Use Poka-Yoke techniques wherever possible to ensure 100 percent inspection. All these steps, once taken, must be reported to the customer to ensure that the customer is satisfied.

In the process of satisfying the customer, the actions taken may include:

1. *Satisfy that particular complainant.* This involves immediately reworking or replacing the part or service, and adjusting the claims of the complainant. Another gesture that pays dividends is to call the customer within the next few days to ensure that the same problem has not resurfaced. This helps reassure the customer that action is being taken to prevent the occurrence of the problem again. Often, satisfying the customer means that a documented action plan for preventing the recurrence of the problem should be submitted at the earliest possible date.

2. *Identify the vital few.* These are the problems that occur more often, making it impossible for the customer to use the product. Based on the identification of the main problems with product quality, it is necessary to analyze the problem in-depth to identify the root cause of the problem. Initially when the process was set up a number of cams reached our customer without the tapped hole, that is, the threads were missing because the operator had failed to backtrack once the tap broke. This would be only detected once the cam entered the engine and this meant a considerable loss to the customer who would end up disassembling an engine at considerable cost. The problem was solved by a two-fold attack on the performance of the tap and by ensuring that all the pieces were checked for presence of threads prior to the part going to the next operation. Once the tool life and performance of the tool were better managed, the need for 100 percent inspection disappeared. If possible, Poka-Yoke devices should be implemented to ensure 100 percent inspection to prevent the occurrence of these defects. Using Poka-Yoke devices is perhaps the best solution, since this ensures that human element for error is eliminated. These devices are particularly useful to effect 100 percent inspection of critical features on the part.

3. *Isolated-incident types of problem.* These can only be dealt with by bringing the problems to the attention of the operator(s) who may have caused them so that their recurrence can be prevented. Here once again it is important to remember to use Poka-Yoke devices to help prevent the occurrence of such isolated defects. These devices do not have to be expensive. The nonquantifiable gains in customer satisfaction are perhaps the more important consideration.

Data analysis is an important factor in the process monitoring customer complaints. This can be done by charting the customer rejects that arise. These customer complaints must be monitored as carefully as possible since difference between usage dates, date of sale, and date of manufacture can cause errors in judgment of performance trends and in correlating cause with effect. With most organizations heading toward just-in-time inventory controls, this does not seem as critical a problem and usually feedback regarding the problem is almost immediate. Data generated from customer complaints should usually be tabulated and charted on a time series chart. Any significant change in the number of rejects should be investigated immediately to find the cause of the problem. This chart should be posted so that all responsible for that particular product are aware of the presence of problems. The various problems associated with the number rejected should also be highlighted so that the concerned are aware of it.

Using Weibull Analysis

One more method of graphically demonstrating the field failure data and life test data is Weibull analysis. This analysis can be used to estimate (with or without confidence intervals) the useful life of an item. The process begins with the collection of "run-to-failure" data, which with some relatively simple calculations produce the information required for plotting on a special kind of graph paper called Weibull probability paper. The plot gives us the following information:

- Percentage of population that can be expected to fall below the specified life.
- The life value below which X percent of the product is expected to fail, where X is the value for which the parts can be expected to fail.
- The slope of the failure distribution line, which provides an indication of the type of failure. Slopes less than 1.0 indicate a decreasing failure rate, that is, the part shows a high degree of early failure but as the part continues to be used, the failure rate comes down. A slope of 1.0 indicates a random failure pattern, while a slope greater than 1.0 is what should normally be expected and indicates "wearout" failure. A whole family of Weibull density functions can be individually distinguished based on the slope. One of the charts obtained is shown in Fig. 13.1.

Field Feedback

Another aspect of customer service is the field feedback. Getting accurate feedback from field service representatives and from customers is an important step in ensuring that the quality of the product meets the highest standards. For this the following steps must be taken:

1. *Provide personnel with well-designed data sheets.* This document has to be carefully created since it is critical to the analysis of failure. All vital information should be contained in the sheet, includ-

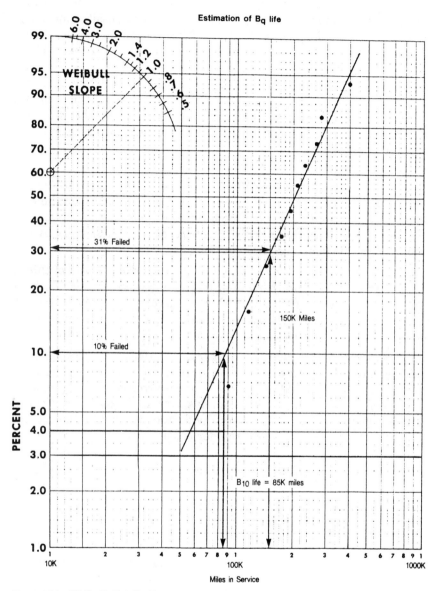

Figure 13.1   Weibull distribution.

ing model number, system, assembly, subassembly, component, and part. If possible, the cause for the failure or the inability of the customer to use the part should be determined. Sometimes it may not be possible to determine the cause of the failure where the failure occurred, in which case it is imperative that the product be sent back for analysis at the manufacturer's location as soon as possible for determining the possible causes of failure. The information sheet should also contain information such as the operating time on the product, description of problems associated with using the product, and related customer downtime. The documentation should also include information related to how the problem was detected and by whom. It is also necessary to document where the failure occurred. In the case of a camshaft which goes into an engine, this means the following: was the part defective so it could not be assembled in the engine or did the failure occur when the customer was using the product?

2. *Provide a glossary of terms to all the people involved so that the reports are uniform.* Usually, providing a brief description of the various parts and the various possible failures can be a basis for communication at a uniform level. This is important to a satisfactory evaluation of the customer's requirements.

3. *Training field service personnel.* The important aspect of this is to show the field service personnel how the data generated by them are critical to the successful operation of the company and to train the personnel in the terminology for satisfactorily documenting the problems found by the user(s).

4. *All data collected should be centrally documented.* Having multiple locations can lead to confusion in terms of where the documentation has to be filed and each location generating conflicting reports. The use of statistical methods for analysis of the problem is critical to preventing the problems. Compare the data generated by the control charts for the particular feature under consideration.

Parameters to Measure Customer (Dis)Satisfaction

There are numerous parameters that can be used when measuring the quality performance of the manufacturer and the field service. These include the complaints, which may be measured in terms of the total number of complaints or value lost as a result of each complaint by the customer. Another measure of quality performance is the value of the returns and the cost of handling the returns. Claims made by the customer can be another measure of the customer satisfaction. Number of failures in use may form an important measure of customer satisfaction. An additional measure of customer satisfaction would be the number of recalls or how many parts/products were defective and were shipped to the customer that now require steps to correct the problem. This is the most critical factor if the product in question poses a threat to human safety or health and these generally tend to be highly publicized and affect consumer confidence.

Perhaps the most important measure of customer satisfaction would be measuring "things gone wrong." In measuring things gone wrong (TGW), parameters have to be set to define what is not right. Any feature that is not correctly produced and leads to premature failure, a customer complaint that is not attended to in a certain period of time, or failure to provide service to a customer within a given period of time are all treated as things gone wrong.

Once again, all the other steps described in the process of implementing your TQM system should normally result in a failsafe system. The chart showing customer complaints, or returns, or any other parameter should have a value of zero on a continual basis.

One of the biggest problems that arises is measuring the response to a customer complaint. A system for measuring the quality of the response must be established. The response to the customer is perhaps the most critical factor in establishing the quality of service and is the factor that makes the difference to the customer. With more and more manufacturers using TQM systems, there is less and less discernible difference between the quality of the products and thus response to the customers is the one factor that can make a difference in getting a jump on competitors. Most manufacturers using TQM systems will eventually be able to reach identical quality levels.

Problems with the Customer Satisfaction System

How to provide satisfactory service to customers is a question that arises from time to time. It is difficult to know how far to go with providing services to a customer. Many customers who do not generate a high volume of business may demand an extremely high level of service and may have a high level of complaints. Inputs must be taken from all these complaints to improve the product to ensure that the reasons for the customer complaints disappear. This requires a manufacturing system that is extremely flexible and can produce a product that meets the individual requirements of the customer.

14

Beyond
Total Quality
Management

Difficulties with Implementing TQM Systems

Before leading to systems beyond TQM, we must discuss some of the difficulties encountered with the use of TQM systems, the biggest of which is not having top management with a vision to see the benefits of a TQM system. Top management with a vision for TQM systems is perhaps the greatest prerequisite to creating such systems, and without their support it cannot succeed.

This leads us to another issue for successful implementation of TQM systems, the failure to inform everyone in the organization regarding the direction in which the TQM system is heading. Any successes due to the TQM system must be publicized, since this encourages individual elements within the company to build on these successes.

Another reason for the failure of TQM systems is lack of adequate training systems. Many organizations tend to cut out training programs due to financial problems created by external constraints. In fact, external training programs conducted by consultants are often the first to be dropped when a company's budget starts to tighten. Another problem with training systems is sending an internal trainer for a two-day training program and then expecting him or her to be able to train all the firm's employees in SPC and other methods of TQM. If you decide to use an internal trainer, then it is necessary to ensure that each level of management is properly trained. Every level of personnel, from top management to the operators should have adequate training in the tools of TQM they are expected to use.

Another reason for failure of TQM systems is lack of follow-through on certain systems, such as FMEAs, which are often not up to date.

Continuously monitoring all existing systems is critical to the successful implementation of TQM systems. To this end each of the systems created should be regularly monitored at the appropriate level. If the operator is not trained in the interpretation of SPC charts, then the charts should be interpreted by the statistician. This frequency may not be adequate for the process control charts to perform their tasks.

Another problem faced with TQM systems is the inability to control suppliers. This is particularly true for small manufacturers, who may have difficulty controlling the suppliers due to the small volume of business they generate. Another problem is mismanagement of the suppliers by large customers, who do not offer appropriate support to their suppliers.

Poor gaging design and/or software failure results in the measurement system failing. This can cause problems to the effective functioning of the TQM system. Proper use of the gaging system and interpreting the results of the measurement system are essential to successful functioning of the TQM system.

Finally, the failure of TQM systems can be due to poor planning and lack of adequate tools for quality planning. Even if management has the vision to see TQM for what it can do for the company, lack of proper planning for creating and using these systems will lead to failure. Once a problem area is identified, then immediate corrective action steps must be taken. Failure to take corrective action at the appropriate time or inadequate systems to find causes and eliminate them results in failed TQM systems. The steps described in the problem-solving process or in any suitably modified sequence of steps must be implemented to ensure that problems are corrected.

Rating Your Quality Systems

With all the difficulties described above in terms of implementing a TQM system, it is necessary to develop a system for evaluating the quality performance of your company. The following questions provide a basis for evaluating action necessary to implement a TQM system. Answering them in terms of your actual performance can form a guideline for managing quality in a manufacturing environment. Depending on the actual situation, this questionnaire may have to be suitably modified. Similar lists can be designed to evaluate the quality performance in service environments.

1. How often is inspection used for sorting?

2. When manufacturing a new product, do clear, written operating procedures exist before the actual production begins?

3. Are the gages calibrated and tested for repeatability and reproducibility?

4. Does a current process routing sheet exist at each operation?

5. How efficiently are customer complaints resolved?

6. Should a customer complaint exist, does a systematic corrective action procedure exist?

7. Are material resources identified correctly? Are the locations of all machines, gages, and parts produced known?

8. Does a system exist for isolating nonconforming parts from the operating system?

9. Does a system exist for evaluating cost of quality?

10. Are new designs evaluated in terms of manufacturing problems before production begins?

11. Is an attempt made to train all employees in defining the quality standard?

12. Are new products and processes tested before production begins?

13. Do proper audit systems exist for ensuring that all quality requirements are met?

14. How well does the supplier management system work?

15. Is attention paid to quality of shipped products?

16. Are production operators trained in basic statistical skills and in operations?

17. Is there a mechanism for recognizing outstanding work by an employee?

18. Is there a mechanism for recognizing outstanding work by a vendor?

19. Are reliability studies performed regularly to ensure that machines continuously produce a quality product?

20. Are preventive maintenance systems in place?

All of these factors have to be evaluated to determine the performance of your company in terms of the quality management system. Depending on the environment in which this system is used, many of these questions may have to be modified or added to ensure that the quality management system is working satisfactorily. Usually a scale for evaluating your performance should be used, with 0 for never, 1 for rarely, 2 for occasionally, 3 for usually, and 4 for always. This means that a maximum score of 80 is possible. If scores estimated by using these methods lie between 0 and 20, extensive improvements in quality systems must be made and efforts to initiate TQM systems must be made. Scores in the midranges indicate certain levels of implementation of TQM systems, while scores between 60 and 80 reveal that you have low levels of scrap, all continuous improvement systems are in place, and "zero defects" is an attainable goal.

Just-in-Time Systems

Once the threshold of TQM has been crossed and the numerous systems have been implemented and have resulted in process improvement, the natural question to ask is what next? It is important to remember here that the manufacturing process does not stop when the product leaves the factory. Distribution and service are still a part of the manufacturing process and should be integrated and coordinated with it. This brings us to the issue of just-in-time (JIT) systems. Successful implementation of JIT systems are dependent on successful implementation of TQM systems. Using TQM systems can set the groundwork to survive and thrive in these difficult times.

JIT systems are based on the idea that the buying and manufacturing tasks should be performed when required, not too early or too late. These systems can only function where the workers feel responsible for the quality of the product, are aware of the sources of error and delay, and plantwide quality improvement systems exist. Implementing JIT systems requires the implementation of a TQM system, where the quality of the part produced by each piece of equipment is known. If any part of the system fails either in terms of the quality of the product or the quality of the equipment used to produce it, then the JIT systems cannot succeed. Implementing JIT systems leads to lower inventories, and the production of defect-free products becomes critical to the manufacturing process.

Since JIT is the next logical step in the TQM process, the practices necessary to achieve this must be examined. All the steps described here as a part of the JIT system are essentially parts of the TQM process and include:

1. *Cutting lot sizes.* The lot sizes are determined by cost and time involved in setting up the machine and carrying cost for the batch. These larger lots mean that there is a greater probability of making defectives and in our inability to detect them. Larger lots mean that

the parts for the next machine are made and they wait until the next machine becomes available. This also calls for elaborate material-handling and scheduling costs. Ideally the line should be perfectly balanced with an operator handing over a new part to the next operator just as he or she finishes the current part..While this may not be practically feasible, it is necessary to minimize lot sizes with successive manufacturing stages set right next to each other.

2. *Cutting setup times.*   This may be in the form of quick-change tooling, conveyors, automation, or operators from neighboring machines helping in the setup process when elaborate setup is required. Machine setup times should not be viewed as a fixed time but something that can be continually improved upon.

3. *Total quality management.*   This is perhaps the most essential step. Without TQM there can be no JIT. If the internal or external suppliers do not supply a quality product, then the customers are unaware of the defects and the JIT system fails. JIT and TQM are closely related since JIT exposes defects in the process and TQM helps eliminate them.

4. *Pull systems.*   The system of queuing parts in front of the next machine should be avoided, and the system should function so that the manufacturing takes place when the next stage of the operation requires the part. The pull system responds to the demands of the customer at the right time and produces the part when the customer orders it.

5. *Flexibility of manufacturing.*   Factories must be built as modules around a stage of production or a number of closely related operations. Each module will have it own control, though there will be an overall control structure. Each of these modules will be maneuverable in terms of its location and relationship to other modules, allowing for rapid changes in design and demand and a low cost for flexibility. An optimal balance has to be struck between standardization and flexibility, which these modules allow. This also requires a different communication and information structure, and all the managers will have to understand the entire process and learn to act and think as team members.

6. *Withdrawing buffer inventories.*   This is done so that sources of delay and potential quality problems are eliminated. This leads to continual attempts to improve the process and smooth out the operation.

7. *Simplifying buying practices.*   This means that the vendor has to be made more responsive to your needs, with a stress on building a long-term relationship.

The People Side of TQM

Before continuing with the systems beyond TQM, let us once again ponder what the successful implementation of TQM systems involves. TQM systems lead to entrepreneurial environments, leading to a creative and dynamic environment that drives the business. One of the requirements for being successful in a manufacturing environment is the initiative shown by the employees of the company. Success of any TQM programs is entirely dependent on the participation of the individual employees, and unless top management has the vision to include each and every employee in the process, it will not have success. TQM systems challenge the members of the organization to be more productive with the existing equipment and facilities. Employees have to be viewed differently to make TQM work. The satisfaction derived from performing the job is the most important motivator. Employees must get the feeling that they are valued and respected. The organizational culture should be such that it encourages employees to contribute and gives them training to do so in an organized way. Once you get rid of discipline as the mechanism to manage your employees, you will give them the motivation to make significant job contributions and the job satisfaction they want. The cost savings as a result of conscientious employees is far, far greater than the upfront costs.

System Integration

Automated information systems lead to instant exchange of data and information. TQM systems provide the basis for analysis and instantaneous decision making based on the electronic interchange of data. System integration is one of the important requirements in the TQM process. The whole manufacturing process must be seen as an integrated process that converts materials into goods. Manufacturing processes are not controlled at all. Most of the parts are independent, supplied by independent suppliers, and this requires system design so that the process can form an integrated flow. TQM systems remove the bottlenecks for system integration and help implement JIT systems.

The working of these systems requires all computer systems to work together, and this leads us to networking computer systems in the operation and also integration of these systems. The computer systems at various ends of the operation have to function together for the TQM system to work successfully.

Kansei Engineering

Almost in a different vein, yet somehow on the same note, the next step in the process of TQM is *kansei engineering*. Kansei engineering is defined as the "absolute awareness" of both reason and emotion. This means each product has to have a personality of its own developed on the basis of the needs of the customer. This means measuring "things gone right." The designer has to be involved in the consumer research aspect of the business, and then translate the needs of the consumer into design parameters, while keeping manufacturability in mind.

The primary consideration for kansei engineering is that many of the considerations for buying a product such as the "look" and "feel" of the product are not articulated into quantified targets to be achieved. Therefore, just meeting all the engineering requirements may not satisfy the customer. Quality function deployment techniques attempt to identify these look and feel characteristics and quantify them so that they can be integrated into the design of the machine.

Kansei engineering also takes us beyond measuring "things gone wrong" to "things gone right." Consumer groups have to be used to understand the tastes in other products and the features of the product that elicit emotion. The product has to be engineered to meet every emotion of the owner. Some Japanese automotive companies during simulated driving sessions for its consumer groups monitor the heart and breathing rate of drivers, who narrate their feelings into a microphone as they bump along at different speeds. These emotions are then engineered to create a personality for each car. Using kansei engineering means that the consumer tastes and preferences have to be monitored even after they have purchased the goods and attempt to incorporate those features into future products.

Flexibility in Manufacturing

Another direction in which management systems will develop is the flexibility of the manufacturing systems, and this is a prerequisite for kansei engineering. If each individual's every reason and emotion has to be satisfied, then the manufacturing systems have to be extremely flexible, to the extent that each lot size should ideally be one. Flexibility in manufacturing will look at the wider view of the ever-changing face of the competition. The flexibility of the company refers to its ability to respond to the changes in the market and must include three areas of excellence:

1. Quick response to the shifts in product mix and volume increases and decreases.

2. Customization of products for specific needs of the customers.

3. Reducing the conception to manufacturing cycle.

Existing systems for manufacturing are not very flexible, and do not attempt to go beyond the quality management philosophy where the customer specifications are met. The future of manufacturing is in flexibility to meet the customer's every "reason and emotion." Many Japanese companies are attempting to be extremely flexible and some have even gone to the extent of getting to manufacturing lot sizes of one. Without the flexibility and speed to address market issues, competitive position will once again be lost to the Japanese, and that has been the tale of American manufacturing for a long time. Managing every aspect of quality in an extremely flexible manufacturing system is the future of manufacturing.

References

The following books and articles were referred to as a part of developing this book to provide its theoretical background. Many of the acceptance standards of General Motors Corporation, Ford Motor Company, and Chrysler Corporation have been used to develop the total quality management standards.

A new era for quality, *Business Week*, October 22, 1990.

Bajaria, H., *AT&T Statistical Quality Control Handbook*, Western Electric, 1985.

——, Quality focused automation, *Tooling and Production*, March 1991.

Banks, J., and Carson, J. S. II, *Discrete Event Simulation*, Prentice-Hall, 1984.

Cranfill, S. M., Seven task manufacturing improvement program, *Manufacturing Systems*, Jan. 1991.

Crosby, David C., How to succeed in SPC, *Quality in Manufacturing*, March/April 1991.

Crosby, Philip B., *Quality Is Free*, NAL Penguin, 1990.

Drucker, P., Buyer's guide to new CMMs, *Quality in Manufacturing*, Jan./Feb. 1991.

Drucker, P., The factory of 1999: The emerging theory of manufacturing, *Harvard Business Review*, May/June 1990.

Geldman, S. B., Supplier recognition award, *Quality*, August 1990.

Gitlow, H., Gitlow, S., Oppenheim, A., and Oppenheim, R., *Tools and Methods for the Improvement of Quality*, Irwin, 1989.

Hwang, C. L., and Yoon, K., *Multiple Attribute Decision Making—A State of the Art Survey*, Springer-Verlag, 1981.

Juran, J. M., and Gryna, F. M., *Juran's Quality Control Handbook*, McGraw-Hill, 1988.

Kaminski, B., Training—key to success in TQM, *Quality in Manufacturing*, Vol. 2, No. 1, Jan./Feb. 1991.

Konz, S., *Work Design and Industrial Ergonomics*, Grid, 1983.

Lenox, H., et al., *Team Oriented Problem Solving*, Ford Powertrain Operations.

Mendenhall, W., and Reinmuth, J. E., *Statistics for Management and Economics*, Duxbury, 1974.

Modic, S. J., *Simultaneous Engineering, Tooling and Production*, Heubcore, Feb. 1991.

Neter, J., Wasserman, W., and Kutner, M. H., *Applied Linear Statistical Models*, Irwin, 1985.

——, *Targets for Excellence*, Supplier Development Administration, General Motors Purchasing Activities, 1987.

Pince et al., *Measurement Systems Analysis*, ASQC, AIAG, Chrysler, Ford, and General Motors, 1990.

Ross, P. J., *Taguchi Techniques for Quality Engineering*, McGraw-Hill, 1988.

Shingo, S., *Zero Quality Control: Source Inspection and the Poka-Yoke System*, Productivity Press, 1986.

Wheeler, D. J., and Lyday, R. W., *Evaluating the Measurement Process*, SPC Press, Inc., 1989.

Yoji, A., *Datamyte Handbook*, Datamyte, 1987.

——, *Quality Function Deployment: Integrating Customer Requirements into Product Design*, Productivity Press, 1990.

Zagarow, H. W., The training challenge, *Quality*, August 1990.

Index

ABOUT THE AUTHOR

H. G. Menon is a manufacturing engineer for Jernberg Industries in Chicago, Illinois, where he is responsible for developing and implementing a total quality management system. He also teaches a course in the engineering program at the Illinois Institute of Technology.